MW00424676

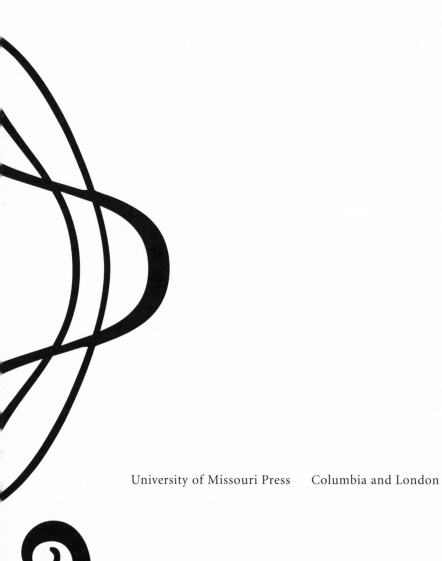

University of Missouri Press   Columbia and London

Thyra J. Edwards

Black Activist in the
Global Freedom Struggle

Gregg Andrews

Copyright ©2011 by
The Curators of the University of Missouri
University of Missouri Press, Columbia, Missouri 65201
Printed and bound in the United States of America
All rights reserved
5 4 3 2 1   15 14 13 12 11

Cataloging-in-Publication data available from the Library of Congress.
ISBN 978-0-8262-1912-1

∞™ This paper meets the requirements of the
American National Standard for Permanence of Paper
for Printed Library Materials, Z39.48, 1984.

Design and composition: Jennifer Cropp
Printing and binding: Thomson-Shore, Inc.
Typefaces: Minion, Chesterfield Antique, and Adobe Garamond

Contents

Acknowledgments

My interest in Thyra J. Edwards as an important historical figure dates back to about ten years ago, when I set out to write a book on Texas labor in the Great Depression with the support of a National Endowment for the Humanities Fellowship. The more I studied Houston's black longshoremen, the more I kept running into Edwards. Over time, her fascinating life story diverted my attention from the Texas labor study, and I decided to undertake a biography of her instead. I would like to thank the NEH for that fellowship. I would also like to thank the Texas State Historical Association for twice awarding me the Mary M. Hughes Research Fellowship to help fund this study. At the annual meeting of the TSHA in 2008, I presented a paper, "Black Labor Leaders and the Civil Rights Struggle in New Deal Texas," in which Edwards figured prominently and generated a lot of audience comments and discussion.

I have tried to write this book in a way that would appeal to a popular audience as well as to scholars. To the extent possible in any book, I have consciously sought not to impose my voice on the narrative too much, but rather to allow Edwards's popular but analytical style of writing to present her voice. On the one hand, she was critical of turgid academic studies that were deeply analytical but useful only to a handful of academics and condemned to gather dust on university library shelves. On the other, she bemoaned the lack of analysis and depth in the growing spate of popular writings on the history and culture of African Americans. In my opinion, her literary style, called "fulsome" by one of her sisters, offered readers an attractive alternative.

I owe a special debt of gratitude to Vikki Bynum—my wife, fellow scholar, former colleague, and now retirement companion in the land of Tom Sawyer and Huckleberry Finn. Edwards has been a constant topic of conversation between us for the last several years, and I have benefited a great deal from Vikki's insights, criticisms, and suggestions. Vikki not only read the manuscript and provided ongoing support, but also tore up the dance floor whenever my band and I—Doctor G and the Mudcats—rocked the Cheatham Street Warehouse with our swampy blues music in San Marcos, Texas. I would like to thank the Mudcats—Sterling Finlay, Big John Mills, Grant Mazak, and Kyle Schneider—for helping me to keep an edge on the beat in more ways than one. I owe a special thanks to my good friend and fellow songwriter, Kent Finlay, owner of the Cheatham Street Warehouse, for encouraging me to put on my other hat as a singer/songwriter.

A couple of years ago, I had the pleasure to meet and host a dazzling performance by Gina Loring, accompanied by beat boxer Joshua Silverstein, on the campus of Texas State University–San Marcos. Loring, a slam poet, hip-hop artist, actor, and political activist, is a great-niece of Thyra Edwards's. Loring provided me with a copy of a brief family history written in 1963 by her grandmother, Thelma Marshall, who was Edwards's sister. She also put me in contact with one of Edwards's cousins, Vee Edwards, of Pasadena, California, who allowed me access to the Edwards family's website, replete with photos and snapshots of the family. I would like to thank Vee and her sister, Ann Edwards, for facilitating the reproduction of several family photos.

I appreciate the research support provided by Frank de la Teja, Chair of the Department of History at Texas State University–San Marcos. Several of my former colleagues discussed my research with me or read portions of it. I would like to give a special thanks to Dwight Watson, Ken Margerison, Rebecca Montgomery, Mary Brennan, Deirdre Lannon, and Tom Alter, my final MA thesis student, who is now in the doctoral program in History at the University of Illinois at Chicago.

A number of scholars have provided leads and references and shared their take on the political activism of Thyra J. Edwards. I would like to thank Gerald Horne, Eric Arnesen, Mike Honey, Beth Bates, Greg Boozell, Tom Dublin, Steve Rosswurm, and Joyce Moore Turner for their collegiality.

Without the help of several outstanding archivists and assistants who facilitated access to manuscript and archival collections, this book would have taken much longer than it did. I wish especially to thank Sam Sims and others at the Chicago History Museum, the repository of the Thyra J. Edwards Papers. Gail Malmgren, Peter Filardo, Erika Gottfried, and Ava Hassinger at the Tamiment Library at New York University provided important help, and so did Virginia Lewick (Franklin D. Roosevelt Presidential Library), Accacia Flanagan (Schlesinger Library, Harvard University), Lia Apodaca (Library of Congress), Nicolette A. Dobrowolski (Syracuse University Library), Margaret Jessup (Sophia Smith Collection, Smith College), Harry Miller (Wisconsin Historical Society), Kathy Shoemaker (Manuscript, Archives, and Rare Book Library, Emory

University), Graham Sherriff (Beinecke Rare Book and Manuscript Library, Yale University), and Nancy Shawcross (Rare Book and Manuscript Library, University of Pennsylvania). I also thank Andrea Cecilia Meyer, a graduate student and researcher who on my behalf searched the Bernard Ades Papers at the Tamiment Library. Alison Orton, a history graduate student at the University of Illinois at Chicago, searched photos for me in the Thyra J. Edwards Papers.

Through the Freedom of Information Act, I obtained the Federal Bureau of Investigation file on Thyra J. Edwards. Unfortunately, the Central Intelligence Agency refused to release materials on her. I challenged their refusal, taking my request to an appeal review board, but to no avail.

I want to thank Editor-in-Chief Clair Willcox, Sara Davis, Gloria Thomas, and other members of the University of Missouri Press staff for their role in preparing my manuscript for publication. The criticisms and suggestions of two anonymous readers for the press also helped to strengthen the manuscript.

Thyra J. Edwards

Introduction

"The Spirit of Aframerican Womanhood"

I assure you that Thyra Edwards is one of the most brilliant young women of the Negro or any other race, in public life today. She has not only a keen analytical mind, but a fine poise, modest charm and a fluency of presentation that will capture the admiration of the most critical.

—A. Philip Randolph, quoted in "The National Religion and
Labor Foundation Sponsors Thyra J. Edwards," ca. 1934

Thyra J. Edwards, the granddaughter of runaway slaves, was an important labor, civil-rights, and peace activist and an internationalist, Pan-Africanist, and advocate of women's rights in the first half of the twentieth century. A Texan who in her early twenties joined the Great Migration to the North, she was among a number of radical black women at that time who put their faith in organized labor and the Communist Party as instruments of civil rights and social justice. She brought not only a "southernness" but also an international dimension to her political activism because of her extensive travels, studies, and associations overseas. For Edwards, the battle for civil rights in the United States was part of the larger struggle against fascism, colonialism, and imperialism in the 1930s, 1940s, and early 1950s.

Edwards grew up on the mean Jim Crow streets of Houston, Texas, in the early 1900s. Houston was a city harshly divided along lines of race and class.

In 1917, during the Camp Logan Riot, Edwards saw the city's streets run red with blood when local police shot down black uniformed soldiers of the United States Army who had rebelled against Jim Crow segregation and harassment by killing or wounding a number of white residents and police officers. The Camp Logan Riot contributed to Edwards's radicalization, but she had hated oppression from the time she was a child, fighting turf wars in which she and black friends battled gangs of white kids on the streets, block by block. She and other black children on their way to crummy, dilapidated school buildings at times had to dodge muddy holes where sidewalks should have been, even wading through deep water in marshlike conditions just to get to school. Racial hatred and violence, hard times, segregation, oppression, disease, Jim Crow medicine, authoritarianism, and exploitation shaped the southern urban setting in which she came of age.[1]

Edwards, although at times reminded by her mother that certain things were off-limits to her in the segregated South, refused to accept second-class citizenship in a racist society. Not even the deep sting of a tyrannical father's razor strap could crush her rebellious spirit as a child. Impulsive and impetuous, with magnificent charm, a restless spirit, and zest for life, she set out on a spiritual quest for freedom that took her around the world. In 1938, a black newspaper in Houston paid a front-page tribute to her as the embodiment of "THE SPIRIT OF AFRAMERICAN WOMANHOOD."[2]

Born in 1897, Edwards was kin to the white, slaveholding family of a former Mississippi governor on her father's side, although the formerly slaveholding family did not acknowledge the kinship. Her maternal great-grandfather was also a white slaveholder. Edwards's maternal grandparents' daring escape from slavery across the Mississippi River at Hannibal, Missouri, provided an important source of inspiration for her activism.

Thyra Edwards's life journey took her from Texas to Gary, Indiana; Chicago; New York City; and then around the world in a peripatetic search for the roots of oppression. She donned a lot of hats on the journey. As an activist, her friendships, professional associations, romantic relationships, and cultural pursuits often grew out of her political commitments. She was a social worker, labor organizer, teacher, and civil-rights activist, as well as a journalist, managing newspaper editor, fiction writer, and world lecturer. She rejected orthodox religion and conventional marriage. She was a theater critic, passionate lover of the arts, excellent cook, and fashion-conscious beauty writer known for her impeccable taste and collection of peasant blouses. She led educational travel seminars to northern and western Europe, Scandinavia, Mexico, and the Soviet Union. Although Edwards took undergraduate courses and passed comprehensive exams at the University of Chicago, she never finished her college degree. A life of travel and intellectual inquiry through field investigations and personal experiences meant more to her. Make no mistake, though, she had a brilliant, analytical mind and contributed to black radical intellectual traditions.

By the time Edwards's life ended in 1953, when she was only fifty-five, she believed that she had lived it to the fullest. At times she had found herself in precarious, sometimes dangerous predicaments, but she had managed to slip out of them. While in Germany in the mid-1930s, she had endured a strip search by Nazis and negotiated her way around the dangerous streets and slums of Stuttgart and Munich, where she slept in the train station. When Hitler's storm troopers, in street solicitations for money in exchange for Nazi trinkets, shoved a cup in front of her face, she had refused to drop money into it. In 1936, she had found many of her Austrian friends in jail as political prisoners in Vienna. Helping as a social worker and journalist, she had risked her life in the Spanish Civil War. With colonies of Spanish Loyalist refugee children and soldiers, she had survived aerial bombings by fascist forces, and in 1937, she had been in Paris to watch the unveiling of Picasso's famous painting *Guernica*.

The same person who as a young girl was warned by her father to stick to the same street on her way to school every day and never to take a different route later walked down the street to the Kremlin, thrilled when she marched in Red Square in a May 1st celebration. Edwards visited Napoleon's tomb; wined, dined, and danced with European politicians and dignitaries; took lovers in a number of countries; and enjoyed nude sunbathing on the Soviet Black Sea Riviera.

Edwards certainly was no stranger to roughing it on many of her travels. In Mexico in 1939, she swigged rum from a canteen that passed from lips to lips of men who were Spanish Loyalist refugees on a special train bound for a remote desert resettlement site in Chihuahua. With her typewriter on her lap, she craned forward to hear their stories as she shared their rum. Whether bedding down in a barn—the only woman among resettlement engineers in the Chihuahua desert—or scrubbing her clothes in a river each day with Maya women in a tropical rainforest village south of Oaxaca, Edwards did not allow primitive conditions or conventional mores to interfere with her intellectual search for the roots of oppression.

Edwards's travels were not merely those of a tourist. They had a political and educational purpose. Her philosophy of civil-rights activism was deeply rooted in a commitment to solving interconnected problems of labor, poverty, imperialism, and economic and racial exploitation. As a women's-rights advocate and trade unionist with a global perspective, she understood that black women faced their own set of special issues in the workplace. She also grasped that the fight against racism in the United States represented only one part of the world struggle against fascism, colonialism, and imperialism. In her outlook on world affairs, she balanced strong Pan-African influences and labor internationalism. Her personal charm, wit, cosmopolitan outlook, beauty, and elegance often disarmed opponents and people skeptical of her abilities. Helen Chappell, a black Los Angeles columnist for the black weekly *Chicago Defender,* called her "the first movement person I liked."[3]

Skilled at building bridges between the liberal and radical communities, Edwards worked closely with Communists in labor and civil-rights struggles, especially in the Popular Front era. She also traveled to the Soviet Union and praised its racial policies, attracting surveillance by the Federal Bureau of Investigation and later the Central Intelligence Agency and other branches of American intelligence. Drawn to the forthright civil-rights stance of the Communists in the 1930s, she was likely a broadly defined, nonsectarian communist in her philosophy, although she denied it under oath. Whatever the case, she remained pro-Soviet in her critique of international affairs but was always intellectually independent and believed in rigorous criticism, democracy, and freedom of expression. She did not hesitate to speak her mind; once she confronted top Communist Party officials in the United States over Popular Front policies that she believed downplayed the war against Jim Crow for the sake of political expediency.

At different times, Edwards lived in Chicago, Harlem, and Greenwich Village, where she became an active figure in public life. In Chicago, she developed friendships with the city's prominent white social workers, especially Helen Castle Mead, Jane Addams, and Mary McDowell. Many of the well-known literary figures and artists of the Harlem Renaissance were her friends. First and foremost among these was the poet Langston Hughes, who kept up a correspondence with her until her death. Novelists Arna Bontemps and Richard Wright, writer/activist Pauli Murray, opera singers Paul Robeson and Marian Anderson, painter Aaron Douglas, sculptor Richard Barthé, and novelist Countee Cullen also numbered among her friends.

Edwards's close friend and mentor A. Philip Randolph, president of the Brotherhood of Sleeping Car Porters, played a huge role in her growth and development. Thanks to him, she received scholarships to attend Brookwood Labor College in New York and the International People's College in Denmark. Edwards and Randolph worked together in labor and civil-rights coalitions, and Randolph was likely the married man, "Philip," with whom Edwards carried on a clandestine romantic affair for several years in the 1930s. For Edwards, it was hard to break off the relationship.

After a brief marriage and divorce in the mid-1920s, Edwards chose to remain single for nearly twenty years, preferring her itinerant lifestyle as an activist to a relationship that might put her in a conventional marriage on terms that she found unacceptable. Until June 1943, she contented herself with casual sexual liaisons and temporary relationships with men who shared her political and intellectual interests. At that time, she married Murray Gitlin, a radical

Jewish writer, activist, and official of the United Jewish Appeal in New York City. She had moved to New York in January of that year to become managing editor of Adam Clayton Powell Jr.'s newspaper, *The People's Voice*. Earlier in her life, Edwards had insisted that she would date only black men, but her experiences forced a reassessment of her attitudes toward interracial relationships. In a published magazine article, she and her husband shared with the American public their experiences as a "mixed marriage" couple in the 1940s.

Rheumatoid arthritis struck Edwards shortly before her fortieth birthday, but it was many years before a specialist diagnosed the condition. In the meantime, the disease's crippling effects periodically incapacitated her. Desperate for relief, she resorted to an alternative treatment of bee stings in Italy, where she and her husband had moved in 1948, when he became director of a branch of the American Jewish Joint Distribution Committee to work in Jewish refugee settlement. The treatment gave her a few pain-free years, but in the meantime she developed breast cancer, which forced her return to the United States in 1952 and caused her death the following year.

Given the international scope and importance of Edwards's political activities, it is puzzling that she has not been the subject of a full-length biography. With a few notable exceptions, in fact, she has flown virtually under the radar of historians until the last decade or so. Social-work scholars Elmer P. Martin and Joanne M. Martin wrote a brief biographical sketch of Edwards for an anthology, and Gwynne Gertz wrote a biographical entry on her for an encyclopedia about Chicago women. A handful of other scholars have called attention to Edwards's important role in what some recently have called "the long civil rights movement." Without study of Edwards, who played such a central part in the labor, racial-justice, and peace struggles of her era, we lose sight of the family, personal, and fuller social context in which her broad-based political activism and intellectual growth took shape and evolved over time.[4]

A number of radical black women who were Edwards's contemporaries have drawn the attention of scholars in recent years, but like many of them, she did not publish an autobiography. Edwards did plan to write one and even had a title, "A Thread from Every Man in the Village," but she never got much past the outline stage because of her hectic travels, activism, and ongoing health problems. While in Italy during the final years of her life, she wrote a philosophical piece of children's fiction, "The Honey Arbor." At the time of her death, Langston Hughes was trying to help her find a publisher for it.[5]

Onah Spencer, with whom Edwards was romantically involved in Chicago for a while, urged her to frame her life story as a novel. Spencer, a black music writer who covered the South Side of Chicago for *Down Beat* and worked for the Illinois Writers Project, believed that a fictional account of her life would have the potential to dwarf Richard Wright's *Native Son* because of the international scope of her experiences. He suggested that if she chose instead to write a nonfictional autobiography, she should title it "A Brown Gal in Seven League Boots" to capture the full sweep of her life.[6]

Edwards's compelling odyssey, characterized by frenetic travel and a relentless quest for freedom, took her far from her southern roots, but she never forgot where she came from. As Texas's most radical black woman in the economic and social-justice struggles of the era, she often returned to Houston to see friends and family, to recruit participants for her international travel seminars, and to promote labor-based civil rights and world peace. Even a conservative black newspaper in her hometown grudgingly conceded in 1940 that "there is little doubt in the minds of Houstonians that Miss Edwards has brought more publicity to Houston in the span of her career than numerous other individuals have done in a longer number of years."[7]

1

Texas Roots of Rebellion
under the Chinaberry Tree

Born in Wharton, Texas, on December 25, 1897, Thyra Johnson Edwards was the oldest of five children, including sisters Thelma, Anna Bell, and Marian and brother George. Her parents—Horace Ferdinand Edwards and Anna Bell (Johnson) Edwards—had married in San Antonio but then moved to Wharton, at that time an unincorporated town on the lower Colorado River, about forty-five miles from the Gulf of Mexico. The family also lived in Glen Flora and Hungerford, other small communities in Wharton County, which was known before the Civil War as part of the Texas sugar bowl because of its slave-based sugar plantations. In Wharton, where she spent her early childhood, Edwards's parents taught in the town's segregated schools and were active in community affairs and social reform.

The images of Wharton County that stayed with Edwards for the rest of her life centered on rural southern culture. Canebrakes, country stores, cotton fields, watermelon patches, and outdoor privies dotted the landscape that shaped her earliest memories. Also prominent in the imagery of her childhood were snuff-dipping farm women in quaint dresses and sawed-off shoes cooking in their lean-to kitchens. Religious fervor, singing, shouting, and "lay exhorting" in the Macedonia Baptist Church, as well as her mother's devout religious views, piano playing, and singing, provided important parts of her cultural upbringing. Edwards later rejected religious dogma, but she grew up reading Bible stories in *Easy Steps for Little Feet,* "aided by the interpretations of my own very devout mother."[1]

As teachers, Horace and Anna Edwards could afford to provide their children with a decent standard of living in Wharton. They lived in a three-room wall-papered house whose furnishings included a piano, jewelry box, bearskin rug, and dressing table, as well as books and the *Ladies Home Journal.* Edwards apparently believed that her mother was driven somewhat by class pretensions. For her mother, home ownership and city living were two of the three most important things in life. To rent, Anna considered a disgrace. In Wharton, the Edwards household included a black domestic servant to help keep house and take care of Thyra and Thelma, who was two years younger, while Anna and Horace were teaching.[2]

Anna Johnson, who had graduated from high school in Galesburg, Illinois, in 1894, first came to Texas with a friend, Daisy Walker. An 1893 graduate of Galesburg High School, Walker eventually left Texas for Alabama, where she attended the Tuskegee Institute, but Anna met Horace Edwards in Texas, married him, and became a teacher.[3]

It was the escape from slavery in Hannibal, Missouri, via the Underground Railroad by Thyra Edwards's maternal grandparents—George Washington ("Wash") Johnson and Eliza ("Liza") Wheeler Johnson—that had established the roots of her mother's family in freedom. For Edwards, the story of their "bold stroke for freedom" remained vividly etched in her memory throughout her life. No doubt passed on and reinforced through family stories, and embellished a bit by Edwards for literary purposes when she began to sketch her autobiography, the compelling account of runaway slaves among her ancestors provided her an important source of inspiration. According to Thelma, Thyra's personality was much like that of their grandmother, whom Thelma described as "a direct-actionist, not too concerned with diplomacy." Thyra would draw on her grandmother's courage in the face of racial oppression and adversity to guide her civil-rights activism.[4]

Liza, born a slave in Virginia around 1841, had come to Hannibal with her owner's family, whose surname was presumably Wheeler. The exact date and town of her birth are unknown. According to Thelma, Liza, who was likely the daughter of her slave master, "was of slightly stocky build, light skinned and straight-haired. Her lips were thin and very firm, her nose was a little heavy but not Negroid in form."[5] According to Thyra, Liza was "white with chestnut braids."[6]

When Liza was about eight years old, her master brought her "to the big house as the sort of nurse-playmate" for his children who were close to her in age. "From that time on," Edwards described, "she slept as she chose, wither on a cot in the alcove of the play room or out in the quarters in her mother's one roomed, dirt floored cabin." Liza's mother did the cooking for the master's family, and Liza's older sister, Fanny, at age twelve, was hired out to cook for the family of a neighboring farmer.[7]

The master's children who grew up with Liza inadvertently helped her learn to read. They often recited their lessons to her and practiced memorization of passages with her in the evenings. As a result, Liza secretly taught herself to read but not to write. She had a fierce hunger for learning, but she had to hide her reading skills from the watchful eye of her mistress. By the time she was married at age seventeen, Liza had devoured all of Shakespeare's works, as well as a number of English classics and books of history and geography.[8]

Liza married Wash, also a slave, who was twenty-five years old at the time of their wedding, and she soon gave birth to their son James. Wash, who stood six feet, six inches in height, worked for a nearby master as a landscape gardener and caretaker of fruit trees. He had been sold from his mother when he was about ten years old. According to Thelma, he was "very black in colour and with a very jolly, pleasant, agreeable disposition." Thyra described him as "a tall, black giant with nobly cut features," including "a splendid high nose, broad forehead and firm mouth." He had "the heartiest and readiest laugh," and he was "the best dancer in the entire county." Although he, too, could read, Wash did not share Liza's intellectual curiosity. According to Thyra, "His great joy was the Saturday night dances at alternate plantations. After that he loved his trees, with a reverence almost religious."[9]

Without warning one night in 1860 or 1861, Wash disappeared. Earlier that day, while planting new cherry trees, he had seen his master showing "a tobacco spitting, high booted planter from Mississippi" around his property. Wash, fearful he might be sold to a new master in the Deep South, slipped across the Mississippi River into Illinois, accompanied by Enoch, one of his half-brothers who belonged to the same slave owner.[10]

Taking advantage of the Underground Railroad, Wash and Enoch made their way first to Monmouth, Illinois, but then moved on until they reached Galesburg, where they established a livelihood and found a place to live. Wash decided to risk a return to the Hannibal area to get his wife and son. At the last minute, however, Enoch, who was single, persuaded Wash to let him be the one to return to the owner's farm at night to get them. He argued that if Wash were captured, Liza, too, would likely be punished.[11]

When Liza married Wash, she was living in a cabin that her master had given her in the slave quarters to accommodate visits from Wash, who then spent most evenings there with her. After Wash ran away, though, Liza's master and mistress dropped his name from all discussions, and Liza and her infant son, James, stopped spending nights in the cabin. Instead, Liza and James "occupied an uncurtained alcove of the broad white nursery of the big house."[12]

One night about two months after Wash vanished, Liza took James, who had the croup, to sleep in the cabin because his cough was disturbing the sleep of the master's son, and she found a surprise waiting there. According to family history, Wash had communicated the escape plan beforehand to Liza through the "grape vine." Earlier on the day of Liza's escape, her mistress had broken the silence about Wash, casually asking, "Liza—wouldn't you like to see Wash?" The mistress's question startled Liza and filled her with forebodings that Wash had been tracked down by bloodhounds, captured, and shackled.[13]

As Liza entered the cabin that night, Edwards recounted, "her strong hands wavered as she struck flint to light the tallow dip in its shallow iron basin." When the candle sputtered out, Liza prepared to relight it, but before she could do it, someone spoke her name "on the shadowy side of the cabin." It was Enoch. According to Edwards's account of what happened next, Liza "stepped again across the shadowed yard, the infant James warmly wrapped in a thick, gray woolen deeply fringed shawl. A shawl I knew well in my childhood. Grandmother always travelled with it, bringing it on those rare long visits she made to us."[14]

Liza quickly grabbed the opportunity put before her. It was nearly daybreak when she and Enoch reached the Mississippi River, where Wash "waited in a canoe-like boat moored under heavy willows." They then safely crossed the river, a watery grave for many runaway slaves from eastern Missouri, and hid in a house that Wash had already discovered to be part of the Underground Railroad. At that point, Wash dropped his slave name, which is unknown, and adopted the name George Washington Johnson. Two days later, after traveling by night, he, Liza, and Enoch reached Galesburg, a virtual colony of runaway slaves where the state's first antislavery society was created in 1837.[15]

In Galesburg, Wash and Liza began a new life in freedom, sometime right before the Civil War broke out. They added five more children to their family. Anna, Thyra's mother, was the youngest, born in 1876. At the time of the 1880 federal manuscript census, the Johnsons' household also included Fanny, age sixteen, named after Liza's older sister; two sons, George and Willie, ages thirteen and ten; and another daughter, Mamie, age seven. James, the ailing infant they took with them on their escape to freedom, died as the result of hardships endured on the journey.

Thanks to hard work and Liza's thriftiness, the Johnson family bought a home and soon owned two other small houses, which they rented out. Wash worked as a wood sawyer, Liza as a domestic. She made jams, canned pickles, did knitting, made rugs, and took care of other household chores. According to Thelma, she was "the moving force in her family." Thyra described her grandmother as "strong, sure, secure."[16]

Wash and Liza's escape from slavery had great significance for Edwards and the family's history. "Romantically," she later wrote, "I used to picture my grandfather as the militant leader of rebellious slaves making a bold dash for freedom. This, my mother realistically assures me, was not exactly the case." Nevertheless, her grandparents' courage, personal convictions, and passion for freedom instilled tremendous pride in her and strengthened her own freedom struggle in the twentieth century. Her grandmother, who "hated slavery and white people," finally learned to write at the age of sixty. Edwards, emphasizing the importance of her grandfather's decision to change his name after crossing the Mississippi River into Illinois, proudly declared, "And so we Johnsons have never carried a master's name."[17]

From the Mississippi side of Edwards's family, as she put it, "freedom is more distant." Her grandfather, George Edwards, was a slave born in Georgia, and her grandmother, Nora Edwards, was a household slave born in Alabama. Thelma described Grandmother Edwards as "very tall, a light brown skin and very pretty, straight hair with a light wave." According to family history, Grandmother Edwards was the daughter of Adam McWillie, a prominent slaveholding planter who was the eldest son of William McWillie, governor of Mississippi from 1857 to 1859. Adam McWillie lived in Madison County, Mississippi, but he also owned a large plantation in Jefferson County, Arkansas. In the Edwards family's memory, he was "a dissolute drunkard" who joined the Confederate Army and promised to defeat the "Damn Yankees before breakfast the next morning." He was killed, however, while commanding a company in the 18th Regiment of Mississippi Volunteers at the First Battle of Bull Run on July 21, 1861.[18]

Edwards's paternal grandfather, George Edwards, had a reputation in the family as "a very harsh man." He and Nora had twelve children, the oldest of whom was Edwards's father, Horace. When Horace, who was born around 1866, was about seven years old, his father had bound him out to a previous master, a physician and his family. Horace worked and lived with them for about seven years.[19] According to Thelma, "They treated him well but would not permit him to go to school. However, they had sons near my father's age who tutored him at home. So he received an excellent though not formal education."[20]

When Horace reached puberty, his status in the family for whom he worked changed. No longer treated as a member of the family, he went back to his own family in Yazoo County in the Mississippi Delta. His father, who became a minister in the Christian Methodist Episcopal Church, was killed in the early 1890s when he was about fifty years old. Horace's mother, who was also literate, kept up a correspondence with her children and grandchildren until her death sometime around 1916 or 1917 at the age of seventy.[21]

Horace and his family, described by Edwards as "nomads," drifted into Louisiana and Texas, where in 1897 Horace married Anna Johnson. In 1910, his mother lived with her daughter, Janie Milton, in the Piney Woods region of east Texas known as the Big Thicket in Hardin County. Janie's husband, John, worked in area saw mills. Also living in the Milton household was Edwards's uncle, Whitfield ("Whit") Edwards, an inventor who owned a butcher shop in the area at the time. By 1920, the Miltons had moved to Independence Heights, a newly incorporated black town later annexed to the city of Houston, where Edwards's cousins—James and Charles—worked on the docks in Houston's ship channel.[22]

Edwards's parents left their teaching jobs in Wharton and moved the family to Houston in the early 1900s. It is not clear what prompted the move; perhaps it was Anna's determination to live in a city. Whatever the case, the move to Houston was hard on the family financially. According to Edwards, the family's income was cut in half, while expenses doubled and Anna gave birth to Anna Bell in 1905. Thyra's father planted a garden and desperately turned to selling wood and "junking" to provide for the family.

The Edwards family lived at 1709 St. Charles Street in Houston's Third Ward, where Thyra would come of age. The Third Ward in 1920 contained the largest number of black residents in the rigidly segregated city. The Third and Fourth wards were the cultural center of Houston's black population, housing a number of black churches, businesses, and social and fraternal institutions and organizations.[23]

The financial condition of the Edwards family in Houston improved considerably when Horace received an appointment as a postal clerk. At that time, he was one of only two black employees in the U.S. Postal Service in Houston. "My mother was proud," Edwards recalled. "It was stable, permanent, dignified work."[24]

Unfortunately for Horace, however, the job was a drag, and it made his explosive temper even worse. The job required him to work a "split watch," being at work from 10 p.m. to 4 a.m., and then again from noon to 4 p.m. He suffered from chronic sleep deprivation, and besides, he detested the work rules, routine nature of his duties, and working under the supervision of a white boss. In short, as Edwards remembered, "He hated the job . . . and grew increasingly irritable and erratic." She emphasized that she and her siblings "always loved" their father, but living with him during this time was apparently challenging. "We were taught parents couldn't err [but] the increasingly [sic] irritableness without tangible provocation bore heavily on that faith." Later in life, she vividly recalled an incident that exemplified his growing explosiveness in this period: "I had thoughtlessly walked thru the front room. My new shoes, which occupied my tho'ts at the time, creaked loudly, woke him. I can still feel the sting of his razor strap, the more heavily Administered because of the abrupt interruption to his already awkward 'split' sleep schedule. It seemed a little harsh, but he was Father."[25]

Edwards also remembered in vivid detail the first time she and her sister witnessed one of their father's disturbing, unpredictable outbursts. "Under a crystalline sky, exquisitely sparkling and far clearer than the famed opaline Northern Lights," she described, "he had started for work & reaching the gate peremptorily thrown his lunch basket into a far corner of the front yard where it struck against a fence post. The night is acid etched in my memory." Inside the lunch basket, and now shattered in pieces, was her father's favorite coffee cup, a gift from Grandmother Johnson. On that particular night, Anna had packed his favorite apple cobbler in the cup and tucked it away in his lunch basket for him. According to Edwards, her father ended up not going to work that night, instead "sulking in the parlor while my mother stayed with him."[26]

For Thyra, this incident was significant for two reasons. First, it dramatized the fear that she and Thelma had felt in the presence of their father: "Although 10 years of our lives that followed were submerged and shadowed by the violence of my father's temper," Thyra recalled, "that pristine night under the stars was the first exhibition we had seen."[27]

On the other hand, Thyra noted, she and Thelma felt a sense of relief when they heard the "crackling sound of breaking china" as the lunch basket hit the post. Their father, a "sentimentalist" who "treasured" the coffee cup dearly, had broken his own cup. He had always "insisted upon drinking his coffee from it twice daily, each time reminding us that should we break it in washing he would 'lash us to the last inch of hide.'" As Thyra reflected, "While Father's temper tantrum somehow seemed the end of the world to us, at the same time the crashing cup sounded a release from a tyrant."[28]

For Thyra and Thelma, the post office job brought an important change in addition to the family's improved financial situation. Up to that point, their father had tutored them at home rather than sending them to segregated public schools, but his taking the post office job "freed" his daughters to attend public school. Despite Edwards's unhappiness as a child and fear of her father's temper, she did learn from his tutoring a couple of very important things that later shaped her political views. She understood as an adult that he had helped to instill in her feelings of "class democracy" and a hatred of "moral snobbery."[29]

Edwards's quest to understand the meaning of race began at an early age. As she put it, "From the time I could crawl on my hands and knees freedom for the Negro people became my own personal problem." She resented the stigma of 250 years of slavery "put upon me and my people by generations of freebooters, imperialists, profiteers and feudal minds of the white race." For her, the struggle for equality meant the same thing that it did to every other black person she knew: "We were a special people, austerely alone, our freedom was separate from everybody else's freedom; our suffering was a thing apart, the most intense and the most intolerable of all suffering."[30]

As an adolescent, Edwards's hostility to whites grew when on her daily walk to school, she at times found herself caught up in racial turf wars. En route to Douglas school, she and other black students often fought "pitched battles" with white students who attended Longfellow, a white school nearby. These were "bitter fights with brick bats and clubs fought block by block down the middle of the street." According to Edwards, "Our boys usually pushed the white boys back inside their section, both sides bloody and dusty. We girls following block by block on the sidewalk, cheered them and brought up fresh supplies of rocks. I don't remember the white girls taking any part." Such battles instilled in Edwards "a relentless hostility and distrust to anyone white and southern."[31]

Even at a young age, though, Edwards's understanding of the connections between race, inequality, and oppression deepened due in large part to the influence of a Jewish rabbi whose family lived on Pease Street on the other side of the railroad tracks opposite her house on St. Charles Street. On one occasion when Rabbi Israel Lurie, a Russian immigrant, overheard an argument between nine-year-old Thyra and his seven-year-old daughter, Josephine, over the plight of black people, he sat them down on his front porch and gave them a history lesson. According to Edwards, he "made me understand that his people had been in slavery for thousands of years, not a mere 250." From that point on, she paid more attention to the complexities of race. "The knowledge that there existed other peoples who had been subjected to discrimination and persecution did not make my own any less intense," she later noted. "But it did sharpen my young mind even at that age to certain strange patterns relating to the whole dark stain of inequality."[32]

The "strange patterns" existed right there in Edwards's neighborhood, friendships, and associations. Despite racially segregated residential patterns, she was in daily contact with whites in her neighborhood. Through the kitchen window of her family's home, for example, she peered out at white railroad workers in the backyard of Irving and Annie Kier, washing their "oil and coal-blackened hands and faces before going into dinner" (p. 51) at the Kiers' home, where they boarded. Annie Kier at times leaned over the picket fence that divided their properties to warn Edwards's mother, busy in the kitchen, not to let her children play with the "sheenies." At other times, Kier from her front porch would caution Rabbi Lurie's wife not to allow her children to play with the "niggers." One of the Kier children, Irving Jr., played with the Edwards children, but only through a crack in the picket fence that separated their yards (p. 51).

As Edwards later remembered, "That picket fence was the line of demarcation. It separated his [Irving's] white world from our colored world. He never crossed it, nor did we" (p. 51). Irving Jr.'s prejudice against Jews went even deeper, for he would leave his backyard altogether whenever the Lurie children were playing with the Edwards children under the chinaberry tree in the Edwardses' yard.

What further complicated Edwards's grasp of the meaning of race and inequality was the "hierarchy of prejudices" in the black community. Black friends scolded Anna Edwards for allowing her children to play with Jews. Moreover, the overlapping variables of gender, race, and class helped to shape the attitudes of black men in the neighborhood toward Annie Kier. Her husband, a mail carrier, was generally well-liked, but she was not. As Edwards explained, "No colored person had anything but contempt for a white woman who worked like a slave keeping a boardinghouse. Any colored woman could do that. The Negro men in our neighborhood boasted that their wives had never set foot in any white woman's kitchen." Kier "was just a white woman who hadn't made good with the larger opportunities white equality offers white people" (p. 51).

As Edwards grew up in the neighborhood, she and Josephine Lurie remained friends, but with important limitations. They shared their dreams, discussed books they read, and pursued a life of play and shared interests. Although Josephine was a close friend of Thyra's, she did not accept other black children whom she met at Thyra's house, and neither did they accept her. And Josephine did not share Thyra's deeply held determination that blacks should enjoy racial equality. As Thyra recalled, "She wished rather that I could be white. That we could go to the movies together, to the public library, that I could attend the same school (for whites only) instead of the old red brick building passed on to the Negroes after the whites had worn it out" (pp. 51–52).

For Edwards, however, the solution was not an individual but a collective one. "I wanted equality without being white," she emphasized. "I wanted equality so that I could go to the movies with Josephine, so that Negroes—all Negroes—could go to the movies." Years later, Edwards reflected that Josephine Lurie "never wished I were Jewish. But then for practical purposes plain white would have cleared the immediate inconveniences" (p. 52).

A pivotal experience that occurred when Thyra and Josephine were attending their respective, racially segregated high schools made them aware of the racial etiquette that limited their relationship in public spaces outside their immediate neighborhood. Until then, they had never had an occasion to meet outside the neighborhood. Thyra usually walked to school, but one day she hopped on a streetcar to get out of a heavy rain. "At the downtown transfer point Josephine and I boarded the same crosstown car," she recalled. "She was with two white girls and she hurried past me on ahead beyond the movable screen that divided Negro passengers from white, turning her head so that our eyes would not meet" (p. 52).

Thyra was disturbed by the incident, and Josephine came over to her house after school to try to explain. Under the chinaberry tree in the Edwards yard they sat, "groping through the tangled pattern of our environment," Edwards explained years later. From her point of view, Josephine should speak to her no matter where they met. Josephine could not explain what had prompted her to avert her eyes and to avoid speaking to Thyra with her white friends present. "But she felt that I ought somehow to understand," Edwards remembered (p. 52).

Although Thyra cut Josephine little slack over the public snub, an incident just a week later caused Thyra to regret how rough she had been on her. On this occasion, Thyra was walking with some black boys when she spotted Josephine approaching them. "This time it was I who turned my head," she confessed. "To acknowledge Josephine's greeting would suggest to the boys that my mother was her mother's cook or laundress—and my mother didn't work for white folks. That moment I sensed the panic Josephine had felt at exposing this unexplainable friendship. I was sorry I had been so hard" (p. 52).

This time, Josephine was waiting under the chinaberry tree when Thyra got home. Achieving what Thyra called a "partial victory," they hashed things out in an attempt to understand their environment of racial segregation. They agreed that from that point on, they would always greet each other, no matter where they were or no matter the circumstances (pp. 52–53).[33]

Edwards graduated from the Colored Public High School in 1915, but her friendship with Lurie extended beyond high school. At the end of Lurie's first year as a college student, she came to see Edwards with a friend, Dan Kelly, and a copy of *The Liberator*, which at that time was edited by Oswald Garrison Villard. Edwards, who taught in Houston's segregated schools off and on from 1915 through 1919,[34] credited Lurie and particularly Kelly for helping to raise her consciousness on labor issues in political discussions they had on that visit. "It was Dan," she noted, "who channeled our groping toward broader efforts for human freedom into the organized labor movement." One of his remarks, in particular, made a lasting impression on her. She recalled that he argued, "People's salvation lies in broad mass movements of their own, trade union organizations under their own leadership. That's how we shall bring equality about. It won't be a gift from philanthropists and reformers" (p. 53).

As Edwards later reflected on what had engendered her rebellious spirit, she singled out the tyranny and explosive temper of her father, which had caused her to chafe under his authority. She recalled how she and Thelma responded to a stern warning that he gave them on the first day of Thyra's freshman year in high school as they set out on the two-mile walk to school: "'From now on, go & come one route,' my father thundered, & for emphasis turning on his heel as he swung the picket gate outward, 'and don't let me catch you off that route these next 4 years.'"[35]

The sisters soon disobeyed the warning. Part of the walk to and from school took them near "one of the richest & loveliest 'white' residential sections of the town & time." The walk past this section opened their eyes to a world far removed from the material realities of black life in Houston at the time. Little by little, the girls veered off the designated route into the white neighborhood in defiance of their father. "We made a daily game of it," Edwards recalled, "shifting our route a block or two each week until we became thoroughly familiar with the families along the way. . . . we peeped in at their weddings and funerals, watched the society columns for their parties and guests lists & visualized ourselves grown up, perfumed & elegantly gowned—free of the made overs my mother ingeniously salvaged from the barrel of odds and ends grandmother Johnson always sent from 'the North' each Xmas."[36]

The walk to and from school in the context of the warning by Edwards's father became a metaphor for her (as well as Thelma's) later life as an activist. From her father's perspective, the warning was simply good advice from a strict parent aware of the potential dangers for young black girls trying to negotiate the Jim Crow boundaries of a harsh urban setting. For Thelma and Thyra, however, the warning created the feeling that they were in a straitjacket. Veering off the designated route and slipping through the wealthy white neighborhood to dream about enjoying the luxuries and lifestyle of its residents had represented to them "our escape from home life that already at 11 & 13 years seemed oppressive."[37]

During the turbulence of their childhood, comforting images of Grandmother Johnson and her escape from slavery helped to get Thyra and Thelma through the rocky times. In the imaginations of the sisters, the Johnsons' house on Mulberry Street in Galesburg, Illinois, became their Underground Railroad station as they planned their own escape from an oppressive home life. "We would endure thro' High School, then escape to grandmother," explained Edwards. "Here we would work, free of the harsh tyranny of Father and of undisciplined, insolent younger brothers and sisters, and attend one of the two colleges in Galesburg."[38]

Grandmother Johnson's occasional visits to Houston brought a feeling of warm comfort to the family home, at least for Edwards. Although her mother believed that she romanticized and idealized her grandma, the visits did bring certain relief to the children. According to Edwards, her grandmother's visits "seemed to bring an orderly way of living into our careless household. Periods of peace and well being during which meals were regularly and careful planned, mending attended, washing and ironing as a natural routine, one's wet feet were dried and changed immediately one returned from the long rainy day." Most important of all, however, "Father lost his irritability. The heavy razor strap which terrorized our young bodies hung unused. In those brief months home took on stability and security."[39]

Edwards was thirteen when Grandmother Johnson visited Houston for the final time, and her hopes of running away to the safety of the home on Mulberry Street in Galesburg after graduating from high school were soon dashed. By the time she finished high school, her grandmother's "mind had slipped into the past" after the death of her husband. "In my Aunt Fanny's house," Edwards noted, "she took to a bed which she quit only 14 years later to find a place near grandfather in the town cemetery."[40]

When Edwards, as a very fashion-conscious adult with special memories of her grandmother's impeccable style of dress, went to Galesburg for the funeral and saw her body in the casket, she was irritated by a lack of attentiveness on the part of those who had picked out the clothes for her burial. Grandmother Johnson's body was dressed in beige, "machine made, factory draped lace." Edwards "felt helplessly resentful that these sons and daughters couldn't remember how she always loved gray—in fine cashmere, her skirt hung in pleats, evenly swinging pleats; a bit of real lace ending with a fine brooch at her throat."[41]

Financial hard times hit the Edwards family again when Horace, known to some in Houston's black community as a person who was hard to get along with, quit his job at the post office. He then sold real estate for a while. In 1912, Anna applied for a position as librarian of the new Carnegie "colored" library in Houston. She emphasized on the application's questionnaire that she intended to promote the library as a social center with which Houston's black masses would feel closely identified. By then, Thyra and Thelma had three younger siblings; Anna Bell was seven, Marian was about six, and George was just a baby. The fact that Anna had a baby to care for at the time helped convince E. O. (Earnest Ollington) Smith, a black school principal and president of the library's board of trustees, not to hire her. Smith rejected her on grounds that she could not devote full attention to the position. He also cited her "disagreeable husband" as a factor.[42]

Smith's problems with Horace Edwards may have been the product of the latter's "disagreeable" temperament, but as we shall see, there were also sharp political differences between them. As Thyra Edwards's social and political consciousness grew, she began to understand her father in a broader context. More and more, she attributed his moodiness and angry outbursts to his political frustrations over the limited options of black people in the Jim Crow South.[43]

Anna opened a laundry service to help make money, but it collapsed, adding to the financial problems of the family. Thyra, after graduating from the Colored Public High School in 1915, proudly earned her first paycheck when she took a position teaching elementary students at Houston's Langston School, but soon lost the job. Apparently, she tried to go to college at that time, but it did not work out—perhaps because of financial considerations. She returned to teaching, this time at the Colored Public High School, but in 1919 she took a position as a Family Visitor with the Houston Social Service Bureau.

The expansion of social services during World War I helped to shape the careers of both Thyra and Thelma Edwards as social reformers. In 1917, Jennie Covington had founded the Bethlehem Settlement, a black settlement house in Houston operated by the city's Social Service Bureau. The settlement provided a number of services for black working-class women—nursery, kindergarten, self-improvement club, and sewing, cooking, and maid-training classes. Uxenia Scott, a black woman from Houston who had graduated from Fisk University's social work program, returned home to take a position at the Bethlehem Settlement. Thelma, who likewise enrolled in Fisk University's social work program, came back to Houston and served an apprenticeship with Scott while teaching at the Gregory School, later succeeding her in the job at Bethlehem.

Thelma's departure to Fisk University in Nashville after high school graduation no doubt had put additional strain on the family's budget. At some point between 1917 and 1920, the Edwards family faced foreclosure and eviction from their house even though the two oldest daughters were both working. Thyra remained in the household, as did Thelma, who was also employed as a caseworker at Bethlehem. According to the census enumerated on January 12, 1920, they lived with the family in a rented house at 2911 Drew Avenue, still in Houston's Third Ward.

For a young black woman in Houston searching for the connections between labor and civil rights in the era of the First World War, black longshoremen in port cities along the Upper Texas Gulf Coast provided a source of inspiration. It was black longshoremen who in 1913 had organized Houston's first local union, number 872, of the International Longshoremen's Association (ILA), an affiliate of the American Federation of Labor (AFL). Despite the limitations of the AFL's racially segregated unions in the South, biracial unionism empowered black longshoremen and encouraged cooperation between white and black unionists in the interest of common economic objectives. Freeman Everett, one of Local 872's officials, resided on Dowling Street in the Third Ward just a few blocks from where Edwards's family lived. Her ties to Everett and other black longshoremen would shape her political activities for the rest of her life.[44]

World War I exposed deep contradictions in the patterns of racial segregation and provided a context for the political mobilization of Houston's black community. When black soldiers from the Illinois National Guard were stationed at Camp Logan in Houston in 1917, Jim Crow ordinances, harassment by many of the city's white residents, and abusive treatment by local police officers provoked a mutiny. On August 23, 1917, about one hundred black soldiers went on a rampage through the downtown area. They marched into the Fourth Ward, where they killed and wounded a number of police officers and bystanders. Four black soldiers were also killed in the riot. Hasty military tribunals led to the hanging of many of the leaders of this rebellion and life prison sentences for others.[45]

Edwards, whose blood boiled over the conditions that led to the Camp Logan Riot and the swift execution of the black soldiers involved, was a teacher at that time in the Colored Public High School, located in the Fourth Ward, where a lot of the violent clashes between the black soldiers and police took place. In 1923, an editorial in the *Houston Informer* criticized the disgraceful conditions in the high school, calling the building a "rat trap."[46] As a teacher in the only high school for black students at the time in Houston, Edwards witnessed firsthand the inequities in the city's "separate but equal" educational facilities. Black schools suffered from overcrowding, higher pupil-teacher ratios, inadequate state and local funding, and discriminatory allocation of resources. In 1910, salaries for black teachers averaged about 30 percent lower than those for white teachers in Houston's schools.[47]

At the Gregory School, where Thelma started teaching around 1919, conditions were particularly appalling. In early 1920, around the time when the sisters decided they had had enough of teaching in a Jim Crow city, the *Houston Informer* featured a front-page story with photographs of the marshy, unhealthy conditions surrounding the elementary school. Because of backwater from nearby Lake Gregory, children and teachers had to wade through mud and deep standing water to reach the school, even several days after a heavy rain. Parents at times accompanied their children to school to ensure that they did not drown. The newspaper reported that although the school was located inside the city's Fourth Ward, duck hunters used the area for hunting, and receding backwater often left a large number of fish for the taking. Disease and demoralization plagued students and teachers alike at the school. According to the newspaper headline, sickness and even death were all too common: "MORE TEACHERS HAVE DIED OUT OF GREGORY SCHOOL THAN ANY PUBLIC SCHOOL IN HOUSTON."[48]

The Camp Logan Riot shook race relations in the city and created conditions that helped to spark a statewide surge of wartime racial activism in which Edwards and her family participated. An investigator sent by the National Association for the Advancement of Colored People (NAACP) to investigate the Camp Logan Riot reported to Field Secretary James Weldon Johnson that conditions were ripe for the organization of a Houston chapter. Assistant Secretary Walter White, following a recommendation by G. N. T. Gray, of the National Alliance of Postal Employees, contacted M. B. Patten, a black mail agent in Houston, about organizing a chapter of the NAACP in the city.[49]

From the outset, however, factionalism plagued efforts to organize the local NAACP branch. Patten initially tried to enlist the support of E. O. Smith, who several years earlier had declined to hire Edwards's mother as a librarian because of her "disagreeable husband." Smith and a number of other local black leaders had formed the Civic Betterment League (CBL) after the Camp Logan Riot. But Smith showed indifference to the suggestion to create a chapter of the NAACP in Houston. Patten then called a meeting of well-known black leaders. At this meeting, on May 31, 1918, a group of about fifty activists led by Patten, Henry L. Mims, C. F. Richardson, and Edwards's father organized Houston's NAACP chapter and requested a charter. Horace Edwards was on the local executive committee and was selected to be vice president of the chapter. Anna and Thyra Edwards also became charter members.[50]

A dispute arose when Smith and other CBL officers also contacted the national office to request affiliation with the NAACP. They, too, applied for a charter, about a week after the other group had, sending a check for $100 before the national office even had a chance to consider their application. Now having to contend with applications from rival factions, the national office tried to resolve the matter in a diplomatic fashion, urging the factions to meet to reconcile their differences in the name of unity.[51]

There were personality conflicts between Edwards's father and E. O. Smith, but the differences between the rival groups went deeper. Unlike members of Smith's faction, who were more conservative and older, the Edwards group endorsed more militant and confrontational tactics. Moreover, Smith was very closely tied to white administration officials in the city. Henry L. Mims, president of the first Houston NAACP chapter and also president of the National Alliance of Postal Employees, pointed this out in a letter to John Shillady, secretary of the national NAACP: "The officers of our local branch are employed in an independent way and unlike Mr. E.O. Smith of the other faction do not depend for a living upon the city administration. It will be impractical and improbable that Mr. Smith will take any steps to remedy crying evils here of which we justly complain because he cannot antagonize his source of income."[52]

According to G. N. T. Gray, the CBL officers were the source of the problem. He believed that the rank and file of the CBL would gladly join the local NAACP chapter, but that the personal ambitions of Smith and other CBL leaders were driving their request for an NAACP charter. Gray clearly suspected ulterior motives on the part of whoever was financing the CBL's initiative. "It is the concensus [sic] of opinion of the men with whom I talked," he told Walter White, "that if E.O. Smith and his associates are forwarding one hundred dollars, the money is furnished by interests inimical to the aims of the N.A.A.C.P."[53]

In the end, Smith's faction dropped its request for a charter, but factionalism continued to plague Houston's NAACP chapter. Another controversy, in the summer of 1919, swirled around branch secretary C. F. Richardson, a cofounder of the *Houston Observer* who had created the *Houston Informer* that year. Richardson, a militant racial activist who had also belonged to the CBL, resigned his NAACP position amid accusations that he had misappropriated funds. Edwards's father, who had become a business partner in the Informer Publishing Company to launch the *Informer,* headed an auditing committee to investigate the complaints. On June 28, 1919, Horace Edwards, in his capacity as vice president, and acting secretary C. A. Paillet notified the NAACP's national office that Richardson resigned as the result of "housecleaning" in the local chapter. Edwards and Paillet requested a certified list of the local chapter's members, noting that Richardson blamed the national office for the "great discrepancy" between the amount of money he remitted and the number of members in the Houston branch. After Richardson met with a committee, he agreed to pay back $136 to clear up the discrepancy. "We will now make a fresh start," reassured Edwards and Paillet, "and will keep a closer watch over our finances."[54]

The NAACP's factionalism exposed divisions in Houston's black community at a time when Edwards was getting her first taste of racial activism. Those divisions could not have surfaced at a worse time, considering the repressive methods being used by Texas officials and white vigilante groups against the wartime-era labor and civil-rights militancy. As the years ahead would demonstrate, the Camp Logan Riot and race riots in Longview, Texas, and other cities around the nation in the Red Summer of 1919 helped to sow the seeds of rebellion in Edwards.[55]

In 1919, after teaching for nearly four years in the Houston public schools, Edwards took a position with the Houston Social Service Bureau as a family visitor. This position put her on a path toward a career in social work, a path that in 1920 led her and Thelma to leave Texas for Gary, Indiana. Social work and teaching in a northern factory town seemed awfully appealing, compared to their options in Houston. Here was a chance to escape Jim Crow and the blood stains in the streets left by the Camp Logan Riot. She and Thelma set out on a similar career trajectory in teaching and social work. The sisters, now in their early twenties, looked forward to devoting their lives to educating and providing social services to black children in Gary. They also shared a determination to work for better race relations in their community. For Thyra Edwards, moving to Gary as part of the Great Migration to the North seemed an attractive solution to the oppressive conditions she was rebelling against, at least for the time being.[56]

2

Social Work and Racial Uplift in Gary, Indiana

Between 1920 and 1932, Thyra Edwards built a national reputation as a social worker, club woman, speaker, and interracial activist in Gary, Indiana. So, too, did her sister Thelma. Although Thyra did not have the formal education that Thelma had at the time they moved to Gary, she took courses in nearby Chicago, where she established friendships and associations with some of the city's most notable social workers and civic leaders. The onset of the Great Depression, coupled with her growing contacts with black labor leaders in Chicago, her interest in national politics, and her first trip to Europe, helped her to frame labor problems more broadly. In particular, she would emerge from her experiences in Gary with a firmer grasp of the connections between labor, social work, and civil rights.

Thyra's plans in Gary included working on a degree in social work at the Chicago School of Civics and Philanthropy in her spare time. In the summer term, 1920, she studied labor problems, family casework, and child welfare. At the end of the term, however, she joined Thelma in Gary, where both took teaching positions in the public schools. Thyra became the playground director and physical education teacher at the racially segregated Virginia Street School.[1]

Thyra and Thelma arrived in Gary in the bitter aftermath of the failed steel strike of 1919. Gary, an industrial town created in 1906 by the United States

Steel Corporation on the sand dunes along the southern shore of Lake Michigan, was home to a large workforce of southern and eastern European immigrants. Named after the company's anti-union president, Judge Elbert H. Gary, the city had been occupied by 1,500 federal troops in October 1919, when the state militia failed to keep order after clashes between strikers and police. The company's use of black strikebreakers, many of whom were recruited from southern states, inflamed racial tensions during the strike, which troop commander General Leonard Wood blamed on foreign radicals. According to Ruth Needleman's *Black Freedom Fighters in Steel: The Struggle for Democratic Unionism,* however, racial hostility between black and immigrant workers was not a problem until the army, local authorities, and newspapers engaged in race-baiting and red-baiting, thus creating a racially charged atmosphere in Gary.[2]

The city had drawn an increasing number of African Americans in the era of the First World War, owing to the Great Migration and U.S. Steel's recruitment of strikebreakers. There were only 400 black residents in Gary in 1910, but by 1920, the city's black population had surpassed 5,000, comprising about 10 percent of the total number of residents at that point. An especially sharp increase in the number of young people took place. The number of black residents between the ages of six and twenty-one shot up from 267 in 1916 to 1125 in 1920.[3]

The population spike produced a demand for black teachers, creating opportunities for Thyra, Thelma, and others. In 1917, there were only four black teachers in Gary's public schools, but by 1920 the number had grown to sixteen. Thyra and Thelma may have been recruited by E. D. Simpson, a black principal who had recommended hiring A. Velma Strickland, a friend of theirs who had also taught in Houston. Thelma, upon accepting a teaching position in the high school, lived as a boarder with Simpson and his wife shortly after moving to Gary.[4]

The Gary school system, which at that time attracted nationwide attention, was modeled on the progressive philosophy of educator John Dewey. Implementation of the "work, study, and play" educational experiment was largely the work of Superintendent of Schools William Wirt. A student-centered, holistic approach to educating children in an industrial society was the organizing principle of the Gary system. The ideal was to put students of all ages in the same school, from kindergarten through high school; to include manual and industrial work; and to have playgrounds on the premises operated by the schools themselves. Only two of the schools—Emerson and Froebel—had fully implemented this ideal, though, at the time Thyra and Thelma took positions in the district.[5]

Wirt, who extended the progressive educational experiment into the 1920s, had no qualms about creating at least a partly racially segregated system at a time when de facto racial segregation existed in most northern as well as southern schools. He had the backing of William P. Gleason, superintendent of U.S. Steel's Gary Works. For black students, there was often little to distinguish the schools from "separate but equal" facilities in other cities. For example, black elementary students attended all-black schools. The Virginia Street School that employed Edwards had opened in 1919, despite concerns expressed by the local chapter of the NAACP over its segregation. Usually channeled into vocational careers, black students in the Gary system continued to have unequal opportunities for decades after the Great Migration.[6]

As a newcomer to the city and as a product of Houston's segregated schools, though, Edwards was impressed by the progressive features of "the most famous school system in the world." By the mid-1920s, the Gary system employed about fifty black teachers, and black principals were in charge of the two all-black schools. Black students made up one-third of the student population of 3,000 at Froebel School, the largest in Gary. A black woman headed Froebel's night school, which was open to black students two evenings per week. "One delightful feature of the schools," Edwards emphasized, "is that they are open day and evening throughout the year and are the community and recreational centers for both young and old."[7]

Edwards admired the progressive features of her new city of residence, too, particularly the carefully laid out streets designed by the city's civic organizations and the Gary Land Company, a subsidiary of U.S. Steel. Writing in 1925, she praised Gary's industrial transformation: "I am inclined to call Gary the eighth wonder of the world. A barren, uninhabited, and uninhabitable waste of sand dunes and thistles has in twenty years developed into one of the largest industrial centers in America."[8]

Residential patterns in Gary reflected the industrial and ethnic composition of its residents. By the mid-1920s, the city's immigrants represented 56 nationalities, and the population had reached 85,000, including about 12,000 African Americans. The overwhelming majority of men in the city worked in the steel mills, which stretched for about ten miles along the northern fringe of the city. Sandwiched between two exclusive residential districts for U.S. Steel's management employees, other business owners, and professionals was "the South Side," or "the Patch," where enclaves of immigrants and migrants from the South lived. Edwards described housing conditions in the Patch: "The houses are crowded tenements with dark basements opening on darker alleyways where they are rank, four-smelling hovels unfit for human habitation. These are punctuated here and there by neat, attractive, well-kept homes, some very small, a few larger (a sort of silent testimonial, these, to the possibilities of gaining a foothold and getting ahead)."[9]

Although racial conflicts did break out at times in the Patch, housing arrangements put residents in close contact with each other on a daily basis. In other words, the color line was not tightly drawn there at that time. As Edwards pointed out, "Europeans, Negroes, and Mexicans frequently occupy apartments in the same building, the Negroes, perhaps, being the only ones conscious that there is anything unusual in such an arrangement."[10]

The steel strike of 1919, set within a repressive national climate of fear and hatred of immigrants, radicals, Jews, Catholics, and African Americans, had left Gary a badly divided city in the early 1920s. The strike had strained ethnic tensions and exposed the underside of Gary, the so-called model industrial town under the benevolent paternalism of the U.S. Steel Corporation. Competing factions fought for control of city government. While some forces tried to foster racial harmony, more repressive, openly racist currents also ran strong in Gary.[11]

By the early 1920s, the Ku Klux Klan had become a major influence in local and Indiana politics. Opposed to Gary's Republican mayor, Roswell O. Johnson, because of his alleged softness on vice and corruption, the Klan put forth its own slate of candidates in the Republican primary in the election of 1924. Black leaders in Gary backed the anti-Klan Lake County Good Government Club, a white organization. After voters in the primary elected nearly all of the Klan's candidates, a battle ensued for control of the county Republican organization. The Klan lost this battle, but its candidates swept into office in the general election in November of that year anyway.[12]

The rise of the Klan in Gary paralleled the growth of civic initiatives to improve race relations in the city. Edwards, after leaving her teaching position in 1921 to become a probation officer with the Lake County Juvenile Court, became increasingly involved in such initiatives. She developed a network of friendships and associations among white and black civic-minded leaders in the city, including her white supervisor, Judge E. Miles Norton. Thanks to a suggestion made to the City Welfare Association by the director of a social settlement for Europeans in the Patch, Gary's community leaders, backed by the U.S. Steel Corporation, took halting steps to promote racial understanding. For example, churches observed an Interracial Sunday, when black congregations listened to visiting white preachers, and black ministers preached to white congregations.[13]

The YMCA in Gary invited a group of seventy-five community representatives to listen to a black speaker on the subject of church and race relations. Those who attended were among the city's top civic, business, and religious leaders, as well as social workers, teachers, and women's club officers, and included state senator C. O. Holmes, Judge Norton, and Mayor Johnson.[14]

After this successful meeting, Edwards worked with Holmes and other leaders to organize Gary's first Interracial Commission in 1924. Until 1929, in fact, she served as the general secretary of the commission, which consisted of fourteen white and fourteen black members, including four women in each group.

The commission organized interracial forums and encouraged community institutions and agencies to promote racial understanding.[15]

For Edwards, efforts to improve housing for African Americans in Gary were among the most important results of the organization of the commission. Working in tandem, white women's clubs and black women's clubs initiated a housing survey of the Patch. The survey revealed that exorbitant rents for African Americans were completely out of proportion to rents paid by whites and immigrants, even though black housing was of much poorer quality.[16]

Edwards singled out the John Stewart Social Settlement Center as an important symbol of racial cooperation. Frank S. Delaney, a black minister of the Trinity Methodist Church, headed the black settlement house, which had been created shortly after the explosive steel strike of 1919 and was backed by the Methodist Episcopal Church and the Illinois Steel Company, a subsidiary of U.S. Steel. Edwards and other black community leaders served on the settlement house's board of directors.[17]

Although Edwards criticized discriminatory hospital care for African Americans in Gary, she praised interracial initiatives in the municipal government, schools, police force, county juvenile court, and YMCA. From her perspective in the mid-1920s, the interracial milieu of Gary had a bright future. "The coming together of the best white and Negro leaders in group discussions," she wrote, "is bringing about in the Negro's mind a sort of restoration of confidence in the whites and in the minds of the whites an awakened respect for the Negro and the potentialities of Negro leadership."[18]

As Thyra's civic activism increased, she and Thelma put down roots in Gary. In the summer of 1924, Thyra, at age twenty-six, married James Malcolm Garnett, the son of Dr. James H. Garnett, a Baptist minister, and Ida Lee Garnett, a teacher. Thyra worked with her father-in-law on a number of civic projects, but little is known about her husband, who in 1918 had worked at the American Sheet and Tin Mill Company, a U.S. Steel subsidiary in Gary. The marriage lasted barely a year, and it is not known what caused the divorce, but Thyra later made clear that she rejected the socially prescribed role for women in conventional marriages. Thelma, who continued to teach in the public schools, married Dr. Vereen M. Marshall, the city's only black dentist at the time. They, too, became very active in black community life. On August 19, 1924, Thelma gave birth to a son, William, who years later became a well-known Hollywood and Broadway actor.

After taking courses in forensics, contract and agency, social literature, and economics at Chicago's Kent College of Law in 1925, Edwards received a promotion that ended her work as a probation officer. In 1925, she accepted a position as a child-placement agent for the Lake County Board of Children's Guardians. As one of only two child-placement agents for the county board, she still worked under the supervision of Judge E. Miles Norton, with whom she collaborated on a number of social-service projects for black children in Gary.

Edwards's civic involvement included organizing Gary's Business and Professional Women's Club (BPWC). As the club's president, she further strengthened her organizational and leadership skills. Because of her dynamic speaking ability, she was in high demand at community, regional, and national forums on economic, social, and women's issues. In 1927, for example, she gave a speech titled "What the Negro Woman Who Buys Expects of the Man Who Sells" at a conference of the National Negro Business League in St. Louis. A reporter who covered the conference for a prominent national black newspaper singled her out for praise as one of the "rarest treats" of the conference.[19]

The National Negro Business League held its functions in St. Louis on the campus of Poro College, founded by Annie Malone, a black pioneer entrepreneur with whom Edwards developed a friendship. Not only did Poro College house offices and manufacturing operations for Malone's hair-care products for black women, it also trained black women in cosmetology and sales and promoted a positive self-image as the key to racial uplift. Poro also served as a community center for a number of civic and religious activities. Malone, a philanthropist, donated money to a number of projects in St. Louis, including an orphan's home for black children.[20]

As a frequent dinner guest of Malone's, Edwards extended her contacts with other prominent black figures in Chicago and beyond. In late 1929, for example, she met the great contralto Marian Anderson, who stopped by Malone's home while Edwards was there. The friendship between Edwards and Malone grew stronger after Malone moved her business operations to Chicago in 1930, and Edwards became a frequent visitor to Malone's South Parkway home after moving to Chicago in late 1931.[21]

Edwards also enjoyed an important network of friends and professional associations among activist social workers in Chicago. One of the most important of these activists was Helen Castle Mead, who had been a suffragist and was a proponent of labor and black welfare reform. Known for her lack of racial prejudice, she was a good friend of Jane Addams's and John Dewey's. Mead, who died on December 25, 1929, was married to George Herbert Mead, a prominent pragmatist philosopher, social psychologist, and sociologist at the University of Chicago.[22]

Through Helen Mead, Edwards met and enjoyed a close personal friendship with Mary McDowell, another distinguished Chicago social activist, sometimes known as the "Angel of the Stockyards." Mead introduced them in Chicago at the Hotel Prado. Until her retirement in 1929, McDowell headed the University of Chicago Settlement, which was a vehicle for her to promote trade unionism, safer working conditions, municipal reforms, and racial harmony. In the early

1890s, she had lived and worked with Jane Addams at Hull House. McDowell was an instrumental figure in the Women's Trade Union League, the Woman's Christian Temperance Union, and the woman's suffrage movement. After Chicago's race riot of 1919, she especially had devoted much of her time to interracial initiatives.[23]

Among Edwards's activities in Gary that were of special interest to McDowell and Mead was the creation of a home for black orphan children. Edwards had laid the groundwork for a children's home in her capacity as child-placement agent and president of the BPWC. In early 1927, she publicized the upcoming opening of the home at a seminar hosted by the Social Workers Round Table, whose president was Zelma Watson, a black, Texas-born social worker and probation officer with the juvenile court in Chicago.[24]

The seminar, held at the Bowen Country Club on the shore of Lake Michigan in Waukegan, Illinois, featured Edwards, sociologist E. Franklin Frazier, attorney Edith S. Sampson, and others as speakers. Edwards pointed out that the children's home was the product of work by club women, civic workers, and county officials. The county had set aside $30,000 for salaries and the purchase of an eighteen-room building near a school and a church. As a reporter for the *Chicago Defender* noted, the facility "will be made as homelike as possible, with nothing suggestive of an institution."[25]

When the Lake County Children's Home opened on December 19, 1927, Edwards presided over the ceremonies, which included a speech by Mary McDowell. Among the speakers, too, was Judge E. Miles Norton, who had played an important role in the founding of the home. Thelma and Vereen Marshall donated a bust of Haitian revolutionary leader Touissant L'Overture to the home. The bust was the work of sculptor Richard Barthé, who had been commissioned by Edwards on behalf of the Marshalls to sculpt it for the new children's home.[26]

In April 1928, 250 guests attended a ceremonial unveiling of the bust of L'Overture and one of Henry O. Tanner, a distinguished black painter. The bust of Tanner, which was also sculpted by Barthé for the new children's home, was the gift of Reverend R. D. and Ida Guy, who were civic-minded members of Gary's black middle-class community. Hosted by Edwards and the BPWC, the ceremony again featured Judge Norton as speaker. He expressed hope that the children's home might become an important center of community life.[27]

Under Edwards's leadership, the children's home got off to a good start. From 1928 to 1931, she was its director. Within the first year of its operation, fifty children had lived in the home, which offered a less institutional living arrangement for black orphans.[28]

Edwards was active in several of Gary's civic organizations, serving as secretary of the Community Council and first vice president of the City Welfare

Association. In November 1928, she was elected vice president of the Gary Council of Social Agencies. As an activist on the YWCA's interracial committee, she also continued efforts to promote better race relations. She cultivated friendships with officials such as Doris Wooten, the YWCA's executive secretary in Cincinnati who in a couple of years would marry Carter Wesley, editor of the *Houston Informer*.

Edwards also helped plan events to celebrate black history in Gary. Annually beginning in 1930, the city's Noonday Business Club, led by Dr. Charles Wood, its president, held ceremonies to commemorate the anniversary of the Emancipation Proclamation. At the first celebration, it was Edwards who read the Proclamation. A community council was formed after the first year's celebration, and she served on the executive committee to plan the program for the celebration on January 1, 1931.[29]

As a representative of Gary's interracial committee, Edwards also traveled to publicize and promote its work. In November 1930, for example, she toured a number of southern states, visiting black schools and other institutions. The tour took her to the cities of Atlanta; Washington, DC; Greensboro, North Carolina; Tuskegee; Talladega; Montgomery; and Nashville. She was a guest at Fisk University, where she attended dedication ceremonies for a new library.[30]

On that same trip, Edwards went to New York City and stayed at the International House as a guest of Anna Cooke's. Edwards fell in love with the city. Cooke bought tickets for them to see *The Green Pastures*, a new Broadway production that won a Pulitzer Prize for Drama. *The Green Pastures* was written by Marc Connelly, a white playwright, but it featured the first all-black cast on Broadway, starring Richard Harrison as "de Lawd." The drama retold biblical episodes from the Old Testament set within a black context in the city of New Orleans. Despite certain criticisms, Edwards wrote a mostly favorable review of the play, which centers around a young black girl who interprets the Bible based on her experiences. The play reminded Edwards of her own religious upbringing as a child in Texas.[31]

Edwards's stature as a social worker grew in national circles. Through the National Conference of Social Work, she broadened her contacts and friendships with colleagues from all around the country, including E. Franklin Frazier, Eugene Kinckle Jones (executive director of the National Urban League), and T. Arnold Hill, who headed the National Urban League's Department of Industrial Relations. By 1928, Edwards had become "one of the most widely known social workers in the country."[32]

Edwards's intellectual horizons expanded when she took her first trip abroad in 1929. Joined by Jewel Herbert, a white friend from Houston, she sailed for London in late summer of 1929. They visited Stratford-upon-Avon, Oxford, and other important sites, linking up with a number of African Americans in

London, including the very wealthy editor of the *Chicago Defender,* Robert S. Abbott, and his wife, Helen. Edwards and Herbert attended a send-off party for the Abbotts, who were about to leave for France, Italy, Austria, and Spain. Among those at the party was Ivan H. Browning, a singer with the Four Harmony Kings who recorded in Europe and the United States and appeared in the Broadway production of *Chocolate Dandies* in 1924.[33]

The European trip helped Edwards frame her understanding of racism more broadly. As she learned, the Abbotts were furious when they left England because of the racism they had encountered at hotels there. Helen could "pass" as white, but Robert was very black. Although they had reservations at the upscale Savoy Hotel, they were turned away because of skin color when they tried to check in. After that, Robert often sat in the car while Helen went into other hotels to take care of the registration, but every time he tried to go past the desk to accompany her to the room, he was stopped and denied admission. After the Abbotts were turned away at thirty hotels, Louis Drysdale, a black, Jamaican-born singer, offered them accommodations and hosted the farewell party that Edwards and Herbert attended.[34]

The extensive trip took Edwards to the main cities and capitals of other European nations, too. Included on the itinerary was a visit to the Tomb of the Unknown Soldier under the monument of the Arc de Triomphe in Paris. Of special concern to Edwards was the ugly presence of bitter nationalist rivalries that were part of the legacy of the First World War. "Travelling through the countries of Europe with all its horror, destruction and human wastage looms forth more terrible than America realizes," she observed. "The feeling between one country and another is more or less tense and peace—world peace is yet an ideal to be sought carefully courted but not yet won."[35]

By the time Edwards's ship returned to New York from Le Havre, France, in late November 1929, the stock market had crashed. When the Great Depression deepened in the early years of President Herbert Hoover's administration, Edwards's intellectual interests and activism turned increasingly to matters of labor and unemployment caused by the collapse of the world economy. At the request of the Chicago Urban League, she filed a report on the need for vocational training of black workers in Gary. She pointed out that the Great Migration had changed the composition of the unskilled industrial workforce in Gary. Even in normal times, she stressed, African Americans in Gary received about 55 percent of charity funds for the poor. In the context of the economic depression, black unskilled workers were the most vulnerable, the first to be fired and the last to be hired. In her report, Edwards called attention to the tendency of employers to replace black workers with machines, and she pointed out the color bar against black workers in many trade unions. All in all, she concluded, "The Negro remains involuntarily a marginal worker."[36]

Near the end of 1931, Edwards resigned her position as director of the Lake County Children's Home to accept a job as caseworker with the Joint Emergency Relief Commission in Chicago. Her sister Thelma Marshall replaced her as director of the children's home, which has since been renamed the Thelma Marshall Children's Home. While teaching at the high school in Gary, Thelma had taken additional courses in social work training at the Chicago School of Civics and Philanthropy.[37]

Despite Edwards's enthusiastic civic activism, her years in Gary had stripped her of illusions about living in the North. She had seen how the economic depression of 1921 and the early years of the Great Depression had devastated working-class families, especially black ones, in a northern industrial setting. She had also discovered that the reach of the Ku Klux Klan was not limited to the South. Notwithstanding her important role in interracial initiatives, the lines of racial segregation in Gary had become but more tightly drawn during the eleven years she lived there. In a critical reflection on her own participation in such initiatives, she later observed sarcastically: "We played childish games, ate rich cakes, tea and jelly and tried to be just awfully nice to each other. Having no common base of interest we had no real conversation—but we chatted and smiled and it might have been Gary, Ind., or Chicago or Cleveland or any one of a number of Race Relations fiascos of which I've been guilty."[38]

By the time Edwards moved to Chicago, she was also ready to reject employer paternalism as a strategy for uplifting the black masses. Her civic activities in Gary had taken place under the long shadow of the U.S. Steel Corporation, the bastion of anti-unionism whose paternalism underlay or at least shaped nearly every institution and initiative in the community. After a decade in which big business and its political allies had nearly decimated organized labor through the Open Shop movement and company paternalism, Edwards had become much more critical of corporations. She had also become more critical of middle-class black leaders who urged black workers to rely on employers rather than unions to protect their interests.

During Thyra Edwards's years in Gary, several significant changes took place in her family. Her grandmother Johnson, with whom she closely identified in so many ways, died in Galesburg, Illinois, in December 1928. Her sister Anna Bell, a teacher who had also moved from Houston to Chicago, in 1930 took a teaching job in Shreveport, Louisiana, where she then married. The marriage of Thyra's parents ended, her father moving to Phoenix, Arizona, where he worked as a real estate agent, and her mother remaining in Houston, where she taught in the segregated public schools. At the time of the 1930 federal census, Thyra's brother, George, was still living at home and attending college, and her mother still employed a black live-in maid.[39]

At the time of Edwards's move to Chicago, she still had not found her political identity. For her, Gary at first was a notable improvement over Jim Crow

Houston, but in time she rebelled against conditions of white paternalism and racial and class exploitation in Gary, too. She left behind an important legacy of social work but was cynical about her own involvement in superficial inter-racial initiatives. Living in Chicago would soon transform her political consciousness. As she dug deeper to find the roots of class and racial exploitation, she would join a community of militant black activists who pushed for civil rights and trade unionism. Her immersion in social work and the politics of labor and civil rights in depression-era Chicago would lead to a radical intellectual awakening.

3

Getting a Labor Education in
Illinois, New York, and Denmark

After moving to the South Side of Chicago in late 1931, Edwards continued her vocation as a social worker but stepped up her labor activism in the community. In the context of the deepening global economic crisis, she gained increasing exposure to radical politics. A growing commitment to labor education soon led her to attend a labor college in New York, and her search for answers to the problems of oppression, exploitation, and militarism then took her abroad for an extended period of study in Denmark.

Edwards worked as a caseworker for the Joint Emergency Relief Commission in Chicago and lived at the Abraham Lincoln Centre, an interracial settlement house that had been created in 1905 by the Unitarian All Souls Church. Headed by Dean Curtis W. Reese, its white director beginning in 1930, the settlement house at 700 Oakwood Boulevard featured a racially integrated staff with activities and social events promoting broad community participation in a city deeply split along lines of race and class. Coworkers and staff at the important cultural and social center became part of Edwards's extended family for the next several years.[1]

One of the most important activist organizations with which Edwards became connected in Chicago was the Brotherhood of Sleeping Car Porters (BSCP). The all-black BSCP promoted an aggressive civil-rights unionism, drawing strong support from the city's black activists, who were increasingly militant in the 1930s. Through her activities at the Lincoln Centre, she formed a relationship with the BSCP's Citizens' Committee and leaders of Chicago's South Parkway YWCA. She also developed a very close relationship with the BSCP's Socialist president, A. Philip Randolph, who for several years was her mentor and was likely her clandestine lover in an extramarital relationship. She also worked with Milton P. Webster, the more conservative vice president of the BSCP in Chicago.[2]

Thanks to Randolph, Edwards received a BSCP scholarship to attend Brookwood Labor College in Katonah, New York. In October 1932, she packed her bags and headed off to the residential labor college founded in 1921 by radical intellectuals devoted to adult education as a tool for strengthening class consciousness and militancy in the labor movement. Brookwood was located on a fifty-three-acre site that included a large colonial farmhouse on a hill slope and dormitories for students. Edwards praised worker education as "the primary tool for securing freedom and training leadership." She complained that "conventional schools ignore that part of current history which really matters."[3]

Edwards and two other black people—Edith Turner and Benjamin McLaurin—were among forty students who lived, studied, and worked together at the college during the term that was scheduled to extend from October to May. Brookwood often hosted conferences on, or in other ways called attention to, the special problems of black workers. Turner was a domestic worker from Indianapolis formerly associated with the YWCA, and McLaurin was a representative of the BSCP who was born in Florida but had moved to Chicago in the mid-1920s. Some of the students were unemployed miners from West Virginia, and some were poor white workers from depressed textile-manufacturing areas in South Carolina. A steelworker from Sweden and a teacher from Norway were also among Edwards's fellow students. So was Zilla Hawes, a graduate of Vassar who had worked as an organizer in Pennsylvania's hosiery mills.[4]

At Brookwood, Edwards received a broad, intellectually stimulating education in the social sciences and humanities. She studied economics and labor history with David Saposs, as well as British labor history with Mark Starr, a former member of the British Labour Party. She also received training from Josephine "Polly" Colby in public speaking and from Helen Norton in journalism. She studied the economic history of Europe and the United States with A. J. Muste, Brookwood's founding director and head of the faculty association. John Dewey visited the campus on weekends, and Anna Louise Strong, an American journalist/activist who had written extensively on China and the Soviet Union, was a frequent visitor between trips to those countries.[5]

Edwards flourished in Brookwood's non-hierarchical structure and residential setting. She and other students sang together, formed theater groups, ate together, and forged bonds of community. On Saturday nights they lampooned President Herbert Hoover in political skits as the election of 1932 approached. During the earliest days of Franklin D. Roosevelt's presidency, they studied proposed New Deal legislation and shared concerns over the rise of fascism in Europe. As Edwards later recalled, she taught one of the students, Bill Baruch, a Russian Jewish fur worker, to read English "while he taught me what to read."[6]

Despite support from several AFL-affiliated unions, Brookwood had a shaky relationship with national AFL officials because of the school's explicit commitment to socialism. In 1928, AFL president William Green, after a secret investigation, had ordered the organization's affiliated unions to sever ties with the school. The withdrawal of union financial support forced Brookwood to rely more heavily on individual benefactors, and the public attack by the AFL drove a wedge between radical and liberal elements on the faculty.[7]

In March 1933, an open split occurred between Muste and more conservative forces on the board of trustees and faculty. Muste, a Christian pacifist at the time he became director of the faculty association in 1921, had moved to the left by the early thirties. Frustrated with evolutionary socialism as well as the conservative policies of the AFL, he moved away from pacifism and embraced the revolutionary doctrines of Marxism. Brookwood's board of trustees criticized his political activities, including his role in founding the Conference for Progressive Labor Action (CPLA) in 1929. The CPLA, which was set up to foster industrial unionism in the AFL, became the anti-Stalinist American Workers Party in 1933, critical of the AFL as well as the Communist Party.[8]

Brookwood's trustees also criticized Tom Tippett, its director of progressive-education extension programs. Tippett, who had worked as a miner in southern Illinois, shared Muste's commitment to conduct field activities to support labor struggles. Tippett had authored a recent book on strikes in the southern textile industry, as well as a novel and a play based on his experiences as a miner. In 1932, the Brookwood Players had done a nine-day tour performing his play *Mill Shadows: A Labor Drama in Four Acts*. Tippett had written the play to dramatize the textile strike of 1929 in Marion, North Carolina. Through his extensive travels north and south, he also helped to infuse the labor movement with folk music as an important cultural expression.[9]

On March 5, when Muste and Tippett resigned their positions and severed ties with Brookwood, the three black students joined many of the white students and administrative staff who ended their stay at the labor college. Although the school term extended to May 1, Edwards, Turner, and McLaurin walked out in support of Muste and Tippett. They did so not only because of their vision of progressive education, but also because of their progressive racial philosophy. At issue were the racist practices of white unions affiliated with the AFL. "Muste stands square on the race question," Edwards insisted. "His position is that all race lines and race discrimination must be wiped out in trade unions, political organizations and in our entire economic and social life. On this score he refused to compromise."[10]

Edwards criticized those who had played a role in forcing Muste and Tippett out of Brookwood. She singled out Mark Starr, noting that "it was Starr who last year jim-crowed the one Negro student traveling and playing with the Brookwood Players." Muste had reprimanded Starr after complaints by white students who opposed racial discrimination. Edwards also put the finger on J. C. Kennedy, the acting director and Muste's successor, who, she complained, was "inclined to compromise" when it came to union racial practices. "He concedes to opponents of the Negro," she emphasized, "that the Negro must build up his living standards to the level of those of the white worker before insisting on admission to white unions. This position is unsound since the Negro is a marginal worker and will be forced to remain so as long as white unions exclude him."[11]

For Edwards, the developments at Brookwood represented a step backward in terms of the school's reputation for progressive racial policies. Until Muste's departure, black students had made significant strides on the campus. One black student served as a student representative on the board of directors, and another was unanimously elected secretary of the student body organization. As noted by the *Gary American,* a black newspaper in Edwards's former city of residence, Gary, Indiana, "Brookwood has in years past stood firmly for equality and fraternity in all activities. . . . Insurgent students are fearful lest Brookwood's old spirit of unity and fraternity may be modified."[12]

When the story first broke about the controversy at Brookwood, the *Gary American* published an article from a news service that featured a picture of Edwards with the caption "On the Fence." According to the article, Edwards was "maintaining a neutral attitude" in the dispute. Furious because of the newspaper's mischaracterization of her position, she whipped off a letter to the *American* expressing indignation over the story. "At no time in my life have I been hesitant, undecided, or even neutral on any vital issue," she insisted. "And I have never been afraid to express my honest opinion whoever might disagree. I know of no more serious indictment against one's courage than the charge of fence-straddling."[13]

In the letter, Edwards emphasized her support for Muste and Tippett in the dispute. She also reproduced a letter from Muste in which he thanked her for "the militant and courageous stand you took on the Brookwood controversy."

Already back at work in Chicago on April 1, she called attention to the consistent opposition of Muste and Tippett to racial discrimination "educationally, economically or in any way whatsoever. My support is openly with any man who takes this position."[14]

Despite the circumstances surrounding Edwards's departure from Brookwood, immersion in progressive labor education had a big impact on her. The experience gave her a deeper exposure to Marxist philosophy and factional disputes on the left, and put her in contact with progressive labor elements critical of the racial limitations of the AFL. She was drawn to Muste's firm stance against racism and his independent, anti-Stalinist Marxism. Brookwood's residential living structure encouraged an egalitarian outlook among students and between students and faculty. Overall, as Thyra emphasized several years later, the experience gave her a more global understanding of race: "Ever since I have felt a kinship with national affairs. I have been able to approach the Negro problem in its world relationship—the only valid approach to any socio-economic-political issue."[15]

Upon leaving Brookwood, Edwards went with Tippett to the mining areas of southern Illinois, where on his recommendation she spent three weeks as an organizer in March 1933 before returning to her job in Chicago. At that time, the insurgent Progressive Miners of America (PMA) was in a bitter struggle against the Peabody Coal Company as well as the rival United Mineworkers of America. Edwards joined Agnes Burns Wieck, a labor organizer who headed the militant Women's Auxiliary of the PMA, in an attempt to strengthen interracial unionism in the coal fields. Wieck, who had received training in a program sponsored by the Women's Trade Union League in Chicago, later recalled, "I sent for Thyra to help among the womenfolk of the Negro miners."[16]

Although the PMA was progressive on racial issues, racial segregation in southern Illinois schools, churches, and restaurants was firmly entrenched. Edwards, Wieck remembered, "had landed in St. Louis from the east, without having eaten a bite. All along her trip she had been told she could eat in the kitchen, which she would not." Furthermore, Wieck added, "When she and I took the bus south, a white woman and a colored woman traveling together had been unheard of."[17]

When Edwards and Wieck got off the bus at the station in Du Quoin, Illinois, they asked a black man walking through the waiting room if he knew how to get to the home of Katie de Rorre, an Italian immigrant and militant activist in the Women's Auxiliary of the PMA. He took them to the house, but Rorre was not at home. Her husband, Joe, invited them in and made supper for them. Also in the house were John Batuello, Pat Ansboury, Joe Burrell, Ray Tambozzi, and other members of the PMA. Joe de Rorre explained to Edwards that his wife was very busy with the movement: "She can express herself better than I can so I'm glad to have her go."[18]

Not until eight o'clock the next morning did Edwards meet Rorre, who did not get home until two in the morning because she was attending meetings in nearby coal towns. By that time, Rorre had already seen her two daughters off to school and cleaned house. She fixed breakfast for Edwards before hurrying off to run an errand. "I was so tickled and surprised to see Mrs. Wieck and glad when she told me she had brought me company," Rorre told Edwards, "so I stopped and bought you some candy."[19]

As Edwards remembered the day, "I had come to southern Illinois to acquaint myself with the present mine war and particularly to see what part Negro miners are playing in the struggle and how they might be effective—and affected. And so I was eager to talk to Negro miners." When Rorre returned from her errand, she brought with her two black men who were militants in the PMA. In a short while, other black miners filled her dining room to discuss PMA issues over lunch. Edwards told Rorre that she would also like to talk to the miners' wives, and when Edwards returned from giving a speech at the miners' hall in nearby Dowell, she found Rorre's front parlor overflowing with the wives of black miners.[20]

At first the black women were polite as they greeted Edwards but held back when they were invited to move to the dining room table for coffee. As Wieck explained, "They never dreamed that they were to sit down at Katie's big table, and when Katie announced that we were all to have coffee, they didn't move from their chairs in the livingroom. Katie quickly sensed it and told them, 'Come on in, all of you and sit down, there's no white folks and colored folks here, we're all just folks' and then they fitted into the new pattern."[21]

At Edwards's request, Rorre arranged for her to speak to a racially integrated general meeting of miners and their wives. That very night, Edwards spoke to seven or eight hundred black and white miners and their wives, squeezed into a local PMA headquarters. After that, racially integrated entertainment and women's and children's programs were held frequently at the union hall. After Rorre converted an old vacant house into a soup kitchen to benefit mining families on strike, the Women's Auxiliary raised money and secured donations from local grocers. Rorre visited black and white schools to make clear that all children, black or white, were welcome to hot meals there at noon.

When Edwards and Wieck visited the soup kitchen, where about 150 children hungrily gulped down their lunch daily, they were thrilled at the sight of black and white children eating together. "Such a thing had never happened in that region before," Wieck gushed. "No Jim Crow rows, no Jim Crow tables, just a lot of children eating together, perfectly natural, as though it were not a new experience." Seeing lunch at the children's soup kitchen, coupled with her other experiences during her three-week stint with the miners, left an encouraging impression on Edwards. "Throughout the coal regions of Illinois," she wrote for a mining publication, "you will find such great spirits as ready with their cash as with their coffee—and with their lives if need be—in this threefold fight against the old union, the operator and the machine."[22]

By April 1933, Edwards was back on the job in Chicago as a caseworker for the Illinois Emergency Relief Commission, which had replaced the Joint Emergency Relief Commission when the latter collapsed because of depleted funds, and she became more deeply involved in radical politics. At that time, the BSCP was asserting a more active role in community networks to fight for economic and racial justice. From the Communist-led Unemployed Council to the BSCP's Citizens' Committee and the YWCA, the BSCP worked with other organizations in coalitions that emphasized militancy and rejected white paternalism. Beginning in 1931, the influence of the Communist Party grew in these networks in Chicago because of its militant support for civil rights, its aggressive recruitment of African Americans, and its political flexibility that anticipated the coming of the left-liberal Popular Front strategy in 1935.[23]

In early June 1933, Edwards was among those who formed the Chicago Scottsboro Action Committee to raise public awareness and money for legal appeals and new trials in the case of nine black teenage boys in Alabama falsely accused of gang-raping two white girls on a Southern Railroad freight train on March 25, 1931. Through the International Labor Defense (ILD), the Communist Party had taken the lead for the past two years in whipping up support for the accused. The NAACP, in contrast, had held back at first, fearful of being tainted in the case. As a result, the organization lost influence in Chicago, but it eventually joined an uneasy coalition with the ILD and other civil-rights groups. Edwards joined Dr. Curtis Reese, of the Lincoln Centre, Edith Spurlock Sampson, a black attorney and probation officer, Melville Herskovits, an anthropology professor at Northwestern University, and several others on the Chicago committee. Robert Morss Lovett, an English professor at the University of Chicago and editor of the *New Republic,* headed the committee, which worked with the National Scottsboro Action Committee to develop a strategy for financing the numerous appeals and retrials of the case.[24]

Around the same time that summer, Edwards drew on her experiences in Gary to organize an Interracial Group at the Lincoln Centre. In doing so, she brought together activists from different organizations with diverse ideological viewpoints to address problems of racism and discrimination in housing, restaurants, and other public facilities. Attracting liberal activists such as A. L. Foster, of the Chicago Urban League, as well as young Communists and members of the BSCP Citizens' Committee, the Interracial Group reflected Edwards's ability to forge coalitions among diverse groups.[25]

Shortly after Edwards formed the Interracial Group and joined the Chicago Scottsboro Action Committee, however, she took advantage of a new opportunity for study that would build on her Brookwood experiences and satisfy her appetite for a more global labor education. Thanks again to the influence of A. Philip Randolph and a scholarship provided by the AFL, she set sail on October 1, 1933, for Elsinore, Denmark, to attend the International People's College for six months. Founded by Peter Manniche in 1921, the college was a folk high school designed to promote cooperative movements and international peace. Edwards's course of study would include Scandinavian literature, sociology, anthropology, and Danish social insurance, labor problems, folk schools, and co-operatives.[26]

Edwards began her long trip by sailing to Plymouth, England, then taking a train to London, where she spent ten days observing the political scene and gathering material for a series of articles she would write as a freelance journalist. When she landed at Plymouth, a letter awaited her from Paul Goldberg, a friend of Chicago black sociologist Dr. Horace Cayton Jr.'s, suggesting that she call him when she reached London. Goldberg, an economist and graduate of Oxford University who had studied trade unions in the United States, worked in the section of the British Ministry of Labour that oversaw the administration of unemployment insurance and health benefits. He also taught night classes for the Workers' Education Association in Reading. His wife, Ruby, was also a Labor Party activist.[27]

After spending a couple of nights with the Goldbergs discussing a range of topics, including the Scottsboro case, National Recovery Administration, NAACP, British African colonial subjects, and the state of international affairs, Edwards accepted an invitation from John Fletcher to visit the Quaker Society of Friends House. She and Fletcher discussed the lectures that she would deliver upon her return from Oxford, which she planned to visit in a few days. Arrangements had been made for her to stay at the International Hostel of the YWCA with a lot of other foreign students.[28]

Unlike on her first trip to England four years earlier, Edwards filled her schedule with activities designed to help her better understand contemporary affairs. "My previous visit to England," she explained, "was a romantic, luxurious pilgrimage concerned and absorbed entirely with the antique—nothing later than Queen Elizabeth. It was lovely, but totally oblivious to contemporary life." Edwards met an Englishwoman who had studied at the International People's College as well as Stella Thomas, a Nigerian founding member of the League of Coloured Peoples in England, who had recently become the first African to be admitted to the British Bar. Also among those she met in England was Nancy Cunard, an English writer who had published an anthology of poems, fiction, and nonfiction primarily by African American authors, among them Langston Hughes. Cunard, who while living in Paris had had a romantic relationship with Henry Crowder, an African American jazz musician, was a radical political activist with a special interest in American civil-rights and anti-colonial movements.[29]

The Goldbergs arranged for Edwards to meet Jyoti Ghosh, a young Indian man who spent a great deal of time visiting them in London. A Hindu scholar at Oxford University, Ghosh was a radical literary figure who would soon become associated with the Progressive Writers Association and its opposition to British colonialism in India. Edwards was not eager to meet him, in spite of their apparent common interests. She confessed that she had "some misgivings," based on previous sporadic contacts with Hindus in the United States. "Their unbending iciness to Negroes," she stressed, "contrasted with the graciousness I had seen them exhibit at the same time to white Americans. . . . I had always felt that the tendency of the Hindu in America was to identify himself with the white man and he felt it accordingly a sharp necessity to shun the Negro even more assiduously than the American white man, who is on surer ground being at home with race predjudice [sic]."[30]

Despite Edwards's misgivings, she and Ghosh hit things off very well as they discussed literature, political theories, art, and race issues. He took her to Oxford University's Rewley House to meet the executive secretary of the Workers Education Association. Through Ghosh, she met a number of Indian students who complained that the British educational system instilled a sense of inferiority in its colonial subjects. There were also pro-British elements among them, whom Edwards compared to "Uncle Toms" and "Good Darkies" at home. They were the ones usually chosen for teaching positions back in India. Edwards lined up with the students who were outspoken in their opposition to British colonialism, "our 'uppity and troublesome' types," as she referred to them sardonically.[31]

Also of special interest to Edwards was the plight of blacks in England. Based on an interview with attorney Stella Thomas for an article that she was writing, and based on her contacts with other black people in England, she observed two, divided camps in the black population there. The League of Coloured Peoples, headed by the magnetic West Indian Dr. Harold Moody, was a conservative-leaning organization that followed along the lines of Booker T. Washington's philosophy in the United States. Moody emphasized the need for culture and refinement among blacks to win the respect of whites. He did not believe the time was yet ripe for economic and political mobilization. "What constituted ripeness of time," Edwards wrote cynically, "he never quite cleared up for me." In contrast, she favored the activist faction that was "openly and intensely interested in shaking the British heel off the necks of the natives."[32]

When Edwards sailed for Copenhagen, Denmark, she did so "on the roughest sea imaginable." The voyage took twenty-five hours because the ship had to cross the numerous straits and sounds around Denmark's tiny islands. After getting "tossed about" on "a tiny little Danish motor ship," she then had to lug her three huge bags and a typewriter on and off trains, "hobbling for blocks to the ferry." It was late at night, and so no porter service was available, but an occasional stranger helped her with her bags. Unable to speak Danish, she eventually figured out that the French agent who booked her trip had failed to reserve a seat for her on a train to Elsinore. After she secured a seat on a train at last, she discovered that one of the tutors from the International People's College was sitting in the seat right behind her. When they arrived in Elsinore on October 28, he carried her bags off the train for her and put her in a taxi to the school.[33]

Arriving on campus a week before classes were to start, Edwards settled comfortably into her room and met a few of the faculty before the rest of the students—mostly Danes and Germans—showed up. She took advantage of the week to catch up on sleep, reading, correspondence, and other writing. She dreaded the arrival of a roommate. "I have listened each day nervously," she wrote to friends, "lest my sanctum be disturbed by the intrusion of another personality. I so like a room alone."[34]

With her characteristic eye for vivid detail and her literary flair, Edwards described in a letter to friends the night her roommate arrived. When she answered a sharp rap on the door that night, she observed "a great, long limbed creature in sandals, gray woolen anklets, a tight fitting very short gray skirt, a sprightly embroidered gray sweater, a tiny crocheted cap at the back of her close cropped head, and evenly tanned and sunburned a neat brown." Her roommate, Emilie Ostergaard, was a Danish Communist who did not speak English. As Edwards recounted the meeting, "She sprung into the room and began pumping my hand up and down, up and down exclaiming yah, yah! Yah, yah! quite gleefully."[35]

As Ostergaard's boyfriend helped to carry her trunk and bags into the room, Edwards quickly emptied one-half of the wardrobe to make room for her roommates' clothes, and then went out for tea. When she returned, she found one of the walls "brilliantly plastered with gay Soviet wall newspapers picturing the overthrow of the dishonest priesthood and the progress of collective farms & in factories." Also on the wall was a hanging that depicted Russian youth dancing to accordions and balalaikas. Ostergaard was also a painter and an embroiderer. "Somehow she seems to me symbolic of Communist youth in its native setting—not the transplanted and artificially forced type of thing we see so often," Edwards told friends.[36]

Both Edwards and Ostergaard were studying German, but Edwards was happy about the language barrier between them. "We grin at each other occassionally [sic] as a gesture of friendly feeling," Edwards noted, but the language barrier protected her privacy and gave her more time for self-reflection, study, and writing. "Since it is a physical impossibility to have a room alone with the school so crowded I am blessed with a creature who cannot speak English."[37]

There were 5 Americans among the 10 female and 168 male students on campus, as well as 2 faculty members from the United States. Rebecca Chalmers Barton taught Negro and Proletarian Literature, and John Barton, her husband, who would later become chair of the Department of Rural Sociology at the University of Wisconsin, taught classes in the social sciences. Edwards described both of them as "splendid." Rebecca, who had written her dissertation on Negro Literature under the supervision of a professor at a German university, was disturbed that her adviser might lose his job under Hitler's regime. Her revised dissertation was pending publication at the time. Edwards praised her course, which she found "important because, while I find little predjudice [*sic*] in Europe and least of all in the Scandinavian countries I do find that the American Press has done a thorough job of convincing the world that the American Negro is an irresponsible clown and a buffoon."[38]

When Edwards had been planning her course of study at the International People's College, she was not impressed when she initially learned that one of the faculty members, Rebecca Barton, had conducted "a study of the Negro." As she put it, "'Studying the Negro' has been one of America's post-war fads." When Edwards discovered further that a book had grown out of Barton's study, she was "bored." After all, she emphasized, there had been "an epidemic of books about the Negro during the last decade. Popular books are read and discussed and discarded with last year's fashions." Moreover, she pointed out that "more serious sociological studies are carefully filed away in university archives as reference works for scholars who are writing more theses to be filed away as more references for later writers of theses. I began to be restless for constructive action."[39]

When Edwards found out that Barton's course centered on social interpretation of black history through the study of black literature, however, she became increasingly intrigued. But when she tried to enroll, Barton told her that since she had already read all of the relevant literature on the subject, there was no need for her to take the course. All Edwards had to do, Barton said, was read her book. Edwards protested, insisting that although she had read all the books, she had not done so critically and analytically. When she emphasized the need to be part of the classroom give-and-take with students from other parts of the world, Barton relented and accepted Edwards into the course.[40]

At a general assembly of students on the night classes began, after all of the teachers had made speeches in German or Danish with interpreters providing translation, John Barton asked Edwards to address the assembly on behalf of the American students. She began by stressing the need for improved international relations in the context of growing tensions, praising Denmark for avoiding involvement in the First World War. She also singled out Danish agricultural cooperatives and the country's social legislation for praise.[41]

In a critical appraisal of the New Deal, Edwards pointed out the contradictions in President Roosevelt's agricultural recovery program to raise prices by reducing supply. "I told them how we, a highly industrialized country, rich in natural resources," she explained, "were bungling along with men starving within the stench of 500,000 little pigs slaughtered at government expense, and dumped on the waste heap to keep market prices up." She also told the assembly that dairy farmers were dumping milk in a desperate attempt to force prices up, and that farmers were "ploughing under wheat and cotton in a land of hungry, naked men."[42]

Edwards had a full program of work and study at the International People's College. She and one of the other American students, a young woman from Winnetka, Illinois, studied German with Elsa Thomsen, "a very sweet Danish girl." She also took a course in gymnastics taught by "a handsome Dane, blond with deep brown eyes," who was "very attractive and . . . aware of it." Edwards worked in the dining room for one hour each day.[43]

The college's location in Elsinore provided a beautiful backdrop. With a room that looked out on the water, Edwards fell in love with the setting that became her base for the next five months. She took advantage of the two railway lines from Elsinore to Copenhagen on many weekends, as well as the short ferry ride to Sweden. Elsinore, a town of about 15,500 residents at the time, featured a town council dominated by Social Democrats and municipally owned gas, water, and electric works. As a freelance journalist for the *Chicago Defender,* Claude Barnett's Associated Negro Press, the American Association of Social Workers, and labor's Federated Press, Edwards conducted research for articles on a number of Denmark's social institutions.[44]

Edwards quickly began to enjoy the sumptuous Danish cuisine. Of course, the pastries, served first with meals, were delicious. In particular, she loved Othello cake, which featured cake, whipped cream, custard, and chocolate icing, along with a good cup of coffee and rich cream. In a letter home describing the cake, she noted that "America would name it 'jazz' or 'nigger heaven.'"[45]

Among Edwards's classmates were several Jewish refugees from Nazi Germany. Many of them could not go back to Germany, their family members' having had their jobs taken from them by Nazi authorities. "All of them are suspicious and afraid to trust each other," she observed, "and so you may engage one in conversation but you can provoke neither discussion or comment when there is more than one. Those who have relatives or friends still in Germany fear that these here may be spies."[46]

A couple of weeks after arriving on campus, Edwards was in the post office when a six-year-old girl pressed her father to ask Edwards if she knew William Pickens, director of branches of the NAACP. That was how Edwards met Dr. Arnold Kalisch, his wife, Erna, and their daughter, Helga, Jewish refugees at whose home Pickens and his family had once stayed while on a trip to Germany. Helga, thrilled to learn that Edwards was a friend of Pickens's, urged her to write a letter to him sending her regards. Kalisch, a linguistics scholar who had been the editor of a socialist newspaper in Germany, now lived with his family in Denmark "in a drear cellar in destitute circumstances."[47]

In a letter to Pickens, Edwards pointed out that Kalisch, about fifty years old, was "too old to start all over again. . . . It's hard to determine for whom it is saddest, the old [Jewish refugees] who cannot begin anew or the young who can find no beginning at all."[48] Pickens replied that he would send a letter to the Kalisch family in Elsinore, including a little gift for Helga. "You will doubtless learn much," he told Edwards, "although your heart will be much burdened with the suffering and injustice which you shall observe. I never thought anything could happen so evil in the world today as the Fascist mischief in Germany."[49]

Edwards found among Danes an eagerness "to know what Negroes are doing."[50] When the December issue of the National Urban League's magazine, *Opportunity,* came out with an article she had written on Stella Thomas, she gave copies to several friends for Christmas gifts. "It was amazing how thrilled they were to have a Negro magazine and a picture of an African girl," Edwards noted. "These Danes are so eager to know about the exotic blacks, honestly to know and to know the many sides of their lives."[51]

In Copenhagen, Edwards attended a performance of *The Green Pastures* by a Danish cast, and she met Roy de Coverley, an African American literary figure from New York who also wrote articles for the *Chicago Defender* while he was in Denmark. The novelty of being black in such a white country made Edwards feel culturally isolated at times. Within two weeks after arriving on campus, she told Pickens in a letter as she anticipated meeting Coverley: "I am beginning to yearn for a glimpse of American Africans."[52]

After seeing *The Green Pastures,* Edwards wrote a letter to Georg Blickingberg, the Swedish actor who starred in the role of God in the play. Because of the language barrier, she had not approached him backstage after the play. Letting him know that she knew Richard B. Harrison personally and that she had seen the play six times previously, she criticized the supporting cast but praised his individual performance: "Until I saw your performance I could never determine whether the *Green Pastures* is a thing peculiarly Negroid or classically human and thus universal. I am now convinced that it interprets the universally human."[53]

After Blickingberg answered her letter, Edwards followed up by asking to meet him some weekend in Copenhagen. She told him how she would love to see him perform the role in the United States with a black cast and choir trained by composer and choir director Hall Johnson. She said she would love to introduce him to Richard Harrison and Mary McDowell, her friend and settle-ment-house coworker who also was a great admirer of Harrison. "One of the beautiful memories of my life is that of Mary McDowell, alone in a dark theatre, after the crowd had gone, talking across the footlights to Richard Harrison."[54]

In December, Edwards got a chance to attend a charity concert by the great contralto Marian Anderson, who was in the middle of a Scandinavian tour at the time. Edwards, who had met Anderson in Chicago in 1929, took three of her Danish friends with her to the performance in Copenhagen and introduced them to her backstage after the concert. One of her friends, Marja Babicka, was an official at the Polish legation, and one, Carl Larsen, was a banker. The third, Anna Hasselris, a collector of antique Chinese porcelains and Javanese prints, presented Anderson with a scarf as a gift.[55]

Shortly after the concert, Anderson wrote a letter to one of her sisters, Alyse, in which she expressed how impressed she was with Edwards. Anderson, impa-tient with her sister for not putting her talents to good use and for not getting focused in life, held Edwards up as someone for her to emulate. In a letter chid-ing her sister's lack of ambition, she commented, "There is a Negro girl study-ing race relations at an institution near Copenhagen in Denmark. I find it such a pity that you are satisfied to sit around and get along any way you can."[56]

To celebrate her thirty-sixth birthday, Edwards eagerly accepted an invita-tion to spend a quiet Christmas holiday with the family of Forstander Rasmus-sen in a small village on the island of Fyn. The invitation came from one of the Rasmussens' daughters, a teacher in Roskilde, near Elsinore. Her brother, who had lived in the United States for several years, was the only one in the family who spoke English. For Edwards, accustomed to quiet birthday celebrations with her family during the Christmas season, the invitation seemed an ideal way to celebrate her birthday and Christmas.[57]

With the help of the Rasmussen son as an interpreter, Edwards had long dis-cussions with Forstander Rasmussen, who presided over the county council that administered unemployment and relief insurance. Rasmussen, an enthu-siastic supporter of Danish cooperatives and social reforms, took her on long walks to show her nearby ancient farms. Of particular interest to her were the small farms that had been carved out of wealthy manorial estates and sold in ten-acre tracts, mostly to young couples. The farms were laid out in a square with four buildings on the four sides, around a court. Edwards was impressed by the attractiveness of "the most charming little white washed brick houses with red tile roofs. . . . Houses and barns are indistinguishable so it makes a very attractive unit. I visited several of them and found cows, pigs, and horses as neatly housed as folk."[58]

Upon learning that Edwards's father had told her the children's story "The Soldier and the Tinder Box," by Hans Christian Andersen, Rasmussen took her to Andersen's boyhood home and museum in Odense. On that same trip to Odense, they visited one of Denmark's finest hospitals, where one of Rasmussen's daughters was the assistant superintendent.[59]

After leaving the Rasmussens' home, Edwards took a train on December 30 to Hillerod in preparation for a New Year's celebration with friends in Copenhagen. She spent the night in Hillerod with Anna Hasselris. Edwards met Hasselris's eighty-year-old mother, who was surprised that the shade of Edwards's skin was not darker than it was. As Edwards noted with amusement, she was "disappointed I am not black."[60] After talking into the night with Hasselris, she took her first bath in ten days, since the Rasmussens' house had heat only in the main sitting room. "Despite my bath fetish," she wrote a friend, "it is amazing how contentedly I settle down to those occassional [sic] intervals when no bath is possible. This time I soaked for half an hour."[61]

The next day, Hasselris and Edwards went to Copenhagen, where they spent New Year's Eve with friends at the apartment of Marja Babicka. Roy de Coverley and Carl Larsen came to Babicka's apartment for the celebration, as did John and Rebecca Barton. Coverley, who wrote a number of skits on black life in the United States, also did some interpretive dancing and lecturing at the University of Copenhagen on black literature. Edwards described Coverley as "very charming and quite a wholesome chap . . . the darling of Copenhagen, petted and adored and much sought after and managing to keep his head very well under what is really extravagant adulation."[62]

With a number of rich, tasty red wines provided by Babicka, Edwards and the others celebrated the eve of the new year with a feast that featured roast duck with prune stuffing. After the meal, Babicka whipped up a number of cocktails. "By the close of the year," remembered Edwards, "we were in amiable spirits and in good Danish fashion stood on the couch and 'jumped into the New Year.'"[63]

"It took much persuasion to get me up next morning," Edwards wrote, but Babicka took her to the Royal Palace Square to observe the royal family's ride from the palace to another palace for a New Year's reception. Edwards and her friend missed the mid-morning reception but showed up at noon just in time to see the king on his return from the reception.[64] It amused Edwards to see "all the Foreign Ministers in their braid and plumes taking themselves quite seriously." For her, "the most interesting phase of it was the crowd gathered there to watch. Only parents who had brought their children to see these live illustrations of Andersen's Fairy Tales. That is all the royal family means to a Dane . . . purely decorative."[65]

As a result of her friendship with Babicka, Edwards enjoyed a special shopping outing during the post-Christmas sales. After Coverley told Edwards, a very snappy, fashion-conscious dresser, that he did not like the hat she was wearing, Babicka phoned her milliner in one of the "smart" shops in Copenhagen. As Edwards explained, "He didn't like the old brown tam I wear with my tweed suit and I simply couldn't wear it with my brown velvet which is quite a stand by when I 'step' in Copenhagen."[66]

Edwards received royal treatment when she and Coverley entered the shop. "When Roy and I walked in the Madame herself came forth to escort us, all the attendants forming an aisle and curtesying [sic] most prettily, until I was seated in a richly carved old chair before a long mirror and a huge and ancient Danish chest with great wrought silver hasps." After experiencing her "usual difficulty" in finding a hat that fit right, she bought an expensive "smart little brown felt, very soft, with an undecided brim that tilts a little over one eye, and a crown that ends in front in a bit of hand shirring." The hat cost five dollars, which gave her "quite a guilty feeling all the next day," but as she told a friend, "I can reduce the quantity of my clothes but I'm not willing to reduce the quality."[67]

Edwards returned to campus after the holidays, impressed by the friendliness extended to her by the Rasmussen family and her friends. "I have never met anything like Danish hospitality," she wrote to a friend in the United States. "And such genuine sincere kindness." As she noted, the language barrier at times created some awkward but good-natured moments in the Rasmussens' home: "It was most amusing when ever the father or mother found themselves alone in the room with me they would look about helplessly and shyly and then rush to call the son or the daughter."[68]

Before classes resumed in January, Edwards caught up on letter writing, including one to A. J. Muste, formerly of Brookwood Labor College, in which she shared her observations on workers' schools and the political and economic conditions in Denmark. Thanks to Ernest Green, the organizing secretary of England's Workers' Educational Association (WEA), Edwards had met Oluf Bertolt, director of Denmark's WEA. She told Muste that Denmark had two resident schools for workers, one of them at Roskilde, which Bertolt had arranged for her to visit soon, and the other at Esbjerg. Bertolt believed that workers' education should contain a definite political orientation, but as Edwards pointed out, "He is not a Marxist, feeling that Marxism is too frequently a cult rather than a living organism." Nevertheless, he seemed critical of the WEA, "which shouts itself hoarse on every hand lest it be labeled either Marxist or political."[69]

Edwards also visited a folk school at Hillerod, where the director seemed embarrassed that there were only twenty-five students in residence at a facility with a capacity of one hundred. Danish trade unions and government insurance made it possible for unemployed workers to attend a school of their choice, but clearly workers preferred the more class-based orientation of workers' rather than folk schools. Edwards reported that workers' schools were overcrowded and had long waiting lists.[70]

Through Muste, Edwards sent her regards to mutual friends who were labor-reform activists and former employees of Brookwood Labor College, including Tom Tippett, Lucile Kohn, Cara Cook, and Bill Truax. Edwards asked Muste to have Cook, the former librarian, send her a copy of the Brookwood Song Book. Edwards wanted to give a copy to the Bartons, who had expressed surprise upon learning that workers' songs were being sung in the United States.[71]

Edwards told Muste that she would like to spend at least a month in the Soviet Union after leaving Denmark on April 1. She said that she could probably scrape together enough money for railroad fare, but stressed that she needed to find a way to take care of living expenses once she got there. Apparently, she had asked Anna Louise Strong, a friend, journalist, and political activist who had recently married a Soviet official, about the possibility of getting a scholarship. Edwards asked Muste if Strong, who had extensive contacts in the Soviet Union, had said anything to him about the possibility of getting a scholarship to help support her stay there.[72]

Eager for news about political developments in the United States, Edwards asked Muste about current attitudes toward the Soviet Union and the Communist Party since Litvinov had helped to bring about the reestablishment of diplomatic relations with the United States. According to the negotiated agreement, the Soviet Union promised in the future to resume payments on its foreign debt, which it had repudiated after the Bolshevik Revolution. Edwards told Muste that she wished "very much I might have returned home long enough to hear your able analysis of that move and its implications. More and more I appreciate the soundness of your position." She also said she would "like to hear what's happening to American radicalism under the Roosevelt manipulations."[73]

Based on her experiences in Denmark, Edwards concluded that although Danes were influenced by American press portrayals of the American Negro "as either a brutal rapist or an irresponsible clown and buffoon," they did not have an emotional investment in racism. Nor did the Danes with whom she had contact question the right of an individual to marry across the color line. After meeting Edwards, Roy de Coverley, and Marian Anderson, Carl Larsen told Edwards that he had found in them "none of the things the American press has promised us. It's like being deceived and cheated."[74]

In early February, Edwards visited a clinic for children of parents with syphilis. When she met Martha Sorenson, who headed the clinic, Sorenson confessed apologetically that she had seen her on a train about six weeks earlier and had rudely stared at her along with the rest of the passengers. "Most of us have never seen a Negro," she told Edwards, who assured her that that was perfectly understandable. "I didn't add," Edwards later wrote, "that when one has been stared down by the furtive, hostile glares of American whites all the days of one's life one could endure without complaint the staring that was merely detached curiosity."[75]

On a trip to England in March, Edwards wrote an article describing what she often went through as a person of color when she stayed at YWCA facilities. When a secretary from the Friends House called to make room reservations for her at the YWCA in London, where only one bed was available in a double room, she asked the person on the other end of the phone line about the room's other occupant, "Has she a color complex? Miss Edwards is a Negro." Then the secretary smiled at the irony of the situation and asked Edwards whether *she* had any prejudice about a roommate. Yes, replied Edwards, prejudice in favor of a single room! "The International Hostel of the Y.W.C.A. is like most of the Y.W.C.A.'s where I have been a guest," Edwards noted; "one pays second-rate prices for third-rate service which is dealt down with an air of charitable condescension. . . . Certainly one never achieves adult status in one of these."[76]

On the third night of Edwards's stay, a woman who already had a room at the hostel changed rooms to move in with her. Edwards described the woman as "a queer, nervous little creature, middle aged, with a defective eye and one leg bulging out of her shoe." Edwards was puzzled by the woman's decision to move in with her, but little by little she found out why she had done it. When the woman was about nineteen, she had been in love with and wanted to marry a black man, but her mother had talked her out of it, promising that a perfectly "nice white man" would surely come along if she waited. She yielded to her mother's advice, but the nice white man never came along, and twenty years had passed since she had said goodbye to the black suitor, who when they parted told her he would return someday. So the woman, now hoping for his return, asked to move in with Edwards. "I think she thought I might have some trace of him," Edwards joked. "I'm afraid I wasn't very helpful. Listening to the woes of others has been my profession for many years—and I'm on holiday now."[77]

Edwards's travels in Denmark included visits to wholesale and retail consumers' cooperatives, speaking engagements on college campuses, and a vibrant nightlife of restaurants, wine houses, and dancing. In Esbjerg, for example, she gave a lecture on the Negro worker to students. She recited poems by black writers and shared bibliographies of important black literature. At night, she often put on her dancing shoes to enjoy Copenhagen's nightlife with friends, including the secretary of the Finnish legation.[78]

The six-month period since Edwards had left the United States complicated her love life because of physical separation. At the time she had embarked on her overseas journey to Denmark via England in October 1933, she was romantically involved with a married man, "Philip" (likely A. Philip Randolph). Apparently, they had discussed working on book projects together at some point in the future. Shortly after settling into her room at the International People's College, she wrote and told him, "My desk here in my room is at a window looking out over the moor and on to the sea. I love that. I can still look at the water as I work. And every day I reserve an hour for walking as outdoor exercise, and always I go down to the sea. I hope when we do our books we can work not too far from the water."[79]

In a letter after the Christmas and New Year's break, she told "Philip" that Charles Wesley Burton, his close friend, confidant, and supporter of the BSCP in Chicago, had written her a long letter with news about "the whole gang." In his letter, Burton had teased her about "Philip's" letters to someone named Edith in order to make Edwards jealous. The teasing "only amused me," Edwards wrote to "Philip"; "I have too deep a contempt for her ever to feel any twinge of jealousy where she is involved."[80]

In an earlier letter, Edwards had confessed to "Philip" that she had had a sexual relationship with a Hindu friend during her ten-day stop in England when she was en route to Denmark. Apparently, "Philip" was not happy to learn the news. "No Dear, I shan't extend any more invitations to paternity," she promised him. "First because I'm quite convinced that you do not like it and that it disturbs you and that I will not do. And second because it really is not so light a matter that one often meets a person one could even remotely consider."[81]

"Philip" was concerned lest the man with whom she had had sex might hold out hope for a more permanent relationship with Edwards. To ease "Philip's" fears, she assured him that that was not the case: "As for his mistaking the immediacy of it he knew that I have two years ahead planned with you including the three mos. when your books are to be written—our three months in a life time—and for no thing in earth would I forego that!" She reassured him of her love for him: "How I hunger to touch you again. Please don't ever let me go away from you for so long a time again. Since I am here I want to see Russia, Vienna and as much as possible and then I shall not come back to Europe again for a long time. Never again will it be my doings that six months separate us. Life is too soon over." Edwards also confided to a close female friend, Etha Bell Rogers: "I still have a hankering to see my married man. Some day I'll give friend wife a wallop in the nose and walk off with him. I really want that more than anything else in the world."[82]

Despite Edwards's reassuring words to "Philip," as the end of her term at the International People's College neared, she made plans to extend her travels even more than she had related to him. Using her contacts and press cards, she planned to conduct independent field investigations of social-welfare policies, public housing, and other institutions in Sweden and Finland before heading to the Soviet Union, where she hoped to stay for at least one, possibly three, months.

On April 6, 1934, as Edwards packed her bags and prepared to leave Denmark, she said a special farewell to Rebecca Barton. The teacher and student had become good friends. "Becky had suggested that when I had my bags all packed and strapped," Edwards later wrote, "I should whistle up her stairway and she'd come down for a final walk." Barton told her she wanted to introduce her to her "favorite and secret walk which I'm sure you haven't discovered. I want to share it with you as a sort of farewell surprise."[83]

Edwards thought she knew every hidden path in the area, but much to her surprise, Barton took her to a hidden garden tucked away on the other side of a tall, dark cypress hedge that Edwards had passed by many times. They sat down on a rough stone as a beautiful swan circled the nearby lake after protesting indignantly that Barton had not brought any cake to feed it on that day. They exchanged gossip and discussed their personal lives, dreams, and future career plans. They also had a deep philosophical discussion of the origins, evolution, and politics of Barton's seminar on black literature.

Edwards's friendships with the Bartons and other faculty, along with her studies and other experiences at the International People's College, contributed to her evolution as an intellectual. Transformed by her studies and cultural experiences, she was now ready to expand her understanding of labor, race, and social policies further yet. As the farewell conversation ended and Edwards prepared to depart for Sweden, though, she looked ahead, numbering, at least for the time being, "my rich Danish experiences and the hearty friends there, in a fast, receding past."[84]

4

Chain Smoking and Thinking "Black" from Red Square to Nazi Germany

Between April and August 1934, Edwards further immersed herself in international affairs through additional travels and independent field investigations in Sweden, Finland, the Soviet Union, Poland, Germany, Austria, and France. She did not leave Elsinore, Denmark, until April 9, but nothing could stop her from reaching Moscow in time for the May 1st festivities in Red Square. She planned to study the role of women and racial minorities in the Soviet Union. Like many African Americans who traveled to the Soviet Union, she came away impressed by the absence of racial prejudice against her there. As a lecturer and freelance journalist with her typewriter at all times, she described her experiences in stories submitted to the Associated Negro Press and other newspapers and journals. Her resourcefulness, experiences, lectures, and writings added to her growing stature as an urbane black intellectual with a sophisticated understanding of world issues.

After leaving Elsinore, Edwards spent about three weeks in Sweden. The first stop was in Trollhattan, located in beautiful mountain country known for its waterfalls. For a couple of days, she was a guest in the home of a newspaper editor. She visited the town's big electric plant and enjoyed long hikes before taking a train to Ludvika.[1]

With a letter of introduction from John Barton, of the International People's College, Edwards was a guest of the Brunnsvik Workers School in Ludvika. The director was Alf Ahlberg, a social psychology scholar whose textbooks were used widely in Scandinavian countries.[2] Edwards described the picturesque location of the school, which "hangs on a high cliff overlooking a great lake and ranges of snow-tipped cliffs, fir forests and frozen lakes as far as you can see."[3] She bedded down in a poets' cottage, where 125 students and faculty enjoyed a cozy setting that inspired camaraderie and intimacy. The experience absolutely thrilled her: "Evenings before a quaint old peasant fireplace, guitar, singing, long talks, long walks thro the frozen forests. All like a fairy dream." As she later told Claude Barnett, head of the Associated Negro Press, in Chicago, "You have never heard anything like the singing of those students, mostly men. At once beautiful, terrible and thrilling. My but I was happy there."[4]

Edwards found romance quickly in such a setting. In the room next to hers lived a young Swedish philosopher and teacher of languages, a "very handsome, dark Italian type" who also played the guitar and sang. On one of her first afternoons at the school, he took her for a "promenade." First, he led her up the highway for awhile and then up into a grove of white birch trees to see an iron mine that had been closed due to the Great Depression. Edwards saw the mine in terms of the suffering that its closure inflicted on workers in the area, but for her new friend, "mines were a rather rude searing of the bosom of the earth."[5]

Edwards and her friend climbed higher in the pines through deep snow drifts until they found two dry, flat stones. Invigorated by the walk and intellectual companionship, they sat down on the stones for a very intimate conversation. They talked "of men and women, of sex, of children, of marriage, of the philosophy of Bertrand and Dora Russell and of those who preach sexual liberty but carefully adhere to orthodoxy."[6]

The subject turned especially to conventional sexual morality and monogamous relationships. "We were agreed," Edwards confided to her friend Etha Bell Rogers in the United States, "that one must have a super sense of physical security and sureness in his partner to condone outside relations. But then we agreed that with so strong and vital a union between two persons there would be little occassion [sic] for outside affairs. And so, dialectically, we disposed of sexual freedom as distinguished from tolerance or from free love."[7]

For the rest of Edwards's stay in Ludvika, she and her Swedish lover grew closer as they visited workers' halls, went for coffee, discussed news and philosophy, and shared poetry. After dinner one night, her companion and Dr. Lindgren, an international relations teacher at the school, invited her to join them for coffee at a country road house about two miles from campus. After a long political and intellectual discussion, her lover, tired of conversation, got up and played American records on the phonograph.[8]

On the way back to campus, they stopped to enjoy dances at workers' halls that were a feature of even the smallest Scandinavian villages. The dances reminded Edwards of a Saturday night in Gary, Indiana, as she danced with both of the men with her. On the walk back to campus "under a dark, star sprinkled sky between avenues of pine, the thawing ice gurgling along the road side," Edwards enjoyed listening to Dr. Lindgren as he recited "bits of Swedish verse to me."[9]

The next day, Edwards curled up in front of the fireplace in her lover's "cozy little apartment" on a lazy, rainy Sunday afternoon. "I enjoy the fire while he plays the guitar and sings to me," she wrote. That night, they attended a "splendid" student performance of "An Enemy of the People," a play written by Norwegian playwright Henrik Ibsen in 1882.[10]

The discussions between Edwards and her lover also explored race and sex. As she confessed to a friend in Chicago, he was "fascinated by my darkness." The new lovers felt close bonds of kinship on political and intellectual issues, but the relationship forced a change in Edwards's attitudes toward the role of race in selecting a partner. Until then, she had ruled out the choice of a white man as a marriage partner for her. "He was quite startled and unconvinced when I said I wouldn't marry a white man," Edwards reported, "and I felt ashamed of my own black chauvinism and had to modify it to American."[11]

Later that night, Edwards, flushed by romance and excitement, found it hard to think about leaving in a few days: "I am really reluctant to continue my journey to Stockholm, which I must do on Tuesday." She felt a real connection with her new lover. What they shared in intimate conversation made a deep impression on her: "It is a relief to really talk to another. So much of the time one only converses with the folk one meets. Most people haven't the courage to face themselves, much less others and speak of the things that occupy much of all our thinking. When I think of all the folk I've met these months and the hours and hours of conversation, often exhaustive and extending far into the night I feel tired and worn."[12]

Despite Edwards's earlier promise to "Philip" that she would not extend any further "invitations to paternity," the intimacy of things shared with her younger lover in Ludvika had drawn her across the sexual color line. She confided to Rogers that she had learned a lot in conversations with so many people since leaving the United States, "but only twice have I talked, naked soul to naked soul. That was with my Hindoo friend in Oxford and my young Swedish philosopher here. A barren record."[13]

Bidding a sad farewell to her young lover, Edwards took off for Stockholm, where she stayed in the apartment of Knud Larsen, a union official and friend of John Barton's. Shortly before she had left the International People's College, Barton wrote a letter introducing her to Larsen. Barton asked if he or anyone else he knew might provide her a place to stay for about ten days while she visited the city. He described Edwards as "the most charming negro student we have ever had here at the college. . . . she is dark and mellow like an African Twilight." Emphasizing her politics, Barton told Larsen: "She is labour through and through and she is on her way through to Russia. . . . She writes for the associated Negro Press and wants to make social education and Labour contacts."[14]

In a letter to Claude Barnett, Edwards described her stay in Larsen's tiny bachelor's apartment in Stockholm as "an amusing and interesting arrangement which I shall tell you of when I get home," but she noted how much she enjoyed her eight days in the city. "I was pampered to death in Stockholm in a beautiful way," she wrote. Kai Anderson, editor of a women's labor magazine in the city, took Edwards under her wing and hosted several intimate parties in her "smart modernistic apartment." At these parties Edwards met a number of important people, including Sven Markelius, an internationally recognized architect who had designed social housing projects with communal-living features in the center of Stockholm. His wife was a journalist who at the time was working in the Soviet Union for six months. Edwards would later meet her in Moscow.[15]

Edwards also met the director of workers' and children's theater, Dr. Matwey Schischkin, who was a foster son of Leo Tolstoi, and Bibi Lindstrom, a sculptor and dancer who worked with Schischkin at the theater. Edwards went to the theater, where she enjoyed a "thrilling evening" of performances. After the young students performed mass recitations and pantomime for her, Schischkin read Russian poems, using a Swedish interpreter, especially for her. Then, with Knud Larsen acting as an interpreter, Edwards recited poems by black poets and explored social themes in the poetry of Paul Dunbar, Claude McKay, and Langston Hughes. She loved the ambience, "the room all dark save for a fire in a tiny corner fireplace over which a copper kettle swung. The students clustered about the floor and Dr. S. and I embracing and kissing each others cheeks."[16]

While in Stockholm, Edwards was "wined and dined at all the smart cafes," including the famous Golden Freedom, where the Swedish-American actor Greta Garbo and the Prince of Wales were entertained. In the House of Parliament's dining room, she had lunch with the Hon. Oscar Olsson, a Social Democratic member of Parliament who played an important role in the adult education movement. Afterward, Olsson took her to his country home to meet his family.[17]

Edwards's travels took her next to Helsinki, Finland. "There is hardly anywhere a more beautiful boat route than the journey from Stockholm to Helsinki affords," she wrote. "Dark pine covered islelets [sic] that link themselves into a coast line so unusual that one is never quite certain one is really out at sea." She was impressed by the city's "spic and span cleanliness" that "startles the American eye accustomed to the filth and exposed garbage of cities in the United States."[18]

In Helsinki, Edwards met Minna Sillanpaa, Finland's first female member of Parliament and former cabinet minister for social affairs. Sillanpaa, who edited a women's magazine for the Finnish Social Democratic Party, had founded the Finnish National Trade Union of Domestic Workers. She was also a member of the Women's International League for Peace and Freedom (WILPF). Edwards compared her to Jane Addams and Mary McDowell, but pointed out the differences. "America's two Grand Old Women were nurtured in homes of comfort and refinement," Edwards wrote, "and deliberately chose to bend their talents and splendid abilities towards making life better for those less fortunately born." In contrast, Sillanpaa was "born an humble country girl. Very early she hired herself out to do the mean chores of cooking and scouring in the homes of the more affluent."[19]

Edwards praised the role of the Workers' Educational Association in helping to educate Sillanpaa and others in the economic and political issues of the day. It was in workers' education classes that Sillanpaa received the training that led her to organize Helsinki's female servants into a class-conscious union. "She is a strong and mighty worker first for the working class," Edwards noted, "and secondly for the Rights of Women."[20]

Sillanpaa's political activities made a lasting impression on Edwards, who was particularly interested in improving the exploitative conditions of black female servants in the American South. In the years ahead, Edwards would hold up the Finnish National Trade Union of Domestic Workers as a model for black servants to follow. Through Sillanpaa and Toivi and Felix Iversen, a math professor at the University of Helsinki and pacifist at whose house she stayed as a guest, Edwards also developed contacts with the Finnish branch of the WILPF. These contacts would reinforce Edwards's commitment to world peace as international rivalries sharpened and militarism increased in the mid-1930s.[21]

Apparently the trip to Moscow was a real hassle for Edwards, but she made it there just in time for the May 1st festivities. "By dent [sic] of sheer insistence I overcame the weighty Soviet bureaucracy and arrived here in the midst of the May Day demonstration and marched around the Red Square," she wrote to Claude Barnett a couple of weeks later. "I think I would never have recovered if I'd missed it. Don't know when I'd permitted my heart to get so set on anything. It was thrilling."[22]

Edwards, who stayed in a private room in the home of a Russian family, was offered a one-year teaching job at the Anglo-American school in Moscow, but she was "not thrilled at the idea of teaching young kids again." What she preferred to do instead was to lecture and organize young student groups. Her options were complicated, though, by the fact that her visa was set to expire on June 1. She had applied for an extension, but there were rules against extending visas in the country. If Soviet authorities did grant her an extension, she leaned toward accepting the teaching job and staying there for a year. "My color is my one hope in winning an extension," she wrote.[23]

When Edwards lectured at the Anglo-American school, she found that the students were very interested in discussing economic and political issues related to the Great Depression. She also noted favorable images of interracial friendship on the walls—pictures of black and white children with hands clasped. Of special interest to children at the school as well as those attending workers' classes was the plight of oppressed, exploited blacks in America.[24]

Edwards's initial contact with the kindergarten children was not good, though. She was wearing an Indian bracelet with engraved swastikas. At one time, of course, the swastika symbol had been commonly used without political stigma, but that was before the Nazis appropriated it. When Edwards realized the impact her bracelet was having on the children, she took it off. As she explained, "The children in the kindergarten ran from me, thinking I wore the Nazi symbol."[25]

By the time Edwards reached Moscow, some of the articles she had written on the trip for the Associated Negro Press already had been published in a number of black newspapers in Pennsylvania, Texas, Oklahoma, and California. "Did Mother and the Aunts like them?" she asked in a letter to Barnett, who was also a close friend and former lover. "I've had one or two comments. The 'unconventional' Bell [her sister] tho't they were shockingly intimate."[26]

Edwards apologized to Barnett for not having finished the Danish/Swedish/Finnish article she had promised him for the Associated Negro Press. At the time she was in the middle of writing a couple of articles for Dr. Curtis Reese's paper at the Abraham Lincoln Centre. She told Barnett that since his and Reese's publications served different readers, she had instructed Reese to pass along her articles to him, too, in case he would like to reprint any of them.[27]

A bit of homesickness overcame Edwards shortly after she reached Moscow, where she spent several days in bed with attacks of diarrhea during the first two weeks. "I'm not sure whether it's the food, the water or my own sheer exhaustion," she wrote, "for I've gone exhaustively since the middle of March." During the period of confinement, she caught up on letter writing, expressing a longing to see friends in Chicago, Harlem, Greenwich Village, Gary, Tuskegee, St. Louis, Kansas City, and Washington, DC. She dreamed of having dinner at Poro College and settling back into her room at the Abraham Lincoln Centre. "It's nice to have a day of enforced idleness," she noted, "so that one can reflect on how deliciously nice life has been, and how charming and loveable one's friends are and how good it will be to see them again. Perhaps I'm homesick and hence not terribly excited about whether I get the visa extension or not."[28]

Apparently Soviet authorities did not grant Edwards's request for a visa extension, for on June 1, 1934, after a month in the Soviet Union, she was in Kraków, Poland. "As you see," she wrote in a letter, "my face is now turned toward home and I have begun the long journey that separates me from the land of the Mormons, Holy Rollers and such like." Also on her itinerary were stops in Vienna and Munich.[29]

Two other Americans had been passengers with Edwards on the train ride through the Ukraine to the Polish border. One of them, an Episcopal clergyman from Long Island, irritated her by his super-patriotism and constant attacks on the Soviet Union. When he learned that Soviet authorities had taken great care to make Edwards feel comfortable, he became upset. A discussion of race ensued. "He tho't I should have resented such particular concern," Edwards wrote. "I told him that after a life time of U.S.A. discrimination I was rather pleased to find a land where my 'objectionable' color was in my favor." The Episcopal minister protested, "But the Scandinavians treated you well, didn't they?" Edwards replied, "Certainly . . . as a drawing room novelty. But here there are no drawing rooms I might add color to. It is not me, but the oppressed and exploited people I represent that they seek to serve and make comfortable."[30]

The other American passenger on the train with Edwards was a young Polish immigrant who had lived in Boston for twelve years. She described him as "a militant, class conscious worker" who "was splendid to me." There were tensions, however, between him and the minister. "The clergy lectured him for swearing and me for smoking," Edwards noted. Edwards and the Polish immigrant ditched the minister during a long wait at the Polish border. When the time came to depart, they slipped into the crowded third-class carriage for smokers, which Edwards described as "worse than our Jim Crow cars and much less comfortable tho' cleaner." As she wrote, "We crowded out with peasants taking their wares to market. Had to huddle ourselves into the midst of sacks of potatoes and lettuce and what not."[31]

When the train reached Kraków on June 1, 1934, Edwards persevered until she found a clean little room in a hostel near the downtown area. The city's charm and beauty impressed her—flowers and gardens everywhere with beautiful parks. She observed a religious festival with people kneeling in the streets and singing mournful songs, and with prayer rugs displayed in the windows of homes. "But I have met nothing so vulgar, rude and suggestive," she stressed, "as the stares of the Poles. I have grown used to being stared at these past 8 mo. But this is a different sort of staring. More harshly curious, less kindly."[32]

Edwards left Kraków for Vienna, where she spent a few weeks at a time of political crisis in Austria. Under intense pressure from the Nazis, Austria's chancellor, Engelbert Dollfuss, had closed Parliament in March 1933, making himself dictator even as he tried to keep the Nazis at bay. His Christian Social Party, which enjoyed close ties to Mussolini and the Italian fascists, had banned other political parties, including the Nazis. In February 1934, just a few months before Edwards arrived, fighting had broken out in the streets of Vienna between the Social Democrats and workers' militias on the one hand and the government on the other. The government had broken the back of the resistance and jailed or driven into exile many of the Social Democratic leaders, and Dollfuss and his party had rammed through a new constitution abolishing the Austrian Republic on May 1, 1934.[33]

Working through contacts and interpreters, Edwards interviewed workers, students, and Social Democrats about the political crisis. She visited the workers' districts in the city, asking questions about the battles between workers and the police and soldiers. Those who spoke to her complained about the weak-kneed tactics of their Socialist leaders, who had vacillated too long because of their fear of unleashing a workers' revolution.

Edwards also slipped into a class at an adult education center, where posters of Dollfuss adorned the stairway walls. The group leader deliberately steered discussions into politically "safe" channels. "With studied caution," Edwards observed, "he guided the group safely onto discussions of American and English folk songs, of harmless cinemas they had seen. . . . Despite his forceful personality from time to time the session lagged with the inanity of the subject matter."[34]

When someone in the class called out that a foreigner was in the room, Edwards stepped forward and introduced herself. When she mentioned that she was on her way home from the Soviet Union, a chorus of voices urged her to talk about Soviet Russia. Before she could do so, however, the leader interrupted, saying they already had plenty of information about Russia. He told her to speak instead about "your own people."[35]

Afterward, several members of the audience approached Edwards to talk about the Soviet Union. They expressed the view that the Soviet Union represented the path of the future. For them, the Socialists had lost all credibility because of their vacillation in Austria. One of the members, Ernsell, who had fought in the workers' February Revolution, made arrangements to take Edwards on a tour of Vienna the next day.

Edwards and Ernsell visited affordable working-class housing projects created by the Social Democrats before Dollfuss had set up his dictatorship. They talked to tenants who complained of police harassment and sharp hikes in rents under the Dollfuss government. Edwards was impressed by the public housing units, including one of the new buildings, which had an attached hospital, clinic, laundry, and kindergarten. After taking her to the housing projects, Ernsell took her to his home to view maps and photos of shelled houses and working-class casualties from the February Revolution. His blind mother, surprised when Edwards greeted her in German, served fresh strawberries and cherries as they viewed the photos and discussed the civil war that had raged for several days in February between workers and soldiers.[36]

About a month before Nazi assassins murdered Dollfuss on July 25, 1934, Ernsell and his mother accompanied Edwards to the train station to see her off for Germany. Ernsell pointed ominously to the "hordes of soldiers swarming the station and pouring out of the trains." He noted that with large increases in rent scheduled to go into effect on July 1, "You ought wait a few days for the excitement.... Somebody's head will pop and the Government is pretty scared." As Ernsell and Edwards exchanged photographs and said their goodbyes, he told her: "My, I'd like to go with you. But we are all sort of held prisoners within the country. Lose your citizenship if you go, particularly if you cross the German frontier."[37]

As Edwards's train slowly pulled out, Ernsell called to her: "You probably won't have it so good in Germany as here. The Nazi are anti-Negro." Edwards, trying to be optimistic and brave, called back, "So I was warned about Vienna, and I found good people here. There are still good people in everyplace and they find each other. Besides, I am an American Negro and inured to Negrophobia" (pt. 1, 3).

Despite Edwards's optimism, she was "trying desperately to pretend I wasn't feeling a bit funny about the week ahead in Germany with no funds" (pt. 1, 2–3). To add to her concerns, she had discovered as she was paying her hotel bill in Vienna that somehow she had lost 150 shillings. With only 125 shillings left in her purse, she was in a quandary. A ticket for the return trip to the United States awaited her in Paris, but third-class train fare to Paris would cost 110 shillings, leaving her with a mere 15 shillings for food, baggage handling, transit visa, and other incidental expenses along the way. She learned, however, that she could get a ticket at a 60 percent discount if she went through the Bavarian municipality of Oberammergau, where the first performance of *The Passion Play* had taken place three centuries earlier. There was an important catch, though: the discount ticket required that she stay in Germany for a full seven days. So, dangerously low on money with no letters of introduction in Germany, she bought the discount ticket, figuring she would deal with the problem of food and lodging once she got there (pt. 1, 1).

More stress awaited Edwards at Salzburg on Austria's border with Germany. When her train stopped, a customs official pointed to her heavy bag stowed on the rack and asked her to lift it down so he could inspect it. She indicated that she would be happy to open the bag if he would get it down for her. In the end, though, the official marked it "inspected" without getting it down off the rack.

The border stop at Salzburg stretched on and on. Finally, Edwards asked a conductor how much longer it would be before the train pulled out. Assured it would be at least an hour longer, Edwards stepped off the train and slipped into a coffee house for a bowl of hot milk to wash down the black bread and cheese she had packed with her from Vienna. When she came back in thirty minutes, she stared in disbelief as her train disappeared through the mountain pass. Officials had finished their business earlier than expected, and so the train had sped off. "There I stood," wrote Edwards, "hatless, gloveless, fortunately holding my purse containing passport, ticket and visa. I tho't of my books and papers scattered on the seat. Would they ever patiently collect all these. But mostly I was troubled lest my bags be opened and the sheaf of notes of interviews with Viennese revolutionists be uncovered" (pt. 1, 3–4).

In Edwards's limited German, she explained to the station master what had happened. He wired ahead to report the items she had left on the train, and thirty minutes later, Edwards found a seat on a nearly empty coach, "an open car," on the next train. She wrote, "None of those snug, private compartments. I remembered that it was on these that one really met the folk types and I began to congratulate myself on missing the express, even at the risk of my bags" (pt. 1, 4).

At the first village where the train stopped, a large group of Nazi men crowded aboard. One of them took a seat facing Edwards, and another, "an old hayseed," sat down at the end of her seat. She carefully eyed all the Nazi ribbons, badges, and insignia on them as well as the "dry, humourless lips" of the "old hayseed." "He might have been a Holy Roller, Jumper or Grand Kleagle of the Ku Klux Klan," she observed. "One could visualize him in the frenzy of religious orgies, or in the solemn business of mystic initiatory rites in some wooded hollow in Georgia or Indiana. . . . This then was the cultural level of these leaders who had set themselves the salvation of a great people" (pt. 1, 5).

Edwards watched an endless, weary round of "Heil Hitlers" as newcomers entered and left her car from station to station. "One looked on as at the ritual of a mysterious sect," she noted, "who, instead of crossing themselves, warded off the Evil Eye with stiffly up-stretched arms and elaborate incantations to Hitler. . . . It kept a restless stirring in and out of the group, a trampling over toes, and one kept one's seat and one's feet with difficulty" (pt. 1, 6).

Amid the rigmarole of continuous "Heiling," Edwards noticed a look of disgust on the face of a traveling salesman, whose name she gives only as "Joseph," sitting opposite her. At some point, she leaned across to him and smiled, "I suppose one does not comment?" After replying, "One dares not," the man got up and left the car, but returned in a few minutes for his luggage. He turned to Edwards and invited her at his expense to move to a first-class compartment with him. He told her that an even larger number of Nazis was getting on the train at the station it was pulling into: "It will be unbearable. . . . Deutschland is theirs and they're inclined to elbow everybody off and out" (pt. 1, 6–7).

After Thyra and Joseph relocated to first class, the conversation turned to race and romance. Joseph, who was about forty years old, invited her to live with him and his mother, but Thyra told him she was married. At his request, she showed him a picture of "her man" back in the United States. He then asked why she did not marry a white man. "Because I love a black man," she replied. "Because most Negro women prefer and marry their own men. And because I'd be ostracized by both white and black if I married a white man" (pt. 1, 8).

Joseph, a former army captain who had grown bitter after serving in the First World War, became Thyra's protector when he learned of her lost luggage, shortage of money, and other travails. By the time the train reached Munich, she had only seventeen marks to last seven days after she exchanged her shillings. Escorted by Joseph, she found that her bags, typewriter, books, and papers were waiting for her at the station. One of her parcels was missing, however, and she had to shell out four marks to pay for a telegram ahead to Paris to notify train authorities about the missing parcel. Joseph quietly paid the tips for Thyra, dismissed the porter, and carried her bags. "I put on my hat and gloves and felt like a woman again," she recalled. "But with a stranger who simply went ahead and assumed charge of one in this fashion one couldn't help feeling like a very frail example of the species" (pt. 1, 10).

After they walked to an inexpensive hotel, Joseph suggested that it would be cheaper if they were to get a double room together. He made clear that they would sleep in separate beds. Thyra thought about it long and hard, finally relenting. He told her she could trust him, offering to step outside the room if she needed to freshen up a bit. She told him there was no need for him to do that. She turned down a dinner invitation from him, though, suggesting instead that they have a picnic in the room with the food she had left from the trip. He called for room service to bring a pot of coffee for her and a large beer for him.

Thyra and Joseph relaxed as they talked and ate. He talked of the war, showing bayonet, shrapnel, and bullet wounds. He condemned the way the French had used their Senegalese colonials in combat as cannon fodder. As he cleared away their dinner dishes and meticulously repacked her provisions after they had finished eating, he complained that he was sick of war. He kissed both of her hands and, to her surprise, said she would sleep better alone. Then he slipped out the door and was gone. When Edwards checked out the next morning, she discovered that he had paid the bill before he left (pt. 1, 10–14).

The train ride from Munich to Oberammergau took Edwards up through beautiful mountain ranges and sparkling lakes. Disappointed that the shrine of *The Passion Play* "flaunted its commercialism with all the vulgarity of an American hot dog stand," she nevertheless spent ten of her last thirteen marks on a ticket to see the play. "But when one has only 13 marks between oneself and the bottom," she mused, "one might as well spend 10 of them for a billet to the Passion" (pt. 2, 2).

When Edwards was unable to find lodging, someone suggested that she walk down to the village of Unterammergau at the foot of the mountains. So away she went, walking down the highway alongside bicyclists and government-owned buses taking crowds to and from Oberammergau. After stopping at several houses in search of lodging, she at last found a family willing to let her stay with them. "Don't you know that Hitler doesn't want Negroes in Deutschland?" the father warned Edwards. "Aren't you afraid to travel in Germany?" (pt. 2, 4). She replied that as an American Negro, she was accustomed to being hated. She expressed faith that since Hitler's "Negro-phobia" was a "new epidemic" in Germany, not everybody would suffer from the disease. When asked how the Soviets regard Germans, she related how the children at the Anglo-American school in Moscow had run from her because of the swastikas on her Indian bracelet. Pleased by the direction of the conversation, the father then revealed to Edwards that he was a Communist whose house had been searched by the police three times.

When a busload of travelers from Stuttgart stopped at the home to buy milk from the family, which had a couple of cows as well as chickens and a garden, several conversations with Edwards took place. The travelers, delighted she could speak enough German to converse with them, asked about her travels. When Edwards mentioned Russia, a woman stepped forward to ask how things were there, but interrupted Edwards when she painted an optimistic picture of Russian conditions: "You will be in jail. Remember you are in Deutschland. Here you must always answer, All is bad in Russialand. All is good in Deutschland, Heil Hitler!" (pt. 2, 5).

Edwards reveled in the hospitality of the family in whose home she stayed for three days. The entire family came out to watch as she climbed on the back of their son's motorcycle for a ride up the mountain road to Oberammergau. Children in the neighborhood came by to stare at her, and the political conversations flowed freely as Edwards savored the breakfast sweet rolls and other food provided by her hosts. She showed her collection of photos of the shelled houses of workers in Vienna and gave a few of them to the father. She also gave him a photo of Lenin's tomb in Moscow, but when she pulled out a number of underground newspapers she had brought with her from Vienna, he warned, "Put them away carefully. Do not show them to anyone else. You will be jailed if the police see these" (pt. 2, 7).

As Edwards prepared to leave, the family slipped the three marks she had paid them for lodging back into her coat pocket. Urged to stay for three months, she explained that her ticket would not allow it, but she promised to return in two years. As they hugged and kissed each other's cheeks, the father pressed her to make sure she would come back in two years: "For, if you are returning, this day the children will mark the calendar. And each day hence they strike off a day, saying, In two years the Nigerin will return" (pt. 2, 8).

A crowded train took Edwards back to Munich, but she still had three days to kill before her ticket would let her leave for Paris. Arriving late at night in

Munich, she sat in the waiting room of the train station and tried to read for awhile. Finally, she stretched out on a long wooden bench in an attempt to sleep. A few minutes later, a nun from the Bahnhof mission invited her and other women and children traveling alone to a room especially reserved for them. Edwards went along. She found another wooden bench in the room and stretched out on it, using her typewriter as a pillow. Within an hour or so, however, the police came through the room, roughly rousing everyone to check passports and railway tickets. After the police intrusion, Edwards slept the rest of the night in preparation for catching her train to Stuttgart the next morning (pt. 3, 1–2).

When Edwards got off the train in Stuttgart at about noon the next day, she met an old American soldier born to German immigrants in Milwaukee. During World War I, he had exchanged American for German citizenship. A socialist who was eager to talk to someone from the United States, he showed Edwards around Stuttgart after she checked her bags for safekeeping at the station. Pointing out two houses that he used to own before hard times had set in, he told her he was living at that time in an apartment but could not make a living. "Of course I don't talk politics," he added. "Seen too many of my friends disappear and fail to show up anymore" (pt. 3, 2).

As they walked through downtown areas, Edwards saw the impact of the government's anti-Semitic policies upon Jewish businesses. Her new friend pointed out shops that had belonged to Jewish owners before being taken over by the Nazis. When Edwards asked just how the government did it, he explained, "Simply send in armed men into the shop. The owner is told to hand over the keys and get out. And he does both. There is no recourse" (pt. 3, 2–3).

When Edwards returned to the train station with two days to go before her ticket to Paris would be valid, she got out her typewriter and began to write. A young German man interrupted her to warn her that police come through the station from time to time and that if she were not careful about what she was writing, she could end up in jail. She listened as he spewed forth hatred of Jews and praised Germany's rebirth under Hitler. He asked her if she was glad she did not have "Jewish blood," and asked about her African lineage. When he claimed that Germans held no grievances against Negroes, Edwards reminded him that unlike in 1929 when she had visited Germany, on this trip she at times had heard racial insults such as *"Niger weibchen"* ("Niger bitch") when she walked down the street (pt. 3, 3).

The young German complained that he had been out of work for three years, stressing that he would like to leave the country but it was too late. In response to his rant that "the Jew is a blood sucking leech" who had ruined Germany, Edwards emphasized that jobs were hard to find in all countries, except the Soviet Union. She told him that his anti-Semitic analysis of the underlying reasons for joblessness was far off the mark. She pointed out that Jewish workers were as poverty stricken and exploited as any others. At that point in the conversation, the young German interrupted to introduce Edwards to a Jewish friend of his who was approaching. Edwards described his Jewish friend as "a gnarled, bent old man with head clean shaven, blackened stubby teeth and protruding eyes set in thick, red rims." The young German emphasized that although the old man was Jewish, he was "a good fellow" and longtime friend (pt. 3, 4).

Upon meeting the old man, formerly a tailor and veteran of the First World War who now lived on relief, Edwards was subjected to boastful, insulting accounts of his sexual exploits with "dark" women from Africa, India, and Greece. The young German apologetically admitted that although he, too, had enjoyed an extensive repertoire of women in the past, he had never had sex with a dark-skinned woman. The old man bragged that sex with "dark" women had "forever dulled" his appetite for his own women. As Edwards noted, "It was an oft repeated chorus in Germany. . . . I waited in bored silence until the recitation should be finished" (pt. 3, 4).

After the conversation turned from the old man's sexual escapades to his war experiences, particularly his killing of a Senagalese soldier with a bayonet, the young German suggested that he, Edwards, and the old man go to a restaurant for a meal. Edwards, who had not eaten in a day and a half, said that if she went, it would have to be at an inexpensive place. So off they went to the old tailor's favorite *rathskeller*. En route, they were stopped constantly by uniformed members of Hitler's elite *Schutzstaffel* who stuck tin cans in their faces, urging them to buy the small Nazi flags they carried with them. Each of Edwards's escorts dropped money into the cans, but she did not. Alarmed, her companions warned, "You will surely get into trouble. It is the Government. One dare not refuse" (pt. 3, 5).

At the *rathskeller*, Edwards's companions drank a beer as they watched her eat a meal of blood sausage and hashed brown potatoes. "I had an unhappy feeling that they hadn't eaten for some time either," Edwards wrote, "tho' they refused to share my meal (pt. 3, 6). When she was finished eating, the old man paid for her meal as well as the beer. Edwards objected, protesting to no avail that he was unemployed.

Afterward, the two men discussed where they might help her find decent lodging at a cheap price. Edwards silently tried to figure out how to shake free of them so she could go back to the mission's waiting room at the train station. At last she convinced them to walk her back to the station, but since it was after midnight, the police would not allow any new entries into the area for shelter. "I had to confess then that I had no money for a hotel and had planned sleeping in the station," Edwards recalled, but "the old man urged his roof upon me." Since the hour was late, he believed he could sneak her into his room without being detected by his landlord, whom he owed a lot of back rent. Desperate, Edwards quickly weighed her options: "I looked at him closely . . . and accepted" (pt. 3, 6).

Uneasy with a sense that she might be in danger, Edwards accompanied the old man to his room, which overlooked an alley in a slum area of Stuttgart. For a while, they looked at his collection of picture cards and clothes that he had made. When it was time to go to bed, Edwards quickly asked for a blanket to use as a pallet on the floor. "But why not in my bed?" he asked. "Because I do not care to," Edwards replied. When he protested insistently that he just wanted to talk to her, she put on her hat as if to leave and said, "Doubtless we have misunderstood each other." He then quickly laid out a blanket and pillow on the floor, muttering, *"Schwarze ist dumm"* ("Black is stupid") (pt. 3, 6–7).

Edwards slept in her tweed suit and heavy coat for warmth in the very cold room. When she woke up the next morning, the old man had two thick slices of black bread and a cup of "vile" tea ready for her. She poured the tea down the basin, ate one slice of the bread, and put the other in her coat pocket for the day ahead. Then, she explained, "He handed me my coat and hat, took on his own, peered carefully out into the hallway, put his eye to a crack in the wall, then beckoned me, we were out and off" (pt. 3, 7).

Despite a bad cold, Edwards was in good spirits once they had left the man's room. At midnight the seven-day-stay restriction on her ticket would expire, and a train was scheduled to leave for Paris at 12:20 a.m. The old man urged her to see a little of the town before she left. He took her on a walking sightseeing tour before waving goodbye and saying he would later see her off at the train station. She returned to the mission's waiting room at the station, where a number of strangers approached her. One of them, a "wild eyed young poet," launched into a tirade against Hitler. A number of unemployed teachers and clerks who had been displaced by the Nazis joined him in the attack on fascism, but likewise blasted the Soviet Union.

The conversations were soon interrupted when a group of Nazis led several hundred visiting members of the right-wing National Youth League of Sweden with their suitcases into the railway station. From the steps, the leader delivered an impassioned oration extolling the virtues of life in Nazi Germany. As Edwards looked on, he invited the pro-Nazi Swedish youth to support Germany in the international arena. Then the large group dispersed out into the streets, where Hitler's storm troopers created a lot of commotion with their "drear" singing and "Heil Hitlers" (pt. 3, 7–9).

As midnight grew closer, Edwards edged into the corridor "to be near that precious train when my hour should arrive." Shortly before she boarded, a young storm trooper dressed in civilian clothes who was on vacation came up to her and asked if she had enjoyed the glorious parade. He told her that he had been without work for three years before Hitler came to power. As she moved through the iron grating to board the train, he was still singing Hitler's praises to her, comparing Hitler to God. When at last she broke free of him and grabbed a seat on the train, she heaved a sigh of relief: "I spent the first half hour digging out a place for myself among the peasants, mostly Czechs going to America, who had sprawled themselves over the seats and their children on the floor between. I had come thro' my seven days bringing nothing worse than a bad cold" (pt. 3, 9).

With the adventures in Nazi Germany safely behind her, Edwards soon boarded ship for the voyage back to the United States. She did a lot of reflecting as she sped toward home aboard the French liner MS *Lafayette*. Past midnight on June 30, 1934, her last night on board, she and a white American couple with whom she had become acquainted on the voyage were standing on deck, talking and staring down at the "marble swirl" below. For the last several days, they had talked, danced, played chess and deck tennis, enjoyed bottles of wine, and lolled and sunned on deck, but Edwards noted that she, as well as they, now seemed "nervous and jumpy. At least keyed and on edge." As she wrote later that night, "I found myself, for the first time during these months, 'chain smoking' and thinking 'black.'"[38]

Edwards and her new friends were preparing to re-enter a racially segregated society. Until now, the couple had avoided the subject of race, but on their last night together, that changed. "And did I only suspect my comrades of thinking black now," Edwards reflected, "or was it that now we were separating there was that last moments urge to get asked the questions they had doubtless tactfully withheld until friendship was established and intimacy and understanding on that plane where friends speak all things to each other. I rather think it was the latter."[39]

It was not only race but Edwards's intellectual curiosity and political radicalism that set her apart from the couple. Her studies and travels abroad had deepened her understanding of race, labor, and world politics, but this couple had spent four months in France without showing the least inclination to learn anything about French culture and politics. Edwards observed in her journal that they had attended an American church in France and made no effort to speak to anyone other than the hotel's head waiter. She complained that they "tho't the most impressive thing in all France was a cute little cottage they saw in Normandy. Yes, they had heard something or other about the street riots in Paris but they understood that was just a part of the Communists' annoying program."[40]

The couple's lack of intellectual curiosity limited their discussions with Edwards, who tried to keep conversation focused on less weighty subjects. Nevertheless, even when they discussed their tastes in music—a topic of great personal interest to Edwards—she bumped up against their lack of understanding of the politics of music. For example, when they told her they loved the music of Richard Wagner, she pointed out that his music and thought served the interests of the Nazis, who had appropriated his legacy. She suggested they read some critical perspectives on Wagner, recommending the work of philosopher Friedrich Nietzsche. The woman in the couple did concede that she had once heard something about Nietzsche, but added that whatever it was that she had heard was not good.

Despite the couple's limitations, Edwards liked them. To her, they were "beautiful" and "good souls." As they said their goodbyes and agreed to stay in touch, Edwards asked them what their plans were. They said they would probably get married, since they both already had finished their educations and visited Europe. They laughed politely but were puzzled when she suggested that they lacked experience for marriage. Privately, Edwards felt pity for them: "To see them you think they have all things to make a man happy. But they have no mind, no understanding, nothing. But I have made them think a little. Only such a little will do no good."[41]

To finish the last bit of writing in her journal later that night, Edwards returned to the subject of how race had come up in their conversations. She noted that although the man (Henrico) had gone out of his way to condemn racial prejudice, "There is something of pity in his feeling." Edwards, of course, did not want his pity: "If only people could restrain that tinge of pity that alters the secure balance of relationship. . . . I feel somehow suffocated by Henrico's overwhelming protestations. . . . I can't quite decide whether I am glad we are landing or whether, now that the subject is launched, I wish we had some days left to study and discuss it." As Edwards had retired to her quarters that night, knowing she would be back in the United States the next day, she felt the overwhelming weight of being black: "God, what a crushing thing this thing of the Negro is."[42]

5

Building a Popular Front in Chicago

Edwards played an important role in building Chicago's Popular Front in the mid- to late 1930s. Because of her recent labor education at home and abroad, she was in demand as a speaker, writer, and labor publicist in community organizations and coalitions, especially those in which the Brotherhood of Sleeping Car Porters (BSCP) was involved. Encouraged by her recent experiences in the Soviet Union, she drew even closer to the Communist Party as a result of its shift in strategy to build alliances with other leftist groups in an attempt to stop the spread of fascism. She helped in the birth of the newly formed National Negro Congress, which pushed the civil-rights agenda to the left, and she endorsed the Congress of Industrial Organizations when it broke with the American Federation of Labor and adopted a more racially inclusive and aggressive unionizing strategy. Because of Edwards's political skills, she was able to help bring radical and liberal groups together in the common pursuit of civil rights, social justice, and world peace.

When Edwards returned from Europe to the Chicago area in the summer of 1934, she took a month off to write, rest, and see friends and family in Gary, Indiana. Soon, though, she settled into her studio apartment again at the Abraham Lincoln Centre in Chicago. She went to see her friend and confidant, Claude A. Barnett, of the Associated Negro Press. At one time they had been romantically involved, and Barnett had even proposed marriage to her, but Edwards had refused his offer. Barnett had married someone else while Edwards was on her way home from Europe that summer. His new bride, Etta Moten, was a distinguished actor and contralto who, like Edwards, had grown up in southeast Texas. Apparently the newlyweds had kept their wedding a secret for a while, at least from Edwards. After the visit, Edwards told Bill Pickens, of the NAACP: "Just left Claude and his bride both beaming happily in the accepted fashion for newlyweds. Etta is a stunner and Claude is a consistently lucky chap. It wasn't quite fair to pull it on us in June and not let us in on the secret until August."[1]

In mid-September, Edwards was the main speaker at a celebration of the ninth anniversary of the BSCP held in the union's headquarters on South Michigan Avenue in Chicago. The program, conducted by Helena Wilson, president of the Colored Women's Economic Council, or the BSCP's International Ladies Auxiliary, also included white social worker Mary McDowell, who endorsed Edwards's call for class unity across racial lines. Edwards discussed the role of black and white women in the labor movements at home and abroad, calling for unionization to achieve common economic goals.[2]

A couple of weeks later, on September 28, 1934, more than one hundred friends and supporters gathered at the University of Chicago's International House for a testimonial dinner to celebrate Edwards's return from Europe. BSCP leaders A. Philip Randolph and Milton Webster gave speeches, and so did Mary McDowell and Poro College's Annie Malone. Frank Crosswaith, a labor organizer for the International Ladies' Garment Workers Union, Dr. Curtis Reese of the Abraham Lincoln Centre, and music critic Maude Roberts George also paid tribute to Edwards, who then entertained the audience with stories of her experiences in Denmark and other European countries.[3]

Edwards, short of cash when she returned to the United States on July 1, 1934, immediately turned her attention to publishing articles as a freelance journalist. Before heading home to Chicago, she had visited with friends in New York City and stopped by the editorial office of the NAACP's journal, the *Crisis,* to chat with George Streator about publishing a few of her articles. Streator, who along with Roy Wilkins was a managing editor of the *Crisis* at that time, commissioned her to write a series of five articles at ten dollars per article. The stories were to be framed around her recent personal experiences and contacts in Europe, with a special emphasis on race and politics.

A month later, Edwards sent a letter to Wilkins, who in the meantime had become the journal's sole editor after Streator and W. E. B. DuBois resigned in a political dispute with the NAACP. She asked Wilkins if he wished to continue with the arrangements she had made with Streator to do the articles. She enclosed the first of three articles about her experiences in Nazi Germany.[4]

Edwards suffered cash-flow problems that plagued her through the fall of 1934 after the *Crisis* did not publish her articles on Germany. Her intermittent employment as a supervising caseworker and intake supervisor with the Joint Emergency Relief Commission and the Illinois Emergency Relief Commission had ended a year earlier, when she left for Denmark. She was in high demand as a speaker at community forums in Chicago, but she apparently did not collect much in the way of speaker fees. She typically asked for twenty-five dollars, but she complained to Bill Pickens in October: "I'm busy and tired. Much talking, little money."[5]

Because of Edwards's interest in labor and the performing arts, she, Claude Barnett, Lillian Herstein, Morris Topchevsky (a white, radical muralist and resident of the Lincoln Centre), and several other Chicagoans helped to bring the Theater Union's play, *Stevedores,* to the city for a month of performances beginning on December 24, 1934. Black dock workers were the subject of the play, which was directed by Paul Peters and George Sklar. With endorsements by the NAACP, Chicago Federation of Labor, the Urban League, Interchurch Association, social workers' groups, and many other organizations, the performance of *Stevedores* was part of plans by the Chicago Drama Union and the Theater Union to establish a noncommercial theater in Chicago to tackle important social and political themes often ignored in commercial productions.[6]

Edwards kept up her contacts with friends on Broadway as she brought together her political and cultural interests. In December 1934, she celebrated her birthday in part by attending a Christmas dinner to honor Nell Hunter, a friend and soprano in the choir of the Broadway production *The Green Pastures.* Hunter was in Chicago at the time to see her mother and sisters. In addition to Edwards, Maude Roberts George, soprano Anita Patti Brown, and a few other close friends attended the dinner.[7]

Edwards's reputation as an authority on black labor grew when the United States Department of Labor's Division of Negro Economics included her in its campaign to focus on the plight of black workers. In early January 1935, Lawrence A. Oxley, chief of the division, held conferences with experts in several states, including Illinois. He encouraged the creation of policy and planning committees comprised of scholars and other race-relations and labor experts. Edwards was appointed to the state of Illinois committee, which was headed by one of her economics professors and a future U.S. Democratic senator, Dr. Paul Douglas, of the University of Chicago. Edith Abbott, a white social worker who had played an important role in creating the Cook County Bureau of Public Welfare, was the only other woman on the committee.[8]

The *Crisis* soon provided a forum for Edwards and others to debate the relationship between black workers, unions, and company paternalism. Women employed by the B. Sopkins and Sons Co., which made housedresses and aprons in Chicago, provided the context. On June 19, 1933, about 1,500 black and white garment workers had gone on strike, led by the Needle Trades Workers Industrial Union, an affiliate of the Communist Party. Most of the workers were black, and they pressed the company to include James W. Ford, a black Communist, in the negotiations. Chicago police attacked the women with clubs and jailed many who were picketing peacefully outside the factory. After two weeks, the strikers went back to work when the company granted most of their demands, including a wage increase and the abolition of racially discriminatory wage rates. The company refused, however, to sign a contract recognizing the union as the women's bargaining agent. Instead, Sopkins organized an Employee Representation Plan, or company union, in response to section 7(a) of the recent National Industrial Recovery Act, part of the New Deal that guaranteed workers' rights to form unions and engage in collective bargaining.[9]

Into the political void created by the failure of the Communists to gain union recognition in the Sopkins plant stepped the International Ladies' Garment Workers Union (ILGWU). In the summer of 1934, the ILGWU sent a black socialist organizer, Frank R. Crosswaith, from New York to Chicago to spearhead an organizational drive against the company union at the plant. The ILGWU employed Edwards as an organizer to work with Crosswaith. In response, Sopkins stepped up a publicity campaign in the black community against the ILGWU and all unions, except, of course, the one under the thumb of the company. Sopkins summoned black preachers from the South Side of Chicago to the shops to urge workers on their lunch breaks to remain loyal. The company enlisted the support of former congressman Oscar De Priest, a black Republican who had represented the South Side. Other prominent black leaders, including aldermen, gave testimonials to the benevolent paternalism of Sopkins. Placards touting company loyalty went up on church doors and in homes and store windows. White foremen at the doors of the plant checked black women at the door to make sure they wore armbands proclaiming their loyalty to the company. Some of the workers even wore the armbands when they went to the cinema or out on a date at night, fearful someone in the community might report them if they did not.[10]

In the March 1935 issue of the *Crisis*, Edwards blasted black middle-class leaders who kowtowed to the Sopkins company. She singled out Jennie Lawrence, a so-called social worker who in cooperation with De Priest and the company collected weekly dues from each worker to help finance company parties at the Republican Party's headquarters on the South Side. According to Edwards, Lawrence also bought flowers for workers when they were sick and took attendance at parties and demonstrations sponsored by the company union. Edwards urged black leaders to quit "clinging to the frayed skirts of the employer." For her, the workers represented "the great uninformed mass of unskilled labor caught between the nether stones of unscrupulous employers and uninformed and unscrupulous race leadership."[11]

The next issue of the *Crisis* featured an article by J. Wellington Evans and a couple of letters to the editor defending the company and attacking Edwards,

Crosswaith, and unions in general. Evans, a cutter employed at the Sopkins plant whose father was pastor of the Metropolitan Church on South Parkway in Chicago, criticized Edwards's endorsement of class warfare. He denied that a company union existed at the plant, and defended Lawrence, who, he boasted, at one time had done volunteer social work and operated a free employment office. Furthermore, he drew attention to the long-standing racist practices of white trade unions.[12]

The *Crisis* published Edwards's response to Evans, whose father, she pointed out, had used his church to host a mass meeting on October 5, 1934, to promote Sopkins's employee-loyalty campaign. Edwards made clear that it was not Lawrence's personal integrity but rather her credentials as a social worker that she questioned. Edwards admitted that racism plagued trade unions, but pointed out that the same was true of business organizations, churches, schools, and government. She emphasized that since employers were organized through chambers of commerce, boards of trade, and other associations, workers, whether black or white, needed their own organizations. In her view, black middle-class leaders who counseled loyalty to employers were selling out the masses: "'Uncle Tom' did not originate in fiction. Nor did he die with the Emancipation proclamation. He is perpetuated and immortalized in the type of leadership that sells the Negro for a few 'sound American dollars.'"[13]

The role of Evans and other black preachers in backing the Sopkins company reinforced Edwards's impatience with conservative black leaders. A year earlier, in contrast, she had praised Ishmael P. Flory, a student at Fisk University who was expelled after he led protests against a lynching close to campus. The protesters also picketed a local Jim Crow theater, preventing Fisk University singers from performing there. When Edwards, who was in Denmark at the time, heard about what happened at Fisk, she sent Flory a letter of praise. They had met in the summer of 1933, when he sought her out in Chicago to praise her work on behalf of the Progressive Miners of America in the Illinois coal fields. To Edwards, Flory demonstrated the kind of aggressive black leadership that the civil-rights movement needed. "It is stupid and futile," she argued, "to wait upon the pussy-footing 'one-step-at-a-time' philosophy of our philanthropic well wishers. Any educational policy that cannot stand the light of exposure is condemned of itself. Let us have done with such educators, be they black or white."[14]

After working as an ILGWU organizer in the campaign against Sopkins, Edwards continued her work on behalf of the International Labor Defense (ILD) in the Scottsboro and other cases. For a few years, Chicago's Communist-affiliated Unemployed Council had been actively protesting apartment evictions on the South Side. In 1935, Edwards worked on the ILD's Newton Defense Committee, which protested the eviction of Herbert and Jane Emery Newton, an interracial couple, from an apartment which they shared with

and subleased from a white woman, Harriet Williams. The apartment was lo-
cated at 615 Oakwood Boulevard, in the neighborhood of the Abraham Lincoln Centre. Herbert Newton, a well-known black Communist on the South
Side who had studied for two years in the Soviet Union, had been jailed in
Georgia about four years earlier for passing out literature protesting lynching.
His wife, Jane, came from a white upper-middle-class banking family from
Grand Rapids, Michigan, that had severed ties with her because of her political
associations. She had attended the University of Michigan for a semester before
going to New York, where she had joined the Communist Party.[15]

Eviction proceedings against the Newtons and Harriet Williams were carried
out in December 1934, not because of nonpayment of rent but because Herbert was living there with two white women. To enforce the eviction, bailiffs set
their furniture and belongings out in the snow, but Communist demonstrators
quickly moved their stuff back into the apartment. Members of the Chicago
police department's "Red Squad" then arrested the Newtons, and a judge sent
Herbert to the county jail and Jane to a hospital to undergo psychiatric evalu-
ation and then a public sanity hearing. From the perspective of the authorities,
the obvious question was, what upper-class white woman in her right mind
would go against her family, turn to communism, and marry a black man?[16]

One of Jane's psychiatrists considered her insane and recommended confinement in the state hospital, but she was released by authorities after another
doctor convincingly argued that she was "not only sane but brilliant." Her husband, while in jail awaiting trial, was hit with new charges, however. Before the
eviction, Chicago's Red Squad had arrested Herbert on charges of "unlawful assembly" for participating in a protest against the federal government and AFL
leaders over hiring discrimination on federal public-works projects. On December 21, 1934, he started serving time in the city's Bridewell House of Cor-
rections after the judge denied his appeal.[17]

The Newton Defense Committee included a number of churches and organizations, especially the ILD, International Workers Order, Chicago chapter
of the American Civil Liberties Union, John Reed Club, and Chicago Urban
League. Several individual members of Chicago's NAACP energetically supported the Newtons, but the local chapter officially avoided involvement. Black
nationalist organizations such as the Universal Negro Improvement Association took no part at all in the case.[18]

In mid-January 1935, the ILD held a racially integrated meeting at the Mon-
umental Baptist Church in Chicago to raise funds to defend the Newtons.
Charles Wesley Burton presided over the program, which included Edwards,
Jane Newton, Dr. Curtis Reese, and several others as speakers. The featured
speaker was Angelo Herndon, the renowned black Communist organizer who
had recently been released from prison after serving two years for the crime of

"insurrection" in Georgia. Herndon, who had been arrested and sentenced to prison for eighteen to twenty years for his role in protests against the cutoff of relief in Atlanta in 1932, in 1935 was traveling around the country on behalf of the ILD.[19]

After Herbert Newton was released from prison, he joined Edwards on the Scottsboro committee to demand freedom for the nine boys in the case. On June 23, 1935, the sponsoring committee held a mass meeting of sympathetic black and white organizations on the South Side. Endorsed by Professor Melville Herskovits, of Northwestern University, the meeting included a community program that included sports and entertainment, a tent show, quartet singing, and dancing.[20]

Edwards facilitated community coalitions of Communists and non-Communists built around civil-rights issues. She helped to lay the groundwork for other Popular Front organizations designed to oppose the spread of fascism. The high-profile positions taken by the Newton and Scottsboro committees reinforced the growing popularity of the Communist Party as a bold champion of civil rights in Chicago and put pressure on the NAACP, which had remained on the sidelines in the Sopkins strike. Given the role of Communists in the growing militancy on the South Side of Chicago, the NAACP faced a dilemma: whether to endorse more aggressive tactics in civil-rights battles and take a firm stance on behalf of black workers or to lose its credibility and influence as a civil-rights organization.[21]

As a freelance writer, Edwards covered the funeral of fellow Chicago social worker Jane Addams in late May 1935. Edwards paid eloquent tribute to Addams's work at Hull House, emphasizing her unflinching devotion to labor reform, women's rights, and world peace. Calling Addams a "neighbor to the whole world," Edwards especially stressed that Addams did not have an "'attitude' toward the Negro," that "she recognized that the distinction of color exposed him more easily to attack and discrimination at the same time adding a moral responsibility upon Americans to work against extraordinary exploitation because of color." Nevertheless, as Edwards pointed out, "Addams was not the pleading advocate of any particular race. Her efforts and her life were directed toward broad, inclusive measures thru which the whole people would benefit."[22]

In her mostly glowing tribute, though, Edwards did not hesitate to offer a critical perspective on Addams's pacifism and gradualist approach to reform. In a section of Edwards's article that was edited out before the article was published in the *Pittsburgh Courier,* she raised questions about the relevance of gradualist, pacifist methods in the context of rapidly spreading militarism and deep social problems arising from the Great Depression. "Whether these techniques are effective, looking at lynching and at permanent unemployment at home, and at the League of Nations and the rape of China by Japan, the aggression of Italy against Abyssinia," she wrote, "is a matter for our times to determine. Each age must select its own tools."[23]

Edwards, drawing on her experiences as a social worker in Chicago, used her writing skills to challenge popular stereotypes about African Americans on relief. In an article published in the National Urban League's magazine, *Opportunity,* she responded to an article by Professor Newell Eason published in the previous issue of the journal. Criticizing Eason's argument that black families on relief refused to accept suggestions of self-help, Edwards pointed out the structural barriers facing black families—wage inequities, discriminatory hiring procedures on public-works projects, and discrimination in relief allotments. She also drew attention to the prevailing notion that black male workers should not be hired if there are white men who are out of work. In response to criticisms of jobs programs established under the Works Progress Administration, Edwards argued that "men and women on relief beg for and accept jobs, project and work relief assignments—even when the wage offered is the mere equivalent of their relief budgets." As she explained, "It restores some of their self respect to handle cash and to purchase direct and be able to shop without the stigma and discrimination attendant upon buying on disbursing orders."[24]

In a hard-hitting rebuttal to Eason, Edwards cited a recent study of a congested strip of about nine city blocks comprised of 1,349 households on Chicago's South Side. Watermelon, ice cream, and fish vendors, as well as window washers and "junk men" desperate to earn even the tiniest sum of money, hawked their wares and services on the area's streets. Edwards called attention to the hardscrabble attempts at self-help on the part of the black vendors. Junk men, she pointed out, "hitched themselves to carts which they have built out of wheels, usually found on dump heaps, and irregular scraps of board gotten from some building in the process of demolition."[25]

To demonstrate further the desperate, impoverished conditions on the strip, Edwards provided readers a glimpse of the colonies of homeless people who lived in an abandoned building where all electrical wiring and gas piping had been removed. "The building appears gruesomely debauched," she observed. "Outside doors have disappeared so that it stands open always. Window apertures are stuffed with rags, old clothes, cardboard, wire netting, wooden doors, anything at hand." Individuals and families tried to carve out their own spaces in a building with rotten floors and rusted bed springs and scraps of iron that barricaded side entrances. "Various styles and sizes of coal stoves are used in the different individual 'quarters,'" she wrote. "In the absence of flues these are piped through holes cut through to the outer walls of the building. Passing on the outside when several 'quarters' have fires the adjoining vacant lot is a series of smoke puffs at various heights and levels."[26]

Edwards criticized Eason for decrying "the wane of parental authority and the loss of prestige by the father" as a result of relief allotments. In the past, she pointed out, "the complete economic dependence of women upon their husbands, children upon their parents, and in turn sickness and old age, parents upon their children has tended to warp every fine, free impulse in familial relationships." The end result was "the nagging wife wheedling an underpaid husband for the little luxuries of life which his inadequate wage cannot provide." Economic dependence "has created the demand upon older sisters and brothers to sacrifice their own education to help support younger sisters and brothers."[27]

For Edwards, the grim conditions of the black unemployed bore a special message for sociologists, who "instead of decrying this overthrow of the tyrant-parent . . . should rather hasten the day when in addition to sickness and invalidity insurance, a comprehensive unemployment insurance act and adequate assistance for the aged will relieve the burden of poor relations on other poor relations." She argued that professional social workers, because they were in close contact with relief recipients and had access to the case files of those on relief since the beginning of the depression, had an obligation to challenge popular stereotypes about those who allegedly were on the dole. "They are thus in possession of the facts to expose and explode these hair trigger conclusions branding the unemployed as maligners, chiselers and indolent and hopeless parasites," she stressed. Rather than blame the victims, Edwards tried to focus public anger on the underlying roots of unemployment and poverty: "Instead of the too ready indictment of the unemployed condemnation should, it would seem, be directed against the political economy that creates these conditions of mass unemployment and its attendant malnutrition, disease, overcrowding, immorality, delinquency and family disintegration."[28]

As a social worker on visits to homeless shelters on the South Side of Chicago, Edwards saw the further ravages of the Great Depression from the bottom up. On one particular rainy winter night, she stopped by a shelter that was a "feeding station" exclusively for "unattached" men and under the supervision of Fraser Lane, a social worker with years of experience. By the time she arrived at 7 p.m., around 1,400 men had already eaten their ration of beef stew, four slices of bread, and choice of milk or coffee in the time since the soup kitchen opened at 4:30 p.m. Edwards, there to "share a meal" with the men, was taken by what seemed to be a never-ending line of the "torn and dirty" and an occasional former college professor, law school graduate, or group of students waiting for their rations: "This evening a long queue of men trailed out into the alleyway in the rain, edging themselves inside to warmth and food. (They formerly came in at the front, but crowding the walks with shabbily clothed annoyed their comfortable neighbors)."[29]

Edwards also paid a visit to what used to be the Royal Gardens Cabaret, which had been converted into a shelter on 31st Street. Less than a decade earlier, as

Edwards noted, the cabaret had been a vibrant center of Chicago's "night life" and "a favored rendezvous of young white women from the gold coast and sleek, brown men" dancing to a jazz orchestra on a crowded dance floor. Now housing long rows of army cots where about 800 men slept, played cards, checkers, and dominos, or otherwise whiled away the hours, the cabaret, like those who slept there, had fallen on hard times, but remembering its past prompted Edwards to observe, "Tonight I somehow felt wickedly glad that for one brief interval black men had lived gaily, extravagantly, lewdly perhaps. Fed, tailored, groomed, perfumed, loved lavishly."[30]

In Chicago, Edwards was emerging as one of the nation's leading social critics and activists, but she also kept up her prominent international contacts. In the late fall of 1935, for example, she hosted a breakfast to honor Oscar Olsson, of Stockholm, Sweden. Olsson, a member of the Swedish Parliament, teacher, and director of Sweden's adult education movement, had met her the year before when she had visited his country. In 1935, he was on an adult education tour of the United States sponsored by the International Good Knight Templars.[31]

In May 1935, the Joint Committee on National Recovery (JCNR), a council of black organizations encouraged by the Roosevelt administration two years earlier, held a conference at Howard University in Washington, DC, to examine how African Americans were faring in New Deal programs. Because of Edwards's expertise on the conditions of black working women in Chicago, John P. Davis, executive secretary of the JCNR, recommended her inclusion on a list of suggested witnesses for a proposed House of Representatives resolution to investigate the status of black labor under the New Deal. Edwards appeared on the JCNR program at Howard University as a discussant to critique the paper "Negro Unemployment and Its Treatment by FERA," by Forrester Washington, director of the Atlanta School of Social Work. During conference discussions, Communist delegates suggested the need for a Popular Front organization to unify the movement to fight racial discrimination and promote the rights of labor.[32]

The National Negro Congress (NNC) grew out of this conference. On July 6, 1935, Executive Secretary Davis sent Edwards material on the proposed organization along with data on the economic plight of African Americans. He then went to Chicago to discuss arrangements to hold a founding conference February 14–16, 1936.[33] A. Philip Randolph had warned Davis on December 28, 1935, that the BSCP's vice president, Milton Webster, was still "extremely skeptical" about the NNC. Randolph recommended that Davis confer first with Edwards and "thoroughly sell the idea to her." As Randolph emphasized, "She is a mighty useful person. She knows what it is all about and knows everybody. I requested her to help you."[34]

Davis gave Edwards the names of people in Chicago who had committed to sponsoring the congress. She joined the presiding committee, which was head-ed by Adam Clayton Powell Jr., of New York. The presiding committee then put her in charge of the Committee on Women's Work. At Davis's request, she served as a discussion leader at the first women's section of the NNC when the conference opened. The topic was "How Can Negro Women Industrial Work-ers Solve Their Problems?"[35]

Charles Wesley Burton, chair of the Chicago Sponsoring Committee and Randolph's close friend and confidant, worked through Edwards to help raise money for the NNC conference. Edwards, whom the committee had chosen as treasurer, hosted a fund-raising reception for poet, novelist, and playwright Langston Hughes, a sponsor of the NNC, at her apartment on January 19, 1936. About ten days after the reception, Davis invited Hughes to serve as a discus-sion leader on a topical session, "The Role of the Negro Artists and Writers in the Changing Social Order." In the weeks leading up to the founding confer-ence, Edwards entertained a number of dinner guests who supported the NNC, including Hughes and white radical economic theorist Scott Nearing. She also accepted a speaking engagement at a women's club in Detroit as a substitute for Randolph, who was confined to his home in New York, too sick at the time to attend the conference.[36]

According to delegate Roy Wilkins, assistant secretary of the NAACP, whose assignment was to report on the proceedings, the founding NNC conference was "unusually democratic in setting up its machinery and in proceedings."[37] About 970 delegates elected Randolph as president of the NNC, Davis as ex-ecutive secretary, and Marion V. Cuthbert, of the Harlem YWCA, as treasurer. Women made up about one-third of the delegates. Edwards, who joined the Executive Council, spoke on the need for consumers' cooperatives. Neva Ryan and Rosa Rayside called attention to efforts to organize black domestic work-ers in Chicago and New York. Other women representing clubs, relief agencies, and a number of civic and educational organizations emphasized the need for broad-based organizing and racial unity.[38]

In a report to the NAACP, Wilkins called attention to the large number of young black and white delegates from working-class organizations "who came at great personal sacrifice and who owed their allegiance only to organizations committed to a militant fight for the Negro. It was not a congress of school teachers, college presidents and others, whose first allegiance was to forces who might be sympathetic with their aims, but who were not in a position to aid them in fighting for their aims." Impressed with the conference's "bottom up" organizational structure, Wilkins, one of its speakers, reported, "Unquestion-ably, the Congress was an expression of the willingness of the masses of the people to sacrifice and fight."[39]

A number of NAACP leaders attended the conference, which was held at the Eighth Regiment Armory, but the prominent role of Communists caused friction from the outset. Officials of the Illinois state militia threatened to disrupt the conference unless Earl Browder, general secretary of the Communist Party USA, was barred from speaking. Browder did not speak, but James Ford, black vice presidential candidate on the party's ticket in 1932, was allowed to appear on the program. Before the conference, Randolph had assured Walter White, his friend and executive director of the NAACP, that the Congress would not be "'sold down the river' to any political group."[40] The presence of Communists and white representatives of radical labor unions at all of the sessions alarmed some of the delegates. Zulme "Nuffie" McNeill, one such delegate, complained to White about all the attention given to southern sharecroppers and the ILD. In her view, the conference was a deep disappointment: "The Congress was supposedly for the sole purpose of benefitting the Negro by considering and discussing his problems and their possible solutions. However, of every ten people at the sessions, two of them were white, and not of the better classes."[41]

Davis continued to press for cooperation, despite tensions over many issues and charges that the NNC intended to replace the NAACP. In Chicago, Charles Wesley Burton, president of the local council of the NNC, complained to him on May 18, 1936, that "several things still militate against us: the 'red scare' has not died down as yet and the Chicago Council of Negro Organizations seems to be working against us, refusing to cooperate with us on the ground that needless duplication and overlapping of efforts will result if both organizations remain in the field."[42] NAACP leader White, who did not attend the founding conference of the NNC, carefully maneuvered to keep the new organization at arm's length, refusing to join it. In a report filed a month after the conference, however, Wilkins warned that Davis was a "showman" as well as an exceptionally intelligent, energetic leader with "a grasp of the economic and civic plight of the Negro second to none of his contemporaries." From Wilkins's perspective, the NAACP should not take the new organization lightly.[43]

Charles H. Houston, special counsel to the NAACP, advised White that the NAACP should reevaluate its position on labor. In a letter written a couple of weeks after the NNC's founding conference in Chicago, Houston told White that he had been in touch with NAACP members Helen Bryan and Marjorie Penny in Philadelphia about plans to hold next year's conference of the NNC in that city. Bryan and Penny both stressed the NNC's wide representation and commitment to organized labor. They believed that the NAACP should do more to reach out to labor unions and the working class. Houston agreed, telling White: "My own personal thought is that we are to do a job for Negro labor similar to the one done by the A.C.L.U. We cannot become labor organizers because we do not have the experience, but we certainly can organize a strong group of lawyers and members to back up Negro labor in its fight to organize, to picket and to strike, freedom of speech and freedom of assembly."[44]

Wilkins, after attending a meeting of the NNC held at the Abyssinian Baptist Church in Harlem on March 2, 1936, was troubled by the black nationalist speeches he heard in the meeting. He complained to Davis that "most of the speakers were concerned with making very ignorant and derogatory remarks about other people and other organizations, rather than reporting upon the progress and state of the movement for the National Negro Congress." Wilkins condemned the expression of West Indian nationalism that resembled the thought of Marcus Garvey. "You were the only person," he told Davis, "who mentioned cooperation with whites."[45]

Wilkins emphasized to Davis that the NNC had a hard job on its hands. "It looks to me from this distance," Wilkins said, "that you have quite a task out for yourself, curbing and holding in line the heterogeneous collections of malcontents, eager to join any movement not so much for what they can do, but for the spite they can direct toward people and movements with which, for one reason or another, they have not hitherto been identified." Wilkins conceded that these racialist, anti-white sentiments might be confined to the Harlem council, but he warned, "I can assure you, as I sat there my enthusiasm for possible alliance of the N.A.A.C.P. with the National Negro Congress suffered severe blows. All the old myths about the N.A.A.C.P. were paraded last night as truths. . . . I am sure the white persons present in the audience last night, and the Negro members of the Communist Party, must have felt something of the same thing that I felt. They were being rebuffed and insulted in a boorish manner."[46]

At a meeting of the NNC's Executive Committee held at Poro College, which provided a suite of rooms for the headquarters of the local chapter of the NNC, Edwards and other members voted to send a delegation to present President Franklin D. Roosevelt, the House of Representatives, and the Senate with demands for full racial equality, the abolition of lynching, and other civil-rights initiatives. An advisory committee of liberals, socialists, and Communists was also created to help Davis implement Popular Front initiatives. Minnesota governor Floyd Olsen, who had been elected from his state's Farmer-Labor Party, sent a black delegate to the meeting who pledged $100 to help underwrite expenses of the NNC's delegation to present the petition of demands to President Roosevelt and both houses of Congress on March 14, 1936.[47]

Much of the civil-rights and labor activism in which Edwards figured prominently in Chicago was spearheaded by the Citizens' Committee of the BSCP. About four months after the founding conference of the NNC, the AFL at last had granted an international charter to the BSCP. Randolph, president of the BSCP and now of the NNC, was still suffering from a prolonged illness, but he came to Chicago from New York for the ceremony in which the AFL president, William Green, formally presented the union charter. Approximately 2,000 Pullman porters and their families and friends gathered at Du Sable High School for the presentation. Edwards, Mary McDowell, economics professor Paul Douglas, Charles Wesley Burton, and Ed Nockels, director of Chicago labor's WCFL radio station, were seated on the rostrum and introduced to the audience.[48]

In Chicago, Edwards worked as treasurer of the local council of the NNC to aid the unionizing drive by the Congress of Industrial Organizations (CIO). Along with officers Charles Wesley Burton (president), Edward L. Doty (financial secretary), Harriet Keys (secretary), and Henry "Hank" Johnson (executive secretary), Edwards helped to put the Chicago Council of the NNC behind the CIO's recruiting drive among steelworkers in the Chicago–Great Lakes area. To promote pro-CIO sentiment, the council organized mass meetings and created volunteer committees to support the area-wide unionizing campaign by the CIO's Steel Workers Organizing Committee beginning in the summer of 1936. Johnson, a black CIO organizer as well as the executive secretary of the Chicago Council of the NNC, was a Texan who, like Edwards, had witnessed the bloody 1917 Camp Logan Riot in Houston.[49]

At the behest of the NNC, the CIO hired Johnson, James McDonald, of the Amalgamated Association of Meat Cutters and Butcher Workmen of North America, and Eleanor Rye, secretary of the labor committee of the Chicago Council of the NNC, to mobilize broad-based community support on the South Side for the CIO's organizing drive in the area. Rye used her position on the executive board of the Fur Workers' Union as well as her contacts with the Chicago Federation of Labor, local members of the Communist Party, and the BSCP's Citizens' Committee to promote coalition politics. Also included in the coalition were the Chicago Urban League, Inter-Club Council of Chicago, women's clubs, and numerous other organizations. Rye also set out to organize Women's Auxiliaries so that the wives of steelworkers might become an important part of the unionization campaign.[50]

Edwards, along with Rye, Johnson, and McDonald, tried to bridge the gap between the NNC and its main competitor, the Chicago Council of Negro Organizations (CCNO), which had been created in 1935 by liberal organizations such as the local chapter of the Urban League, NAACP, and other fraternal, civic, and church groups in the city. Edwards and Johnson belonged to the CCNO as well as the local council of the NNC, but the competing councils were suspicious of each other. On May 13, 1936, Rye complained to John P. Davis, executive secretary of the NNC, that the CCNO was "trying to steal the thunder from us and in many instances are succeeding quite well." She pointed out that the CCNO had failed to include the NNC when it called a joint conference with the Association of Workers in Public Relief Agencies, of which Edwards was a member, to discuss the administration of relief in the city. The NNC sent Edwards, who at the time was assistant district administrator of the Chicago Relief Administration, to try to persuade A. C. McNeal of the CCNO to include the NNC in the conference, but Edwards's efforts were to no avail. Rye complained that McNeal, who was also president of the local branch of the NAACP, "fought it bitterly."[51]

Tensions also plagued relations between the CIO and the NNC, which hoped, of course, to get financial help from the CIO in exchange for cooperation in the unionizing campaign among black steelworkers in Chicago and Gary. Davis consistently chided Johnson for not keeping him informed of his activities and for not bringing in more contributions to the NNC. "I am working to get ten thousand dollars allocated by C.I.O. toward Negro work in steel under auspices of Congress," Davis reminded him. "I don't stand a chance to get this unless you, Eleanor, and Mac stick by me with weekly complete letters on the activities of the labor committee. . . . Our Negro organizers must prove that they can bring in members—and especially must Eleanor plan her work and produce."[52]

After repeated complaints from Davis that the NNC, due to its desperate financial predicament, was on the verge of being evicted from its national office in Washington, DC, Johnson, frustrated, urged him to come to Chicago in September 1936 to meet with a few key people to better explain the purposes and functions of the NNC and to set up a budget. Davis claimed he did not have the money to travel to Chicago, but Johnson emphasized the urgency of the situation. Johnson told him that the CIO was contributing $100 per month to the Chicago Council of the NNC, and that he and McDonald were contributing another $108 from their salaries to the local NNC. Disgusted at the way the NNC was being conducted, Johnson complained: "I am not satisfied with the present arrangements and it is hardly possible that I could be satisfied until a distinct change is made in the set-up in Chicago."[53]

Infighting between Johnson and Rye also took a toll on the NNC and the CIO's campaign in the local steel industry. According to Johnson, Rye was undermining the unionizing drive by impugning his motives. "Eleanor has damaged the Congress considerably," he bitterly insisted to Davis. "Instead of using the contacts and prestige which I had built up for the Congress through my work to further strengthen and build an organization, she has gotten the rumor around to more than one or two people with whom I have been working very closely that since I have been working as an organizer for the C.I.O. I had gotten the 'swell head,' and wanted to become the big leader of the National Negro Congress in the Chicago area, while she did all the work, and that she was going to see to it that I did not use her to build up my prestige." Johnson, attacking Rye for creating other unnecessary antagonisms among black steelworkers, complained that "if a check is not put on her little mouth she will do the Congress damage nationally." Finally, he claimed that Rye had told Neva Ryan, of the Domestic Workers Association, that the NNC had secured jobs with the CIO for him and McDonald on a specific stipulation that each kick back $1.50 per day to the NNC. "All of the other things she has done are excusable and follow the natural course of things," he wrote to Davis, "but when she begins to infer that the National Negro Congress is making a racket out of a serious campaign to organize steel workers, I think a stop should be made to that kind of propaganda."[54]

International travel pulled Edwards away from the organizational demands of the newly formed NNC in the last half of 1936, but when she returned, she quickly went to New York City in an effort to soothe tensions with NAACP leaders. She worked with Communists but maintained her close relationship with Randolph and other socialists as well as liberals. She invited Juanita Jackson, special assistant to Walter White, to a meeting on behalf of the NNC on January 29, 1937. The meeting, to be held at the YWCA on West 137th Street in New York City, was sponsored by Max Yergan, a former YMCA missionary who had been radicalized by his experiences in South Africa. Edwards, hoping to ease NAACP fears, tried without success to get Roy Wilkins to attend the meeting. "I'll try to come down early," she wrote to him, " . . . to clear the issue of 'duplication.'"[55]

As national chair of the NNC's Women's Committee, Edwards was working for the New York Federation of Councils while Davis was offering to help the NAACP in its campaign for anti-lynching legislation. Davis suggested to White that he contact her, Randolph, and Marion Cuthbert to set up a meeting with them to explore ways the NNC could help the NAACP in its battle against lynching.[56]

The Greater New York Federation of Councils hosted a banquet for Edwards in mid-December 1936 at which she and several others on the program spoke. Afterward she went back to Chicago for her birthday and holiday season but returned to New York on behalf of the NNC on January 4, 1937. Working with Yergan and James H. Baker Jr., who chaired the Greater New York Federation of Councils, Edwards helped to organize and coordinate a Popular Front program that had several components. Baker arranged a dinner and meeting at the West 135th Street YMCA on February 5, 1937, to discuss housing and support for an upcoming conference of maritime workers. Edwards, who had spent the last five weeks appraising the local council's activities, was there to discuss recommendations to improve and strengthen its work. Two weeks later, Yergan, chair of the Committee on Housing campaign, sent a letter asking key friends and agencies to attend a meeting on February 26 to draft plans for a campaign to publicize the need for adequate housing in the black community.[57]

Back in Chicago, however, the NNC continued to sputter amid growing tensions between the local council and the organization's national headquarters. In April 1938, Davis told Ishmael Flory, secretary-treasurer of the Joint Council of Dining Car Employees in Chicago, that he and Randolph "just had a long, long talk" about problems in the Chicago NNC. According to Davis, Randolph had persuaded Charles Wesley Burton, president of the Chicago Council, to resign "for the good of all concerned." Davis, who had written a letter to William Patterson to get more information on the council's problems, urged Flory that "everything possible be done to make Dr. Burton feel that he is still a part of the council and that all patience be used in working with him even after he relinquishes the chairmanship. I know he has many weaknesses, but he also has a number of good points, not the least of which is an absolute loyalty to the Congress, and I feel certain that he can be of a great deal of service to the local council."[58]

Apparently Burton did not resign immediately. In October 1938, he still remained as president of the local council, preparing for an upcoming Midwest conference of the NNC to be held on October 28. Tensions between him and Davis had surfaced, though. In a letter, Burton expressed disappointment that Davis had not come to Chicago to help finalize plans for the conference. Complaining about the lack of progress by the NNC in Chicago, Burton responded to Davis's steady complaints about a lack of money by assuring him they could probably raise enough money for him to travel to Chicago. Burton told Davis that Edwards, Flory, William L. Patterson, and others had pledged money to buy a train ticket for him and pay for a hotel and week of maintenance if he would come to Chicago a week ahead of the planned conference.[59]

Shortly after the conference, the Chicago Council of the NNC underwent reorganization. A couple of months later, Flory informed Davis that Dewey Jones, one of the New Deal's race-relations advisers in the Works Progress Administration, had accepted the candidacy to replace Burton as president of the Chicago Council. Optimistic about the reorganization, Flory reported to Davis that he was especially exploring ways to beef up the labor section of the NNC and to extend the sweep of the Popular Front in the city.[60]

Edwards's role in the Chicago Council of the NNC soon diminished. Because of her growing overseas travels and expanding intellectual horizons, she devoted more and more of her time to world peace in the late 1930s. She remained committed to the Popular Front but increasingly focused on its application to international politics and coalitions. The war against fascism would soon take her to Spain, where a raging civil war would absorb most of her time and energy for the next few years.

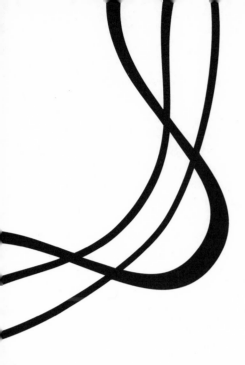

6

Conducting Educational Travel Seminars to Europe

Mussolini's invasion of Ethiopia in 1935 and the outbreak of the Spanish Civil War in 1936 underscored the importance of the Popular Front to check the spread of fascism. The grave threat to world peace posed by Hitler and Mussolini reinforced Edwards's determination to link civil rights at home to the struggles against imperialism, theories of racial supremacy, and fascism in Europe. As she had suggested in her eulogy of Jane Addams, the rise of fascism posed a threat to world peace for which pacifism had no solution. Without a radical social restructuring to get rid of exploitation and poverty, the use of force might be necessary to defend the world against those who sought to spread racial hatred and fascist institutions through conquest.

To broaden the perspective of African Americans on international affairs, Edwards initiated educational travel seminars overseas. She planned summer tours abroad to educate participants on the serious economic and political problems confronting the world. In particular, she set out to make clear what was at stake for African Americans in the hate-filled political machinations of fascist dictators. She hoped to promote peace, Popular Front coalitions, women's trade unions, and the National Negro Congress overseas, just like she had done in Chicago.

On December 17, 1935, Edwards began to recruit for the first of her educational summer seminars. She planned it to coincide with the Third International Conference of Social Workers in London scheduled for July 12–18, 1936. She was offering an eight-week seminar at a cost of $525 per person that would consist of a week each in England, Denmark, Sweden, Finland, the Soviet Union, and France, with two weeks in transit and return via Paris. The seminar would not only educate the participants but also underwrite Edwards's overseas political activities as a social worker and writer.[1]

Edwards planned to retrace the steps that had taken her to the International People's College in Denmark in 1933–1934 with her seminar participants. The emphasis would be on showcasing class-based cooperative institutions and public-housing initiatives. In England, for example, she planned to take seminar participants to visit housing experiments, the Ruskin Workers' School at Oxford University, and a cooperative school at Manchester. The seminar's focus in the Scandinavian countries would be on folk schools, land reform, consumers' and producers' cooperatives, and public-housing innovations. In the Soviet Union, Edwards planned trips to Kiev, Moscow, Kharkov, and Leningrad, where members of the seminar would visit collective farms, factories, and museums and attend the Bolshoi and Children's Theatre.[2]

An interracial group of twenty-three seminar enrollees sailed with Edwards from New York on July 3, 1936. Most were teachers and social workers, and most were from Chicago, including A. L. Foster, of the Urban League, Dr. A. Wilberforce Williams, a physician and health columnist, Viola Neely, assistant district supervisor of the Cook County Bureau of Public Welfare, Margaret Kirkland, a teacher, and Imogene Rousseau, a social worker. Pauline Lubin, a friend of Edwards's from Houston who was a librarian and representative of the Texas Federation of Colored Women's Clubs, also was part of the group.[3]

A number of friends came down to the dock that morning to see Edwards off. She was there early to count heads for a scheduled noon departure. Richard Barthé, her friend the Harlem Renaissance sculptor, brought her flowers. So, too, did Agnes Burns Wieck, with whom Edwards had worked in the coalmining struggles in southern Illinois. She gave Edwards a bouquet of roses and letters of introduction to European women whom Edwards intended to interview for a new magazine, the *Woman Today*. Both Edwards and Wieck were on the advisory board of the magazine, an antifascist publication devoted to women's rights, the organization of women into trade unions, and international peace. At that time Wieck was working with the American League against War and Fascism and lobbying for minimum-wage laws for women in the workforce.[4]

Edwards designed a rigorous routine for the seminar at a time of increasing travel by African Americans to Scandinavian countries and the Soviet Union. Some members of the seminar complained about the regimentation, but Edwards was determined to uphold the educational value of the seminar as she drew on her previous experiences, training, and readings. She gave lectures on the history and social and political institutions of the countries they visited. On the second day at sea, she began the lectures and discussions with an analysis of England's imperial policy and its role in institutionalizing race hatreds and oppression. Other groups on the ship joined the discussions. On the final day at sea en route to Europe, Edwards asked Countee Cullen, a prominent Harlem Renaissance poet, to read from some of his poems. She had recruited him for the seminar after trying for two days to get up enough courage to ask him. "But he was so charming in his response," she noted, "that I felt ashamed."[5]

As a contributing editor of the Woman Today, Edwards published a couple of articles on women's issues based on her travels that summer. One of the articles grew out of an interview with Kai Anderson, editor of a progressive women's magazine in Stockholm whom she had met in her travels there in 1934. Reunited over breakfast for the first time in two years, the two women discussed sexism, birth control, low-cost housing, government support for prenatal care, and the role of Housewives' Clubs in visiting factories and supporting consumers' research to coordinate production and consumption. Anderson told Edwards, who belonged to the Illinois Housewives Association as an assistant on national and international affairs, that her magazine also emphasized cultural and recreational issues important to women, ranging from class distinctions in beauty and clothing to vacations for mothers and housewives. Under the coordination of Housewives' Clubs, Anderson emphasized, housewives had joined professional and trade union women on travel excursions to Denmark, Norway, and the Soviet Union.[6]

Edwards briefed Anderson on the formation of the National Negro Congress and its vigorous commitment to the labor movement. They agreed that the struggles of all minorities were part of the worldwide struggles on the labor front. "Until I knew you two years ago," Anderson said, "I had never met and talked with a Negro woman. At first it was strange and interesting, a novelty. Now we have spoken about all these things, we have understood all these things together. It is as though you were my sister working beside me."[7]

The cultural exposure enjoyed by seminar participants grew out of and reinforced Edwards's political activism. In the Soviet Union, for example, she took the participants to several performances of the Moscow Theatre for Children, which she described in the Woman Today. She was impressed with the children's knowledge not only of technique and form but also of the work of classic Russian writers. She noted especially their love of the poetry of Alexander Pushkin.

In addition to attending performances inside the theater, directed by Natalia Satz, Edwards and the seminar participants accompanied members of the children's theater to a tuberculosis sanatorium, where she observed a performance for the patients. As she acknowledged, the children's theater also served a frank political purpose—to help consolidate and extend Soviet socialism.[8]

On August 16, 1936, members of Edwards's seminar left Kiev for Paris en route to New York, but she went back to Moscow alone for a prolonged stay. Her visit was marred by illness. Besides suffering from stomach flu and bronchitis, she developed a serious infection in her right ankle after she fell off a street car. She suffered only a tiny abrasion, but an infection set in, spreading nearly to the bone before she sought medical help. "I had it drained and it is now healing nicely," she later told Claude Barnett, "but with a deep, ugly scar that may send me to cotton stockings. What a blow to my vanity!"[9]

Edwards hoped to stay longer in the Soviet Union, but her Soviet tourist visa was soon to expire. At her request, Barnett wrote the Soviet Embassy and Consulate in an attempt to get her a correspondent's visa as a reporter for the Associated Negro Press (ANP), but to no avail. A correspondent's visa would have given her more flexibility, let her stay longer, and therefore would have given her access to cheaper housing rates. Edwards was eager to plan next summer's seminar while she was there, but Soviet authorities refused to grant a correspondent's visa for the ANP since the previous issuance of her tourist visa had automatically voided her eligibility for any other type of visa.[10]

Because of the physical demands of the seminar, Edwards had missed the deadline for sending Barnett a series of articles she had promised for the ANP. By the time she sent three articles, promising that more would soon follow, the seminar participants had already returned to Chicago. Barnett pointed out that the participants spoke favorably about their experiences, but he chided her about the articles: "Why were you so late in sending your material? It came as a sort of anti-climax to our stories of their [seminar members'] return."[11]

Edwards defended her tardiness with the articles: "Why didn't I send them earlier? My Dear, I had 23 people in Europe!" She pointed out how exhausting and hectic it had been to take care of all the logistical issues that came up as the result of leading such a large group abroad. As she also noted, she had been sick with bronchitis for a week in Moscow after the participants left for home. The news from Barnett that seminar participants were giving public talks on their experiences pleased Edwards a great deal, though. She emphasized that "satisfied customers" would do much to encourage participation in next year's seminar. "And, incidentally," she noted to Barnett, "I did give them a corking trip. You know how the Race is, and they were no exceptions. Having no previous experience to go by, they were very critical and watchful of white groups led mostly by University prof[essors] of international prestige. And in every

instance they found that our group had visited more institutions, been entertained in private homes and by groups and altogether had a more intimate
glimpse of the countries and people visited."[12]

All of Edwards's previous travels and new friendships in Europe benefited
those who participated in the seminar. She may have lacked the formal educational credentials of other seminar directors, but her knowledge, self-con-
fidence, dynamic energy and personality, and extensive contacts opened a lot
of doors for members of her group. "I gave them a good show—an intimate
one that few tourists ever get," she boasted to Barnett. "My European friends
were royal to us." She added, "Funny, you know. In 1929 Jewel [Herbert] and I
spent 3? mos. in Europe and only once were we guests in a home. Now whether
its Vienna, Moscow, London, Paris, or Copenhagen my program is as crowded as tho' I was in New York or Chicago. It seems quite natural when I stop to
think of it."[13]

Edwards complained, though, that the seminar was so demanding and grueling that "I actually forgot I was a person. I felt entirely depersonalized and
completely mechanized." She had worked at a frenetic pace right up until the
day she had left for Europe. As a result, she had packed at the very last minute
without time to shop for the trip. "It was wild, really—I'm only just now getting
straightened out and organized," she said. Seminar members teased her that she
used to have a reputation as a "pretty keen dresser," but that now she had become "pretty careless save on occasions."[14]

The teasing had captured Edwards's attention: "I began to realize this matter
of good dressing was as much a matter of time and attention as of money for
I've been working the past 2 years but I'd been trying to do so many things that
I just hadn't taken the time shopping and planning required." So, when she later
got to Vienna, she went on a shopping spree in one of the city's finest clothing
stores. As she explained, "Well, anyway I got to thinking it over and realized that
being past 35 it was hardly the part of wisdom to go hayseed."[15]

Edwards told Barnett she would be back in the United States in early December and would likely "hang around" New York, Boston, and Washington, DC,
most of the month. She mentioned that she would be doing some work for the
Woman's Section of the National Negro Congress. She asked him to see what
he could do to help her schedule some paid lectures in the area. "Really when
I read this letter and see all the things I'm asking you to do I am a bit appalled
at my audacity," she admitted. "But of course it is no new thing to you and perhaps I too take your tolerance and indulgence for granted."[16]

Edwards sent Barnett new pictures of her in a beautiful, multicolored hand-
woven robe and hand-embroidered needlepoint cap that she had recently
bought in Uzbekistan. "I bought the cap off of the wearer's head," she told him,
"And I picked the robe up by accident." She urged Barnett to use the pictures

however he thought best to advertise her winter lectures and next summer's travel tour. Appreciative of all that he had done for her, she wrote with a subtle reference to their past romantic relationship: "I think your autobiography ought to be titled 'Careers I have helped to shape.' Your autobiography would embrace the biography of so many, many contemporaries. And that's not being cryptic and I'm not alluding to women. In fact I'm really feeling quite sweet and mellow. I can't decide whether I'm getting old and foolish or just relaxing a little."[17]

Like Louise Thompson, W. E. B. DuBois, Langston Hughes, and many other African Americans who had visited the Soviet Union, Edwards enjoyed the fact that her skin color was not a handicap in the country. A number of black radical intellectuals and artists, impressed by the Bolshevik Revolution in 1917, had traveled there in the 1920s and early 1930s in search of an alternative model to racial segregation in the United States. They had come away favorably impressed by the comparative absence of racism toward African Americans. Edwards wrote a letter to her friend Robert Abbott, publisher of the *Chicago Defender*, emphasizing the lack of racial prejudice that she encountered among Russians. She told him of the summer seminar's success, stressing the magnificent reception they had received in the Scandinavian countries and the Soviet Union. She urged him to visit the Soviet Union soon, noting that as a black newspaper publisher, he would receive a warm reception. "I think you would be particularly interested in the experiments here," she wrote optimistically, "particlarly [sic] in regard to the liquidation of Race prejudice. Perhaps nowhere in the world is there such a mixture of races and for the first time in history racial friction has been destroyed."[18]

After leaving Moscow, where health problems had plagued her, Edwards cruised down the Volga River and through the Caucasus to get some rest and relaxation with friends on the Soviet Black Sea Riviera. For a week, she lolled on the beach in the sun, bathing in the nude. In a letter to Barnett, she told him how wonderful it felt to bake in the sun with "some splendid specimens—as well as some pretty flabby numbers." Some of the bathers were "sunburned blacker than I," she said. "And I was trying to bake a few shades darker. It's more popular here. I'd love to be one of those velvety black gals. I could tuck this end of the world in my breast pocket. And even a mere brown skin has no cause to complain."[19]

When Edwards left the Soviet Union for Austria and then a short trip into Germany, however, danger quickly swept away the temporary feelings of sunbaked contentment. The forces of repression, militarism, and authoritarianism had strengthened their grip on power in parts of Europe. On October 31, 1936, for example, she wrote from Kitzbuhel in the Tirol region of Austria that "in Vienna I found most of my friends in jail."[20]

Edwards did not really want to go to Germany, in part because she was a bit pressed for time. It would be tough to squeeze in even a brief trip because after she had undergone X-rays and tests in Vienna, a doctor had recommended three weeks of rest in the Swiss Alps to help clear up a long-standing problem in her right bronchial tube. Ever since influenza had confined Edwards to bed for three weeks during a winter she spent in New York a few years earlier, she had suffered bronchial problems from time to time. A rest cure in the Swiss Alps would require her to shorten her stay in Vienna, Geneva, and Paris, but as she made clear, "I'd do more than that to be rid of this trouble. I was very ill at Tuskegee last time but Mary Williams nursed me like a baby until I was able to come home. My Dr. assures me that 3 weeks in a place of an altitude of 3000 feet will absolutely cure me."[21]

In 1934, though, Edwards had promised the family of Communists with whom she stayed in the Bavarian Alps village of Unterammergau that she would return in two years. She was determined to keep her promise and see how the family was faring at the hands of the Nazis. Besides, the village was located in a picturesque setting. "It's really quite charming," she wrote to Claude Barnett.[22]

In August, Edwards crossed into Germany to visit the family for a couple of days. The family, although delighted to see her, feared that her presence might invite a police raid. Conditions had deteriorated even more since Edwards's visit two years earlier. Her skin color added to the danger, especially since she was there shortly after African American track star Jesse Owens had embarrassed the Nazis by winning four gold medals at the International Summer Olympics in Berlin. She reported that "things are more tense in Germany and people who entertain foreign guests are immediately suspect and liable to police raids."[23]

Edwards spent much of her time in Unterammergau with Leon, the host family's handsome son who was a craftsman in a nearby factory. They discussed politics and the class implications of his upcoming marriage. Leon was unhappy at the time because his parents had arranged for him to marry a wealthy girl he did not love. The wedding was to be held on November 30, 1936, but Leon's heart belonged to a very poor girl in Hanover. "Poor chap," Edwards observed, "he sighs so heavily."[24]

On a Saturday afternoon, Leon took Edwards to see some friends she had met two years earlier, and they enjoyed an exciting reunion of wine, music, and intimate conversation. As Edwards fondly remembered, Leon "dressed up in his beautiful peasant clothes, green hat with a beautiful cock's plume at the back, green suit with elk horn buttons," and walked with her two miles down to the next village. His friends, "very merry mountain fellows," were thrilled to see her again after two years. "And so they brought out wine and cake and the guitar and the melodian [sic]," she recalled, "and I had to have my picture made in their funny short leather breeches. It was jolly."[25]

Leon and Edwards afterward walked to a coffee shop, where she lent him a sympathetic ear as he poured out his feelings about his arranged marriage. "And then we walked the 2 mi. back with the moon over the snow tipped Bavarian Alps," Edwards wrote. "And then we stopped and kissed back of the barn before we got to the house. Tender, innocent, very lovely." Flushed with the excitement of the moment, Edwards nearly missed her train out of Germany because of her time behind the barn with Leon. As she later confessed, "I'm still feeling red in the face and wondering if I'm getting old and silly—or just relaxing. Anyhow it was nice."[26]

From Unterammergau, Edwards headed for the rest cure in the Swiss Alps, but she ran into trouble with Nazi authorities when she reached the border. Her skin color attracted the attention of Nazi officials. "I was arbitrarily arrested and searched at the border," she complained. "And when I say searched I mean having one's clothing entirely taken off and the seams examined, the toes and what not."[27]

After the Nazis released her to cross the border, she holed up at the rest cure in the Swiss Alps. She spent three weeks doing nothing but eating three meals daily, walking two hours every day, and sleeping a lot—all of this, of course, in hopes of getting rid of the bronchial disturbance that plagued her.

While in Austria, Edwards had received a press card from the Associated Negro Press, and she hoped to use the card to arrange an interview with Ethiopian emperor Haile Selassie in Geneva, where he was presenting his case against Italy at the League of Nations. She wrote a letter to the Ethiopian Legation requesting an interview with Selassie for the ANP and one with the empress for the *Woman Today.*[28]

As a journalist, Edwards frequently wrote articles that did not conform to copy guidelines. Barnett reminded her that newspapers often had a 500-word limit on articles, and he scolded her for the excessive length of her stories, some of which ran from 2,000 to 2,500 words. In a letter to her, he pointed out that the *Pittsburgh Courier,* for example, had rejected a batch of her articles on that basis. "I plead guilty to forgetting that stipulation," Edwards admitted. "You ought to tell me what to cut. That is less description or less conversation. Belle has told me I have too 'fulsome' a style—whatever that means. But she is also shocked at the intimate stories I tell."[29]

While Edwards was in Europe that summer, the peace movement at home tried to mobilize a new coalition of groups against war in Europe. Sponsored by the American Friends Service, the recently created Emergency Peace Campaign (EPC) launched a nationwide campaign to discourage pro-war sentiments in the United States. Edwards was among those recruited by the EPC's Speakers Bureau. In a letter that was forwarded to her in Vienna, Fred Atkins Moore asked her to subscribe to the campaign. She replied, however, that she could not afford a yearly contribution of twelve dollars. "At present I am spending with nothing coming in," she wrote. She did offer, though, to give a couple of free speeches on behalf of the campaign upon her return to the United States.[30]

Edwards told Moore to check with A. Philip Randolph about her schedule. She expected to be in New York between December 15 and December 22, and then in Philadelphia and Washington, DC, to do some work for the NNC. From December 15, 1936, to April 1, 1937, she would be available to give a couple of speeches for the Emergency Peace Campaign. She told Moore that because her friends in Vienna had been jailed and she had been strip-searched by the Nazis on a short but "very disagreeable" trip into Germany, "I'm quite in the mood to go on a rampage against armaments."[31]

After Edwards returned to the United States on December 7, 1936, her work with the NNC focused more and more on international affairs. The Greater New York Federation of the NNC held a banquet in Harlem in her honor December 15. A coalition of Communists, socialists, and liberals gathered to hear her perspective on the state of affairs in Europe. Among those who attended were Rev. Adam Clayton Powell Jr., Benjamin J. Davis Jr., Frank Crosswaith, Bessye Bearden, Aaron Douglas, Lester Granger, and Assemblyman William Andrews.[32]

After criticizing the League of Nations' failure to come to Ethiopia's aid, she praised financial contributions by Soviet workers to the Ethiopian defense fund. She pointed out the implications of fascist expansion in Africa, emphasizing that Mussolini's aggression was encouraging Nazi Germany's lust for Liberia, the last "semi-independent" African nation. "You should see how proudly the Soviet people place Negro heroes alongside their own," Edwards told the audience. "For example, on the wall paper of the Kharkov factory, the workers have placed the picture of Emperor Haile Selassie next to the pictures of Maxim Gorki and Lenin."[33]

Edwards suffered a long bout with the flu that winter in Chicago, but soon afterward went on a spring speaking tour in Texas. The trip brought her back home to see her mother and other relatives in Houston in late April 1937. "I'm glad to get down here for a little sunshine," she wrote to Claude Barnett. "I have been so slow regaining my strength after the flu."[34]

Edwards stopped first in Marshall, Texas, where she gave a lecture at Wiley College. At a YWCA forum in Houston, she discussed labor conditions overseas, holding up Denmark's system of unemployment insurance as a model. She also pointed out that Danish workers had given $50,000 to Ethiopia in an unsuccessful effort to repel fascist Italy's invasion in 1935. In response to questions, she praised the CIO's racial policies, pointing in particular to the International Union of Mine Mill & Smelter Workers in Birmingham, Alabama. She also attacked company unions, which especially plagued the Texas labor movement. Later on the trip, she spoke to students at the Houston College for Negroes, and she spent the week of May 5–11 as a guest lecturer on the campus of Prairie View A&M College.[35]

In scheduling her trip from Chicago to Texas, Edwards ran up against the craziness of trying to book first-class travel from a northern state to cities in the Jim Crow South. "I managed to get Pullman into Marshall," she told Claude Barnett, "and the promise that return accomodations [sic] would be awaiting me in N.O. [New Orleans]." The promise came from an agent for the Illinois Central via telephone, so Edwards asked Barnett to "get a letter for me or whatever magic it was you used to adapt so that I'll be sure of having the accomodation [sic] handed over to me when I get to N.O." She was scheduled to leave New Orleans to return to Chicago on the 14th of May.[36]

Barnett's secretary, Irene Roland, confirmed that a reservation was being held for Edwards in the open car at the New Orleans station. According to instructions, Edwards was to go to the city ticket office and ask for the reservation. "As an interstate passenger they will sell you in the open car if necessary since that is a positive law," wrote Roland. "They will probably put you in a compartment."[37]

When Edwards went to the ticket office in New Orleans to claim her reservation, however, she got the runaround. Told to return when the ticket agent was in, she did so only to learn that there was no space on the train for her. Edwards then went to her sister Anna Bell's house in New Orleans and called the station to request space. The agent first asked her phone number, "I assume to locate the neighborhood," Edwards noted. After she provided her sister's phone number, the agent immediately reserved a space for her on the Pullman. Anna Bell and her husband were the only blacks who lived in their white neighborhood, so the agent assumed that Edwards's phone call came from a white person. Edwards's brother-in-law, who was "exceedingly light," went to the station and picked up the ticket for her.[38]

When Edwards got to the gate, however, the Pullman conductor looked at her, took her ticket, and told her she could not use it, referring her then to the station agent. The agent insisted on giving her money back. "When I refused to take it," Edwards wrote, "he threw it at me through the window. I went off refusing to pick it up and telling him I could wait and get the money from the Chicago office. I then, of course, boarded the Jim Crow coach, my luggage having been put in the Pullman." The story did not end there, however, for when the conductor came for her ticket, he gave her back her original Pullman ticket and told her that she could now have the original first-class seat she had reserved in Chicago. Edwards relayed the incident to Barnett: "I have had this experience with the I.C. out of New Orleans on another occassion [sic] and since I shall probably be travelling South next winter would like it called to their attention."[39]

As a result of Edwards's bout of two months with the flu and her Texas tour, she dropped the ball on publicity work for her second travel seminar abroad in the summer of 1937. She decided to go through with the seminar anyway in order to maintain continuity and build interest in it. She asked Barnett to write a letter to the State Department requesting ANP credentials for her to enter Spain to cover the Civil War when she got to Europe.[40]

Edwards timed the second seminar abroad to coincide with the conference of the Anti-Imperialist International Congress in Paris in the summer of 1937. By then, the Spanish Civil War had been raging for a year as the democratically elected Popular Front coalition government of Loyalists fought desperately to avoid its overthrow by right-wing forces under the command of General Francisco Franco and aided by Mussolini and Hitler. The bombing of Guernica by Hitler's planes had led to the town's fall to Franco's forces just a few months before Edwards arrived in Paris in 1937. At the opening of the Loyalist-sponsored Spanish Pavilion of the Paris International Exposition in July, Edwards and her seminar participants were among those who witnessed the unveiling of painter Pablo Picasso's representation of the bombing of Guernica. There she met and established a lifetime friendship with Otto and Hermina Dumont Huiswoud, Harlem Communists originally from Dutch Guiana and British Guiana, respectively. Also there with Edwards in Paris were William Patterson and Louise Thompson as well as Jacques Roumain, a Haitian Communist, and the radical Afro-Cuban poet Nicolás Guillén. Langston Hughes, on assignment as a correspondent for the *Baltimore Afro-American* to report on the role of Americans in the International Brigades in Loyalist Spain, was also in Paris at the time to attend the Second International Writers' Congress.[41]

Members of Edwards's summer seminar returned to New York at the end of September 1937, but she remained in Europe to attend a conference of the International Cooperative Alliance. She also attended the World Conference against Anti-Semitism and Racism, but according to the *Pittsburgh Courier,* she planned to return to the United States on the fifteenth of October, in time to attend the second annual conference of the National Negro Congress in Philadelphia and to organize a Christmas tour to Mexico.[42]

Because of Edwards's growing interest in the Spanish Civil War, however, her plans to return to the United States in time for the NNC conference changed. While in Kiev on August 5, 1937, she had written Claude Barnett to ask him to write the State Department to request that she be granted credentials to represent the Associated Negro Press in Spain. Chester Franklin, owner and editor of the black newspaper the *Call* in Kansas City, had already applied to the State Department on her behalf for permission to go to Spain as a correspondent for his newspaper. Her passport was about to expire at the time, and she wanted to go to Spain to cover the civil war before returning home.[43]

Edwards kept her plans hidden from John P. Davis, executive secretary of the NNC, until the last minute. On October 2, 1937, she notified him that the Social Workers' Committee to Aid Spanish Democracy had asked her to go to Spain to report on colonies of children's refugees uprooted by the civil war. Writing from Paris, she told Davis she would leave for Spain the next day and therefore would be unable to attend the NNC conference in Philadelphia. She did not plan to sail from Le Havre, France, to the United States until the third of November, just in time to present her report to the November meeting of the Social Workers' Committee.[44]

Edwards's trip into the thick of fighting in war-torn Spain would soon raise her consciousness and shape her political commitments even further. With world war looming on the horizon, she saw the defense of Spain's Republican government as critical to efforts to halt the spread of fascism. For the next few years, working to mobilize resources on behalf of Republican Spain and to educate African Americans as to why they should support democratic forces there would absorb much of her time and energy.

7

With Loyalists in the Spanish Civil War

Along with Constance Kyle, a white Chicago social worker and member of the National Negro Congress, Edwards left Paris for Spain in early October 1937 on behalf of the Social Workers' Committee to Aid Spanish Democracy. For Edwards, the Spanish Civil War represented the central battleground in the war against fascism. Risking her life on the ground in Spain, she devoted her skills as an activist social worker, journalist, and fund-raiser to the defense of Spain's elected Republican (or Loyalist) government, a Popular Front coalition. Upon her return to the United States from her month-long stay in Spain, she would tirelessly direct much of her political energy toward fund-raising and promoting support for the Loyalists, especially in the African American community.

The two social workers bore credentials from the Spanish Minister of Public Instruction. Kyle, a member of the staff of the Illinois Research Department at the University of Illinois Medical School, was in Spain to coordinate distribution of money and supplies sent through the North American Committee to Aid Spanish Democracy. Edwards's mission was to report on the conditions of Spanish children at Puigcerda, Barcelona, and Valencia who had been evacuated from bombarded areas after their parents were killed. She was also to visit

the International Brigade in which many African American men were serving as volunteer soldiers. Among supporters and friends in Paris to see her
and Kyle off as they departed for Spain were William Patterson, of the International Labor Defense, Mary Thygeson Ford, of New York, Dr. A. Wilberforce
Williams, of Chicago, Harold Weinstein, a history professor and author at Columbia University, Peter Rhodes, of the United Press, and Ione Boulanger, secretary of the Children's Commission on the Comité Sanitaire International.[1]

To enter Spain through France at that time was difficult, at times dangerous,
even though France's Socialist prime minister, Leon Blum, headed a Popular
Front government akin to the one under siege in Spain. Blum, under British
political and financial pressure and perhaps fearful of igniting a civil war in his
own country, adopted a policy of neutrality, much to the dislike of Communists.[2] As a result, anyone who tried to enter Spain clandestinely or get medical
supplies to the Loyalists through France was subject to arrest and prosecution. In theory, then, France's borders with Spain were closed, but many of the
French people were overwhelmingly sympathetic with Republican Spain and
willing to help get volunteers and supplies secretly into the country.

Under such circumstances, volunteers such as Edwards and Kyle who waited
in France never knew the exact moment at which they might leave for Spain.
They had to be ready on short notice. When the time finally came for the two
social workers to undertake the difficult trip, they simply had to grab whatever they could to take with them. As Hermina Huiswoud, who was in Paris
with Edwards at the time, later recalled: "Americans, accustomed to travel with
much luggage, had no idea what difficulties awaited them getting into Spain so
that Thyra, being no exception, had to leave her two suitcases behind."[3]

From Barcelona, Edwards soon sent Claude Barnett a press release about
her activities with Kyle in Spain, as well as a couple of stories on her experiences there. She sent pictures along with the stories. Describing Kyle as "a splendid type," Edwards was exuberant about the larger purpose of their mission
in Spain:

> We travel, work and live together. It is interesting mainly because we are not on
> an inter-racial, save the Negro crusade but rather on an inter-national commis-
> sion concerned with freedom and democracy for all kinds of people. Just now the
> Spanish people happen to be symbolic of all the rest of us. And certainly there
> isn't going to be any freedom and equality for Negroes until and unless there is a
> free world. But I'm really not trying to indoctrinate you.[4]

Edwards and Kyle stayed at the Rosa Luxemburg children's colony well up
the side of the mountain of Tibidabo on the outskirts of Barcelona, which suffered nightly aerial and naval bombardments by fascist forces. The social workers

were impressed by the discipline of the fifty-eight children when the nightly air-raid sirens blew. "You have only to see this once to realize what stable intelligent supervision the children are given," wrote Kyle to the executive secretary of the Social Workers' Committee to Aid Spanish Democracy on October 19, 1937. "As soon as the siren blows all lights are out in the city and the regulation calls for closed blinds. Not one of the fifty-eight children becomes excited despite the heavy explosions from the anti-air craft batteries." When the children, evacuated from Madrid in November 1936, had first arrived at the home, however, they "went into a panic every time they heard a commercial plane go over in the morning."[5]

In a letter to Dr. Herman F. Reissig, of the North American Committee to Aid Spanish Democracy, Kyle called attention to the nightly pattern of bombardments. "Thyra has just reminded me that our nightly bombardment is now ten minutes overdue," she wrote. "It is horrible to see the people coming up to sleep in the metro stations to get away from the factory district near the bay." Kyle pointed out that the working-class population bore the brunt of the bombardments: "The planes come in from Malorca [sic], circle around and drop bombs on the poorer homes down there, with a few farther in for good measure. For those in the safer districts, it means all lights out and the work stopped. We do what we can with a dim light behind carefully closed blinds, using not more than a farm lantern turned very low." Just as Kyle wrote the above line, however, sirens blew and a raid began. She added a final paragraph with the help of a candle: "The children were just lined up to brush their teeth, but they're getting into bed in orderly fashion."[6]

At the Luxemburg colony, as well as the Thomas Jefferson Home, where they had spent four days the previous week, Edwards and Kyle lived with the children as they followed a daily routine of classes, meals, and outdoor play. They also reported on important shortages of rationed bread and milk as well as coal to heat the homes. Dependent almost entirely on foreign contributions of material and cloth, women busily ran sewing machines in the central clothing rooms of the colonies to try to keep the children adequately clothed. Kyle called attention to the desperate plight of the refugee colonies: "What the local people have to give is nearly depleted, and any really substantial gifts will have to come from abroad this winter."[7]

When Edwards and Kyle reached the small, picturesque Catalonian town of Puigcerda in the Pyrenees Mountains on the border with France, the Prefect of Police assigned them a civil guard to protect them. By now the war had been raging for more than a year, and in newspaper articles Edwards called attention to growing shortages of fuel, sugar, butter, and other supplies. There were now about 1,500 refugees in the small town, Edwards reported. She and Kyle trekked up to the top of a nearby mountain to visit a former estate now being used to house Loyalist refugee children. Edwards noted with sarcasm that the aristocrat who formerly owned the estate was "now wintering in Paris where he can more easily contribute his funds to Franco's bombing raids."[8]

On October 20, the American social workers met with other foreign relief workers in Valencia, where Edwards also attended a convention of the National Assembly of Spanish Women against War and Fascism. As a delegate representing the National Negro Congress, she was invited to speak. When she rose to her feet, about 3,000 women and children gave her a lengthy standing ovation as they shouted, with clenched fists raised, "Viva la Raza Negra!" Leading the ovation was Dolores Ibárurri Gómez, or *La Pasionaria*, a communist icon whose impassioned speeches helped to rally Loyalist forces in the defense of Madrid. "It was an overwhelming and tremendous expression of solidarity with the Negro people," Edwards wrote in regard to her reception at the convention, "and with all peoples struggling for freedom and full emancipation and education and progressive development. . . . For in truth Spain is the battlefield on which all our destinies are being fought just now, and fought with such relentless courage and such clarity of direction."[9]

Edwards met and became friends with a number of writers who were in Spain at the time. Among them was the Scottish journalist William Forrest, who covered the Spanish Civil War for a couple of London newspapers. It was perhaps through Forrest that Edwards began to work for the London News Agency, too, at this time. Nicolás Guillén, the black Cuban poet who had met Edwards in Paris, was also in Valencia when she was there. Edwards sent one of his poems to Claude Barnett, noting that she was doing a translation for Guillén and that she would try to help him get it published in England. "But battling with publishers is really a terrible job," she complained.[10]

In Madrid, where Langston Hughes was at the time, too, Edwards met the famous Republican military commander El Campesino and interviewed black recruits among the Americans who volunteered to fight for Republican Spain in battalions known collectively as the Abraham Lincoln Brigade. El Campesino was a Communist who at that point had still managed to help keep Madrid from falling into the hands of General Franco's forces. The eighty black soldiers in the Lincoln Brigade had responded to the Moscow-based Communist International's call for volunteers to aid the Spanish Republic about a year earlier. As historian Robin D. G. Kelley has pointed out, the Communist Party emphasized black-white unity but accommodated race consciousness. The political philosophy of most of the black volunteers blended Pan-African nationalism and class-conscious labor internationalism. Most were Communists or leftist supporters who linked Mussolini's invasion of Ethiopia to General Franco's war against the Loyalist government.[11]

Among those Edwards interviewed was Basilio Cueria y Obrit, a Cuban captain of a machine-gun company of the Spanish 46th Division. Cueria, a professional baseball player who had moved to New York and joined the Communist

Party, was a machine gunner in the Abraham Lincoln Brigade when Edwards interviewed him. "In our trenches we fight fascism," he told her. "If we're defeated the working class of the world is defeated."[12]

When Edwards left Spain for France at the beginning of November, she barely managed to reach Le Havre in time for her return voyage to the United States. Thanks to a lot of resourcefulness and the frantic help of her friends Otto and Hermina Huiswoud and Peter Rhodes, she recovered the two bags of luggage she had left behind at a hotel in Paris. Her friends, who had retrieved the bags from the hotel, received a telegram from Edwards saying she was en route from Spain and asking them to meet her at the train station in Paris with the bags. After searching and searching for her at the Paris station, Rhodes looked up and caught a glimpse of her leaning out the window of a train bound for Le Havre, eating a sandwich and yelling at them to send her luggage to the United States. Instead, the Huiswouds decided to take the bags on a train to Le Havre, where they rented a taxi and then pulled up dockside just in time to hand Edwards her bags before she boarded the ship and set sail for home in a deluxe suite in first class, even though she did not have a first-class ticket. As Hermina later recalled, the entire incident, including Edwards's talking her way into a first-class deluxe suite, typified Edwards's talent for resourcefulness: "What a gal, that Thyra! That was a day's experience, that was."[13]

After Edwards's return to New York on November 8, 1937, she soon hit the lecture circuit and published more articles on the Spanish Civil War. In one of those articles, she described the killings of Milton Herndon and Joe Dallet— Chicago brigade volunteers—on the battlefield in Spain while she was there. Both Dallet and Herndon had been killed during the Aragon offensive at Fuentes del Ebro on October 13. Herndon, a twenty-five-year-old black Communist labor organizer and steelworker from Chicago, was the younger brother of well-known Communist organizer Angelo Herndon and an officer in the machine gun corps of the MacKenzie Papineau Battalion of the 15th International Brigade when he was killed. The brigade was comprised of Canadians, Americans, Spaniards, Finns, and a sprinkling of Irish volunteers.[14]

While in Spain, Edwards had interviewed an educator who was part of the Republican government's "brain trust" of advisers about General Franco's use of Moors as shock troops against Loyalist forces. A few months after she returned to the United States, she published an article about it, "Moors in the Spanish War," which appeared in the journal *Opportunity*. Edwards, who had heard and read stories about alleged atrocities committed by the Moors, set out to put the sensationalized racial assertions of such accounts into a broader context. "Doesn't it seem a bit strange," she asked, "that the Fascists, who claim to be racial purists, should be bargaining to reintroduce the Moors?" The adviser, denying the existence of racism in Spain, replied that "the Moorish question is in no respect a race question in Spain. It is a political and religious question. The tradition of hatred between the Moors and the Spaniards dates back to old wars."[15]

The Spanish adviser emphasized that most of the Moors used as "shock troops" by Franco were dead. Only a few Moors were now fighting in Spain, he assured Edwards, and they were mere adventurers fighting for money and whatever loot they might take home with them. When asked by Edwards if the Loyalists would be willing to grant Moroccans self-rule, he replied that they would have already done so but were bound to friendship with France. According to him, France feared that if Spain granted self-rule to Moroccans, similar demands for self-government would spread to adjoining French colonies in Africa.[16]

After taking a week off in New York to visit Margaret McKinney Severson (formerly of Winnetka, Illinois), whom she had met at the International People's College in Denmark, Edwards went to Howard University for a speaking engagement. On November 14, she took a train to Washington, DC, where she had been invited to campus to address a president's conference on black land-grant colleges. She was to discuss with attendees a scholarship program for black undergraduates to travel and study in Europe. Friends also arranged a reception in her honor to discuss conditions in Spain. Dr. Robert Weaver, a black economist and former adviser on black affairs in FDR's Department of the Interior who now served with the Federal Housing Authority, hosted the reception. Prominent black scholars such as economist Abram Lincoln Harris and sociologist E. Franklin Frazier were among those gathered to honor Edwards, as was poet Sterling Brown. She stayed in the home of Judge W. C. Hueston, former president of baseball's National Negro League, whom Edwards knew from their days in Gary, Indiana. The reception reflected Edwards's prominent stature as a black authority on international affairs.[17]

Upon her return to Chicago, Edwards set out to raise money for Spanish refugee children and drum up support for the Loyalist cause. In February 1938, Helen Abbott, the wife of *Chicago Defender* publisher Robert Abbott, hosted a tea to bring publicity to the need for funds to build a children's home in Spain. Edwards was there, along with a number of other prominent Chicago women who were social and civic leaders.[18]

As a field representative of both the American Medical Bureau to Aid Spanish Democracy and the North American Committee to Aid Spanish Democracy, Edwards embarked on a speaking tour in many states to educate black college students and the public on the importance of a Loyalist victory in Spain. On February 17, 1938, she kept an audience of students and members of the community spellbound at Shaw University in Raleigh, North Carolina, as she described conditions in war-torn Spain and spoke of her European travels. A

couple of weeks later, she spoke to students and faculty of the North Carolina
Agricultural and Technical College in Greensboro. Sponsored by the YWCA
and the Delta Sigma Theta sorority, she also gave a lecture entitled "Opposite
Trends in World Government and Its Effect on Youth" at Fisk University in
Nashville in March.[19]

The speaking tour took Edwards home to Texas again, with a stop at Wiley
College in Marshall, where she gave a lecture hosted by the International Relations Club. Her speaking engagements were sponsored by the National Religion
and Labor Foundation, a coalition of labor unions and interdenominational
religious activists created by the Federal Council of Churches in 1932 to educate congregations and communities about labor issues and to promote economic and social justice. In a Houston lecture hosted by the Wesley Chapel
Sunday School, A.M.E., she shared her travel experiences with the audience
and highlighted the basic needs of black workers for jobs, decent wages, credit, old-age pensions, and other forms of social insurance. Her lecture stressed
the common interests of black and white workers in their struggles to satisfy
these needs.[20]

Edwards's CIO connections did not prevent Freeman Everett, a black longshoreman who lived in Houston's Third Ward, where Edwards had grown up,
from arranging for her to speak at a mass meeting of black trade unionists and
their families, most of whom were AFL longshoremen. Everett, who served as
master of ceremonies at the meeting, was president of the International Longshoremen's Association's black Local 872, which remained loyal to the AFL.
Edwards emphasized the need for interracial cooperation in struggles against
employers. She praised workers' cooperatives and credit unions, and called on
white-collar members of the black middle class to support organized labor.
In particular, she urged Houston's black teachers to organize like their white
counterparts in the city, pointing to how teachers in Gary had received higher
salaries and better working conditions after they organized. In response to a
question about domestic workers, she pointed to the success of unionized domestic workers in Chicago, New York, and Finland, and she urged the formation of women's auxiliaries through which women could support the union
activities of their husbands.[21]

Edwards's speech stirred controversy in Houston's black community. A few
weeks later, C. W. Rice, black editor of the very conservative *Negro Labor News*
and a self-styled labor leader who backed company unions, blasted her and Everett, calling her "one of the most shrewd Negro propagandists for the CIO."
According to Rice, Edwards had pulled a fast one on Everett and Houston's
black longshoremen. Rice, who warned about the influence of Communists
and other CIO radicals, claimed that a few ILA leaders had refused to go to the
meeting because of Edwards's political affiliations. "Not only are Negro labor
leaders being deceived through shrewd propagandists about labor organiza-

tions," he asserted, "but leaders in religious, civic and other community activities, are being misled on this question."[22]

Edwards was a featured speaker at other community forums in Houston, too, before heading to San Antonio, where her parents had been married. In San Antonio, she spoke to black students at the junior and senior high schools as well as St. Philips Junior College. The local branch of the YWCA hosted a lecture by her, and San Antonio's black newspaper gave her a hearty endorsement.[23]

In Waco, Edwards was the featured speaker at the Texas Conference of Social Welfare (TCSW) in late April 1938. About 200 black and white delegates jammed into the room to listen as she praised Houston's ILA locals in her speech. W. W. Whitson, the outgoing president of the TCSW who headed the Social Service Department in Houston, had extended the speaking invitation to her, the first black speaker in the conference's history. Edwards also praised the CIO, singling out what farmers in the small black Texas community of Littig in Travis County had accomplished through cooperatives and CIO leadership. She exhorted delegates to engage in political activism to achieve the full integration of African Americans into American political, social, and intellectual life.[24]

After leaving Texas, Edwards went to Mexico, where she met with educators and government representatives to lay the groundwork for two travel seminars later that summer. Mexico and the Soviet Union were the only two nations openly providing direct aid to the Spanish Loyalists. The social changes brought about by the Mexican Revolution, particularly the reforms of Mexico's president Lázaro Cárdenas (1934–1940), attracted her. "Landless peons and peasants, hitherto as destitute and hopeless as our own landless tenant farmers and share croppers," Edwards said, "are now receiving land, education, health services, under a president who democratically rides the countryside on horseback, talking personally with peasants and working men of their needs and wants, and of how best to meet them."[25]

In planning the seminars to Mexico, Edwards set a grueling pace for herself once again. The first seminar lasted from June 12 to July 2, 1938, and the second from July 3 to July 25. On the itinerary were trips to schools, cooperatives, archaeological monuments, anthropological sites, and cultural landmarks. Edwards arranged to have Dr. Salomón de La Selva, a Nicaraguan poet and labor activist who at the time was employed at the National University in Mexico City, host a roundtable discussion on a number of topics related to the history and culture of Mexico.[26]

As Edwards expanded her global understanding of colonialism, imperialism, and fascist expansion at the time, she urged African Americans and Mexican Americans, both of whom she regarded as colonial subjects, to recognize their common struggles. Among black Texans who signed up for the seminars in

Mexico were the *Houston Informer*'s editor, Carter Wesley, and his wife, Doris, both of whom were friends of Edwards's. Mary Juarez, dean of Prairie View A&M College, also signed up. "With so many brown people occupying high official positions it [Mexico] is one of the few countries," Edwards wrote, "where one moves about a happy part of the landscape, free from curious stares."[27]

After the Mexican seminars ended in late July 1938, Edwards took up where she had left off in the campaign to raise money as a field organizer for the American Medical Bureau to Aid Spanish Democracy and the North American Committee to Aid Spanish Democracy. In early June, she and other Popular Front activists in Chicago hosted a reception to honor Salaria Kea, a black nurse from Harlem who had returned from Spain after she had been wounded on the battlefields as a volunteer nurse. Edwards, having arranged for Kea to speak at a meeting of the Chicago and Northern District of black club women, also organized a tour to raise funds for an ambulance to be marked "From the Negro People of America to the Heroic People of Spain." Her friends Langston Hughes, Paul Robeson, and Richard Wright, as well as other prominent black intellectuals, were among those who contributed to the campaign.[28]

After Robeson had donated $250 for a down payment, committees in Chicago and New York quickly formed to get the fund-raising drive rolling, but they did not do too much until Edwards, Kea, and Ashley Bertram Totten, an officer in the Brotherhood of Sleeping Car Porters, launched the tour to raise the rest of the money for the ambulance. Edwards used her vast contacts around the country to mobilize groups and educate African Americans as to what was at stake for them in the Spanish Civil War. She, Totten, and Kea would accompany the ambulance on tour, starting in New York August 15, after the ambulance participated in a World Youth Conference reception parade. The tour to a number of eastern, southern, and midwestern cities would end back in New York on September 25. "In this way," she explained to John Davis, executive secretary of the NNC, "we hope to raise money enough to pay the balance on the ambulance and, in addition, a reasonable amount for some effective participation for the American Relief Ship Campaign."[29]

Edwards asked Davis if the local committee of the NNC in Washington, DC, would arrange a high-profile reception for her and Kea, and she asked him for sponsorship help in Baltimore, Richmond, Norfolk, Washington, Cleveland, Detroit, and a number of other cities. Davis gave her the names of officers to contact in a couple of cities, but told her that the NNC could not do much, in part because so many members were out of town. Those who were in town, he stressed, were too busy in a petition drive to protest police brutality in the nation's capital. He also warned that representatives of the Washington Committee to Aid Spanish Democracy were skeptical that they could commit to helping her in any substantial way.[30]

Despite Davis's refusal to commit NNC resources, Edwards, Kea, and Totten made final preparations for the tour. A "desperate attempt" to take the ambulance to Randall's Island to coincide with the opening of the World Youth Conference failed because the garage where the ambulance was getting a mechanical checkup got behind schedule and did not have the ambulance ready in time. The three took two large "American Relief Ship for Spain" signs that had been used in the peace parade in New York and rigged them to the ambulance to publicize their mission when they were able to begin the tour.[31]

Setting out early in the morning on August 16, Edwards, Totten, and Kea stopped first at the Port of Cape Charles, Virginia, where Kea was shocked when she went to buy ice cream bars and the vendor refused to sell them to her because she was black. "'Won't serve' is an old story," Edwards noted, "but 'won't sell' was a little new even to me." They then boarded a ferry for Hampton, Virginia. "We had to coax Salaria out of the freight room," Edwards wrote, "as she was afraid of another rebuff. We found a comfortable Jim Crow (segregated) deck and the waiter brought us sandwiches out of the dining room."[32]

In Hampton, Edwards and Kea set up an exhibit on the Relief Ship Campaign in the hall where the Association of Colored Graduate Nurses was holding a convention. With the ambulance parked outside, they spoke to individual nurses and handed out literature to publicize the need to aid Spain. They did the same on a boat ride on the night of August 17. Edwards appeared before the executive board of the National Medical Association, which was also in session at the time. The board approved her request to address the convention, which was being attended by about 900 physicians and surgeons and their wives. In the meantime Edwards and Kea spoke to the nurses' general session, where they raised money from cash contributions, pledges, and the sale of pamphlets. Several nurses representing local associations around the country promised to raise milk and medical supplies when they returned home.

The campaign fared much worse, however, when it came to the doctors. After a lot of pressure and lobbying, Edwards spoke to the conference of doctors on August 19, but the president was completely unsympathetic: he gave her only a minute and a half to make her appeal for funds. The conference members did vote in favor of an appropriation from their treasury and sent the authorization to the executive board, which then stonewalled the dispensation of funds. "I hung around and finally at 8:00 at night was told the executive board had appointed a committee for further investigation," Edwards complained. "Later I learned from the presiding officer of the board that the question was never presented. Simply sabotaged."[33]

A few individual physicians did donate $4.50, but there were no follow-up or working committees put in place. Dr. Louis T. Wright, of Harlem Hospital, who had promised Edwards before she left New York that he would give a public endorsement, did so in his speech to the convention. He devoted the opening part of his speech to the Spanish Civil War and the need for cooperation to support the Loyalists. His speech stimulated discussions but did not lead to concrete support of any substance. Edwards pointed out that several southern physicians showed more interest and understanding of the campaign than others.

Edwards noted that in contrast to the physicians, however, "a tiny little white haired Negro woman, accompanied by a badly crippled and paralyzed young man . . . was thrilled at the ambulance and asked 'could anybody be allowed to give as little as a quarter.'" The woman, who carried a display of the boy's painting and weaving, headed an orphanage with thirty children. She had taught the children about Africa, including the Italian invasion of Ethiopia, and also about the war in Spain. At her request, Edwards, Kea, and Totten drove the ambulance out to the orphanage so the children could see it. After Edwards talked to them about the children's colonies in Spain, the kids pooled their pennies and donated a dollar. Thrilled, Edwards reported: "The experience was more overwhelming than any experience we've had."[34]

As a result of a meeting with about forty students at the Hampton Institute, the students there formed a committee to support the Relief Ship Campaign. Estelle Thomas, the assistant dean of women, agreed to be their sponsor. The students pledged 1,000 cans of milk to accompany the ambulance on the ship scheduled to sail for Spain on October 30. A Norfolk newspaper photographed the students with the ambulance. As Edwards pointed out, the students "felt some pride in being the first committee to aid Spain set up on a Negro campus. I feel we'll get some results there if our follow up is close enough." In contrast, an attempt to set up a faculty committee did not get anywhere; only two faculty members agreed to participate, but both refused to assume leadership.[35]

One of the best meetings on the tour took place during the week of September 17th in Covington, Kentucky, where Mrs. F. A. Rothier hosted a reception. Rothier—nearly deaf—was a very wealthy, elderly white Kentuckian who lived by herself in one of the state's pre–Civil War mansion estates. Although she did not donate to charities, she did support "the most unpopular causes presented." She had contributed to the legal defense of a black youth who was legally lynched for alleged rape. She was also responsible for establishing playgrounds for black children in Covington. When she learned about the ambulance publicity campaign, she responded, "I don't know anything about international affairs, I've never turned my attention to them. But if the Negroes with whom I've been fighting all my life are now interested in this I see no reason why I shouldn't help them here too."[36]

Nearly forty people, including about six whites, responded to invitations sent out by Rothier. Among the blacks who attended was a bishop of the Methodist Episcopal Church, M. W. Clair, who agreed to serve as chair of a committee that was set up. They pledged about thirty-five dollars, collecting three dollars of it on the spot. The committee agreed to canvass schools and churches for milk and to approach a local Procter and Gamble soap factory for a sizeable donation of soap for Spanish Loyalists. Edwards reported that when staff from a local newspaper came out to take a picture of the ambulance, "they were a little disturbed when Mrs. Rothier insisted on posing beside it with the very handsome, very black Bishop Clair. But she has wealth and family and there was nothing to do but go thro' the motions of photographing tho' it's doubtful they'll publish it."[37]

Despite difficulties and frustrations, Edwards continued her work in the fund-raising drive. By mid- to late September 1938, she was back in New York with the ambulance in time to accompany it to a mass meeting in Madison Square Garden to protest Hitler's invasion of Czechoslovakia. At that time she also appeared with Douglas Jacobs, campaign manager of the $250,000 American Relief Ship, aboard the *Queen Mary* in New York Harbor to see her friend, William Pickens, of the NAACP and the Negro People's Committee to Aid Spanish Democracy, off on a trip to investigate children's colonies, relief efforts, and American-supported hospitals in Republican Spain. On November 12, she spoke at a meeting of the Urban League in Springfield, Illinois, sponsored by the YMCA and black women's clubs, to raise money for Spain.[38]

On September 26, Edwards was an invited speaker at a reception in Chicago for delegates to a national meeting of twenty-eight Women's Economic Councils called by the Brotherhood of Sleeping Car Porters to organize an International Ladies' Auxiliary. Along the same lines set forth by BSCP president Randolph, who opened the meeting by discussing the ominous state of world affairs, Edwards condemned militarism and fascism. She pointed out that Hitler had broken up trade unions and attacked liberal internationalists long before he initiated his systematic campaign against Jews. Urging vigilance, she denounced fascism's prescribed role for women, warning delegates that "fascist powers immediately dissolve women's groups and send them back to the kitchen, church and cooking. Most women would like to have these things, but certainly as an optional matter. The fascists believe that women have only one purpose and that is to bear children."[39]

Calling attention to endangered democracies around the world, Edwards included Japan in her attack on imperialist nations. She singled out Japan's aggression in China and criticized isolationist sentiment. To combat past friendly attitudes of many African Americans toward Japan, she pointed out: "I think in passing we ought to mention Japan's role because we have in the past turned our attention to Japan as a black hope. I don't know why. Japan never came out to offer us succor, but we had a kind of pride that a dark people was strong."[40]

In a message that touted housing as a "social right," and health insurance as a "state responsibility," Edwards praised the role of ladies' auxiliaries in recent sit-down strikes led by the CIO, and she noted that women had been shot down on the picket line a few months earlier in the Memorial Day Massacre outside Republic Steel's plant on the South Side of Chicago. She emphasized the need for trade unions to adopt an educational as well as a political philosophy. For a trade union movement to succeed, she argued, labor should incorporate theater, art, music, and literature into its educational programs. Furthermore, she insisted that "it must have a political philosophy whether it be in Labor's Non-Partisan League or the American Labor Party."[41]

Other speakers included Mary McLeod Bethune, of the National Youth Administration, and Chicago union leaders Agnes Nestor (Glovemakers) and Lillian Herstein (Teachers). As historian Melinda Chateauvert has pointed out, Edwards and Herstein, a Socialist, were trying to encourage women to move beyond the "helpmeet" role endorsed by Randolph and supported by Nestor and Bethune. For Edwards, an ideal woman in the labor movement was a class-conscious woman fired by passionate political activism: "We had the fallacious idea that a black boss would be superior to a white boss when what we want is a democratic order with no boss with his heel on our necks."[42]

The meeting's proceedings reflected a commitment to Popular Front politics. For example, the Committee on Constitution and Resolutions adopted a resolution by Randolph pledging support for the Spanish Loyalists. The resolution urged President Roosevelt and the United States Congress to repeal an embargo on arms shipments to the Spanish Republic.[43]

Despite several appeals to the National Negro Congress for financial and logistical support for the ambulance fund-raising tour to benefit Loyalist Spain, Edwards received little help from the organization. Executive Secretary John P. Davis's lack of support reinforced growing tensions between Davis and Edwards, and between Edwards and other top black Communists over programmatic issues at a time of growing financial difficulties for the organization. In December 1938, the NNC stepped up a coordinated campaign to solicit financial contributions from liberal groups to resolve a deficit of several hundred dollars. At an executive council meeting of the NNC on December 8, Edwards, Davis, Randolph, Yergan, James Baker, and James Ford donated $100 and pledged to get loans from friends to cover the deficit. Edwards agreed to request a loan in the amount of $100 from Blanche Lowenthal, a wealthy supporter of left-wing initiatives in Chicago whom she planned to see soon at the conference of the American League for Peace and Democracy (formerly the American League against War and Fascism) in Washington, DC. Davis checked with Edwards a few days later to make sure she had "rushed off" the letter.[44]

Members of the NNC executive council also agreed to a proposal by Yergan to hold a concurrent conference of the American League for Peace and Democracy and the Negro People's Committee to Aid Spanish Democracy (sometimes called the Negro People's Committee to Aid Spain). The proposal, unanimously adopted, had the endorsements of YWCA national board members Marion Cuthbert and Isabel Lawson, as well as Channing Tobias, of the YMCA. The American Medical Bureau to Aid Spanish Democracy, on that basis, agreed to finance the conference, promising not to try to override any recommendations by the NNC. The Committee to Lift the Embargo on Spain also agreed to participate in the conference, which was scheduled to take place January 6–8, 1939, in Washington, DC.[45]

As preparations were being made for the upcoming conference, Edwards got into hot water with Davis and other black Communist leaders as the result of differences over programmatic issues related to the American League for Peace and Democracy. Davis and others decided to focus on police brutality instead of the broader issue of segregation and class in the nation's capital. Edwards disagreed with the decision to bow to Jim Crow in the set-up of the conference and to ignore the issues faced by the black working class. "I still feel to have the League ignore the question of segregation, etc. in the set up of their Conference," she complained to Davis, "will be inviting a broad attack from the Negro press which will cloud the pertinent and extraordinary issues for which the Convention is called. I also feel that stressing police brutality against Negroes in Washington is narrowing the basic issue of police brutality and ignoring their attacks of workers on picket lines, in strike zones, hunger marches and unemployment demonstrations."[46]

After a defensive response by Davis, who argued that criticisms of police brutality had restrained the police from "extending their brutality to the field of workers rights," Edwards continued to express opposition to the programmatic decisions made by the League. Concerned that Davis took her criticisms personally, she tactfully wrote, "My reference to the danger of narrowing the emphasis on 'police brutality against Negroes in Washington' was in no wise overlooking the splendid work you have carried on there." Nevertheless, she reminded him, "We are, I believe, discussing a national conference of the American League for Peace and Democracy and so, it is still my feeling that emphasis must be broad while including the specific." Edwards told Davis that she had voiced her concerns to officials of the League and in a public speech at a preconference dinner the week before. She reassured him that she was not trying to say which issue—police brutality or segregation—was more important. "What I am saying," she argued, "is that . . . some technique or policy should be carefully studied and agreed upon before the convention. Otherwise we do run the risk of broad publicity that will cloud the primary issue of the Conference and will tend to precipitate the very thing you want to avoid—namely having the Conference get so involved in the segregation issue that all else will be submerged."[47]

The conflict extended beyond segregation to Edwards's immersion in programs that highlighted the significance of the Spanish Civil War to black people. Apparently she and officers of the American Medical Bureau to Aid Spanish Democracy and the Negro People's Committee to Aid Spanish Democracy, on whose executive committee Edwards served, tried without success to include a session on the Negro in Spain at the conference of the American League for Peace and Democracy. When that failed, the Negro People's Committee to Aid Spanish Democracy continued to press the issue with the American League for Peace and Democracy, which finally relented on January 3 and accepted a call for a mass meeting to be held, but only after the conference ended on January 8, 1939.[48]

Held in the Lincoln Congregational Tabernacle on the evening of January 8, 1939, the Negro People's Committee to Aid Spanish Democracy's mass meeting, "Relation of the Present Struggle in Spain to Democracy and Its Meaning to the Negro People," featured a number of prominent speakers, including Howard University professors Alain Locke and Doxey Wilkerson. William Pickens, who had just returned from a trip to Spain on behalf of the committee, and Max Yergan were also among the speakers. The featured speaker was Dr. Arnold Donawa, a Harlem dentist and oral surgeon who had treated wounded Loyalists at a base hospital in Villa Paz, Spain.[49]

A couple of weeks after the conference, Louise Thompson, a black Communist activist, took Edwards to the woodshed after criticism surfaced of Edwards's procedure and program for the conference. According to Thompson, James Ford, the Communist Party USA's vice presidential candidate in the election of 1936, was unhappy with her behavior at the conference. Thompson told Edwards that the criticism centered on her tendency to cry "white chauvinism" when plans and programs did not go according to her wishes.[50]

Furious, Edwards fired off a letter to Ford, defending herself, and she sent Thompson a copy. First, she questioned why Ford had not expressed the criticism in a face-to-face meeting with her. She questioned why Thompson was even brought into the matter. "I got much the feeling," Edwards complained, "that she was the case worker assigned on my case." Edwards reminded Ford that she had conferred repeatedly with him and a number of important Popular Front leaders, including Davis, Randolph, Yergan, John Sherman, Channing Tobias, Harry Ward, Bob Minor, Steve Nelson, Herman Reissig, and Clarence Hathaway, about the conference. Edwards emphasized to Ford that since Thompson had not been present at any of those meetings, "it would have seemed more logical and productive of positive analysis had such an interview been assigned to any one or more of the above persons—already familiar with the particular situation in question."[51]

Edwards told Ford that she did not understand why he and Randolph, as executive officers of the NNC, did not take the matter up with her directly. After all, she kept them regularly informed about all of her public activities through memoranda and personal conferences. "I would have welcomed an opportunity," she said, "to talk these things over with either or both of you."[52]

In regard to Edwards's alleged charge of "white chauvinism" on the part of conference leaders of the American League for Peace and Democracy, she emphatically denied that she was guilty of the charge. In fact, she philosophically rejected the tactic of charging white chauvinism as "the easy tool of persons who lacked logic, reason or understanding or the ability to state and support a case and if necessary withdraw it. For such people the easiest escape is the cry, 'chauvinism.'" Edwards found the complaint against her along these lines to be insulting: "It is not a technique adaptable to my program. The Conference method is mine."[53]

Edwards reminded Ford that the proposal to have concurrent conferences of the Negro People's Committee to Aid Spanish Democracy and the American League for Peace and Democracy originated with Yergan and Tobias and was supported by Marion Cuthbert and Isabel Lawson of the YWCA's national board. She reminded Ford, too, that he had attended the meeting of the Executive Council of the NNC at which the proposal was unanimously adopted. On that basis, the American Medical Bureau to Aid Spanish Democracy agreed to sponsor the conference and promised not to override recommendations of the NNC. "The endorsement, and financing of our Conference by the Medburo executives brought the discussion to one of jurisdiction and slanting as between the League and the Bureau. It was therefore at no time reduced to merely a Negro-white [issue]."[54]

Edwards objected to the American League's programmatic approach to "the Negro question" as well as the way black delegates to the conference were treated. In fact, she had earlier complained directly to Ford, Randolph, and others that the League's "expressed position and policy this year indicated a less vigorous and more apologetic position than that of many established conventional groups" such as the YWCA, American Association of Social Workers, and the interracial committees of the Federal Council of Churches. As she reminded Ford, "I further observed that a popular front policy that maintains itself at the expense of subordinating the Negro question instead of bringing it forward and integrating it into the whole pattern—the Negro people coming forward on broad issues simultaneously with their own special problems—was open to question and certainly subject to attack by the Negro People."[55]

The other criticism of Edwards was that she failed to devote full attention to finding a solution to the problem that grew out of "the League's failure to effectively provide for Negro delegations so as to save them insult and inconvenience." In other words, she was criticized for failing to do anything about the problem that she had called attention to. Black delegates to the conference complained about being relegated to "the usual backstage role" and the subsequent isolation of their concerns. Edwards told Ford that she attended the backstage meeting that night but refrained from serving on a committee appointed to commend the League's business agents for the job they did to make preparations for black delegates to the conference. She also missed a speech she was supposed to give in order to work on a committee to formulate a League policy on the question.[56]

The friction with Ford and Thompson reflected Edwards's independence and growing frustration with Communists in the NNC and other Popular Front organizations because of their failure to make strong commitments to race- and gender-specific remedies for minorities and women. Tensions over such issues had been growing for at least a year. Edwards was getting more support from liberal groups than from Communist-led organizations. On October 2, 1937, for example, she had resigned as chair of the NNC's Committee on Women's Work. She had assured Davis of her continued support for the NNC and willingness to work with him at that time, but in reference to his request for a committee report, she had complained in her letter of resignation, "There is no report to be submitted in this connection as neither program nor work has ever been defined or agreed upon. There has been no budget, neither estimated nor actual. In short there has been no such committee. It is therefore obvious that there is either no need for a chairman or grave need for a new chairman." Edwards expressed eagerness to meet with Ford and other leaders to discuss the work for Spain among African Americans. She emphasized that without the mobilization of substantial support, the venture should be abandoned: "We have certainly not felt any support either from the Negro Commission or the Negro Congress," she complained. "The work has been a tremendous strain and expense—too much to devolve upon an individual."[57]

The fall of Madrid on March 28, 1939, and the defeat of the Spanish Loyalists soon tightened the grip of fascism in Western Europe, but Edwards's commitment to the Loyalists would continue. Stalin's repudiation of the Popular Front sent many Communists ducking for cover, especially when the Nazi-Soviet Pact on August 28, 1939, sent shock waves through the ranks of Popular Front supporters. The coming outbreak of World War II in Europe would bring Edwards's European travel seminars to a halt, but not her personal travels. She did not abandon the Loyalist cause, instead turning her attention to the plight of Loyalist refugees in Mexico.

Thyra Edwards, circa 1920.
Photo courtesy of Chicago History Museum

Anna Bell Johnson Edwards, mother of Thyra Edwards.
Photo courtesy of Vee Edwards

Horace Ferdinand Edwards, father of Thyra Edwards.
Photo courtesy of Vee Edwards

Nora Edwards, paternal grandmother of Thyra Edwards.
Photo courtesy of Vee Edwards

Thyra Edwards, circa 1928.
Photo courtesy of Chicago History Museum

Thyra Edwards wearing a cap and robe made in Uzbekistan, circa 1936.
Photo courtesy of Vee Edwards

Thyra Edwards, *seated third from left*, with other black attendees at the Anti-Imperialist International Congress in Paris, 1937. Photo courtesy of Joyce Moore Turner

Thyra Edwards addressing a group of Chicago women to raise money for a children's home in Spain, February 1938. Photo courtesy of Chicago History Museum

Thyra Edwards, *left,* and nurse Salaria Kea on a fund-raising tour for the American Medical Bureau to Aid Spanish Democracy, with the ambulance they raised funds to purchase, New York, 1938. Photo courtesy of Chicago History Museum

126

(*Opposite top*) Thyra Edwards with Douglas Jacobs, *left,* manager of the Relief Ship Campaign, and William Pickens, of the NAACP and the Negro People's Committee to Aid Spanish Democracy, 1938. Photo courtesy of Chicago History Museum

(*Opposite bottom*) Thyra Edwards, *left,* and two other women running a "country store" as a fund-raiser for the Negro People's Committee to Aid Spanish Democracy, New York, 1939. Photo courtesy of Chicago History Museum

(*Above*) Thyra Edwards handing out flyers for a performance by her friend opera singer Paul Robeson to benefit Loyalists in Spain during its civil war, circa 1939. Photo courtesy of Chicago History Museum

(Top) Vee Edwards, first cousin of Thyra Edwards. Photo courtesy of Vee Edwards

(Bottom) Gina Loring, visiting in 2009 the children's home in Gary, Indiana, founded by her great-aunt, Thyra Edwards, and renamed in honor of her grandmother, Thelma Edwards Marshall. Photo courtesy of Gina Loring

8

With Health Problems and Spanish Loyalist Refugees in Mexico

By the summer of 1939, Edwards, disturbed by the Spanish Loyalists' defeat and the outbreak of war in Europe, was facing ever-worsening health problems. The relentless pace of her political activities on behalf of Republican Spain had exhausted her, and to make matters worse, the Popular Front was dead as an official strategy of the Soviet Union. Because of internal tensions between socialists, liberals, and Communists in the National Negro Congress, Edwards's relationship with A. Philip Randolph had become strained. As a result, she planned to go to Mexico in late summer to get rejuvenated, reevaluate her personal life, write an autobiography, and gather material for articles on Loyalist refugees. At this stage of her life, she hoped to carve out a career as a writer.

Shortly before Edwards's fortieth birthday, December 25, 1937, she had been on a speaking tour when she suffered strange, crippling sensations of pain, dizziness, and paralysis. Dazed and frightened, she could barely lift her limbs. "My feet were weights, my legs collapsible, my head crowned the spinal column in pain and unease," she remembered. "Sleep translated itself into a procession of nightmares: I was sucked into a vortex; my skull was being scraped raw and my arms lay paralyzed."[1]

Edwards had kept her physical problems a secret on the trip. "In this condition I toured a good half of the United States," she recalled, "confiding to no one that I felt my physical equilibrium crumbling under me." Once she got back to Chicago, she underwent a series of tests and X-rays at a private clinic but was told by doctors that there was nothing seriously wrong with her—just a little inflammation of the appendix, congestion in her bronchial tubes, and "the usual neurasthenic symptoms of an unmarried woman approaching middle age." As Edwards explained, the conditions amounted to "an aggregate of symptoms totaling up to mere nuisance value."[2]

Reassured by the doctors' report, Edwards had resumed her political activism, even though she suffered crippling attacks periodically. On July 28, 1939, she escorted Franz Karl Weiskopf, a Czech exile, writer, and publisher of an antifascist newspaper in Prague who had recently fled to New York via Paris, to a meeting of student activists affiliated with the American Student Union (ASU). The ASU operated five summer leadership institute groups, one of which was at Locust Farm, where Edwards and Weiskopf spoke. In fact, the Locust Farm group named their working unit the Thyra Edwards Group to honor her activism, inspiration, and efforts on behalf of racial unity. At the meeting on July 28, Edwards and Weiskopf spoke on the topic of culture in the progressive movement. Edwards urged the ASU to examine the political implications of art and culture in order to assess art's overall aesthetic value.[3]

Edwards pressed ahead with plans to spend six months in Mexico as a freelance writer to cover the resettlement of Spanish refugees there and to write an autobiography. On August 1, 1939, she packed her bags, grabbed her typewriter, camera, and recorder, and dashed to the train station. En route to Mexico, she stopped first in New Orleans to see her sister Anna Bell Douglas, at whose home her mother was also visiting at the time. Afterward, Edwards went to Houston to spend a day and night visiting with her brother and his family.[4]

Edwards took her time on the journey to Mexico City, which took about two weeks. She got there in late August. "I was not feeling at all well," she wrote on September 1st, "and my first week here I felt almost discouraged about myself. Queer, sharpe [sic] penetrating pains that involved the area of the head plus complete exhaustion." During the second week, however, she felt "quite myself again" after she "took things easily, did nothing, lay in the sun most of the day and only went out for a few hours in the evening—usually to the theatre."[5]

In Mexico City, Edwards boarded in the home of Elizabeth Cervantes. The house was built around a patio that Edwards described as "a tropical garden." For five cents a day, she got a room and breakfast. In the afternoon she usually lit out downtown for "a banquet of a meal" at a cost of between thirty and fifty cents. All in all, with carfare, theater tickets, and other expenses, she managed to get by on two dollars a day.[6]

Friends arrived in Mexico City soon after Edwards got there. Melva Price, an activist teacher who worked with her on the Negro People's Committee to Aid Spanish Refugees (NPC), came from New York, and John P. Davis, of the NNC, arrived from Washington, DC. Davis ended up boarding at Cervantes's house, too. As Edwards wrote, "John moved out here to my patio house and my land lady fell quite in love with him. She put her arms around him and kissed him when he left. He was quite moved by it."[7]

Shortly after Edwards left the United States en route to Mexico, Hitler and Stalin had signed the Nazi-Soviet Pact and subsequently invaded Poland, so she, Price, and Davis had a lot to discuss in regard to politics, including the future of the NNC and the NPC. In addition, Mexico's reformist government of Lázaro Cárdenas was nearing the end of its term, and the right-wing opposition was beginning to crystallize around the candidacy of General Juan Andreu Almazán to oppose Manuel Ávila Camacho, the candidate of Cárdenas and the ruling party. Edwards, Price, and Davis attended a big political demonstration held on the Plaza de la Revolución by supporters of Almazán. Edwards claimed that Almazán hired 18,000 peasants to make the demonstration look larger than it was. Although extensive violence was expected, the demonstration turned out to be "quite mild" as President Cárdenas convinced progressive organizations to avoid the area.[8]

As a result of the Nazi-Soviet Pact, which infuriated liberals and socialists who had cooperated with Communists in the Popular Front's defense of Loyalist Spain, Edwards had to confront the impending dissolution of the NPC. Before she left the United States, she had resigned her paid fund-raising position with the NPC. Edwards's friend, Pauli Murray, acting executive secretary in her absence and, like her, an alumnus of Brookwood Labor College, contacted her in Mexico to complain that donations had dried up because liberals feared a Communist takeover of the committee. Murray disapproved of the Soviet Union's actions, but insisted that she was "willing to keep an open mind on any part of the international situation because of my intellectual independence. . . . I have absolutely no respect for the Communist Party and its tactics, but given a job to do, in which I believe that we are helping human beings, I will do it in cooperation with the communists or anyone else."[9]

With Murray under pressure from financial sponsors, the viability of the NPC was in doubt. Pointing out that National Chairman Lester Granger, for example, had refused to renew his support until the executive committee met to clarify where it stood on the Soviet-Nazi alliance, Murray asked Edwards to express her views on the matter as a member of the executive board. Murray made clear that "my disrespect for the Communist Party does not apply to communist individuals. They are judged on the basis of their individual honesty and sincerity. . . . As long as I believe the Negro People's Committee is not dominated by a particular political line, I will give my best; when I become convinced that this is not true, I will have to resign in the interests of my own integrity and that of the Committee."[10]

In reply, Edwards emphasized that the NPC's executive committee and sponsor roster of fifty members included only three Communists—Louise Thompson, Angelo Herndon, and William L. Patterson, and she pointed out that none of the three had become involved with the NPC as representatives of the Communist Party. In the case of Herndon, it was his brother's death as a brigade volunteer on a Spanish battlefield that caused him to get involved with the NPC, and both Thompson and Patterson had been motivated by their own experiences in Spain to support the work of the committee. Furthermore, Edwards was emphatic that at no time had a policy of the NPC been adopted without open discussions that included Granger, Channing Tobias, Reverend William Lloyd Imes, and other liberal committee members who were now concerned that the NPC might become a mere tool of the Communist Party.[11]

Edwards did endorse Granger's call for a meeting, though, to discuss the NPC's policy in regard to the Soviet-Nazi alliance. "I think it is an excellent idea," she told Murray, "that our sponsors and executive board members call a meeting at this time for joint thinking and clarification in the light of the International scene. This is a healthy indication of genuine working interest." Complaining that contributions to the NPC and other organizations to aid Spain's people had been limited by allegations that such organizations were appendages of the Communist Party, Edwards warned that such "unsubstantiated" charges threatened to derail important humanitarian work on behalf of refugee victims of fascist expansion and worldwide militarism. She expressed her "sincere hope that our Committee will not be deflected by the confusion inherent in the current war and world turmoil. More than ever we need unity and clarity of thinking."[12]

In an attempt to broaden its appeal, the NPC had expanded its humanitarian mission to help Ethiopian, Chinese, and other refugees, but its financial problems worsened despite Murray's determined efforts to host major fund-raising events and despite Edwards's urgent attempts to help her from afar. By November 1939, Murray had developed a sense of hopelessness about the survivability of the committee, and the pressure had slightly strained her friendship with Edwards. Murray had worked herself into a near state of exhaustion in a desperate attempt to raise money, but a major fund-raising event in New York City turned out to be a financial flop, thanks in part to persistent red-baiting by local media. She assured Edwards that she and a handful of people around her, including Melva Price, had done everything they could to ensure the event's success, but to no avail. "I don't believe even you could do it," she told Edwards in exasperation.[13]

Murray let Edwards know that she was about to resign. In her view, the Soviet-Nazi alliance had crippled fund-raising, and the financial condition of the NPC no longer supported a salaried position. "I feel that the appeal of Spanish refugees is too narrow an appeal at this crucial economic situation in the experiences of Negroes to make possible the financial returns necessary to run the Committee."[14]

As a result of the collapse of the NPC, Edwards would have no job to go back to in the United States, but she had come to Mexico to pursue a writing career. With plans to write an article on the resettlement of Spanish refugees in Mexico, Edwards had set out to interview resettlement officials and gain access to the refugees as soon as possible. She bore letters of introduction from Joe North, an American writer who had covered the brigades in Spain, and from Constancia de La Mora, former head of the Republican Foreign Press Office who at the time of the fall of the Republican government was in New York on a diplomatic mission to appeal for aid. La Mora, who would soon move to Mexico, had become popular in left-liberal circles in New York on account of her work on behalf of Loyalist refugees.[15]

When Edwards arrived in Mexico City, she did not know which Mexican official's door to knock on first, but on the first of September, she called on Mexico's representative on the Committee to Aid Spanish Refugees. When the Mexican official, a Spanish Republican who had lived in Mexico for many years, saw the names of La Mora and North on her letters of recommendation, he quickly cooperated, explaining to Edwards the details of the resettlement project. A vast tract of uncultivated land (340,000 acres) in the Chihuahuan Desert, formerly owned by the politically powerful Terrazas family, was to become transformed into a city by the refugees through irrigation and mechanization to support production of olives, wine, and wheat, as well as cattle raising and a lumber industry. Edwards learned that a trainload of 300 selected Spanish refugee families, mostly artisans, engineers, and technicians, would stop in Mexico City the next day en route from Vera Cruz to Chihuahua. It would be the job of this group to build temporary shelter and clear the hacienda tract to make a place for other refugees who would soon follow them to the Chihuahuan Desert.[16]

Here was Edwards's chance. She asked for authorization to board the train and travel with the refugees. A bit stunned, the official warned how grueling the trip would be, riding in crowded coaches with children, some of whom were still sick from conditions in French refugee camps. Besides, he reminded her, there was nothing waiting for them in Santa Clara but a vast, uncleared tract. The official suggested that she take a plane and meet the refugees in Chihuahua, but Edwards kept pressing him. At last he relented and told her he would arrange for her transportation with the refugees. "At the door he placed both hands on my shoulder," Edwards proudly recalled, "with a gesture that made me feel completely one of them."[17]

Edwards hurried back to the house where she was staying and got ready for the trip. She whipped off a letter to home, telling of her plans. "It means 72 hours of hard travel, 3rd class, in crowded coaches of several hundred refugee families and single men," she said. "It will be a little hard but I'll get material for a pretty good article and one can best write about something one has shared, not just looked at."[18]

Especially considering Edwards's health problems, the trip was a rugged undertaking. She planned to stay with the refugees a couple of weeks, and then go to Vera Cruz, where several thousand more refugees would be waiting eagerly to resettle in their new home. From there, she would return to Mexico City to pen an article about the settlement. "Santa Clara I understand is a great pine section," she noted, "and so cold that my landlady says in all seriousness the backsides of the horses freeze."[19]

The leader of the expedition, *El Jefe,* whom Edwards met at the train station the next morning, was Emilio Fortanet, an experienced engineer and the former commander of the 29th Division in the Spanish Republican Army and former chief magistrate of Barcelona. There were about twenty-five others, mostly young men, with him. The Mexican government had reserved a coach for them. One group of refugees from Vera Cruz would shortly couple onto the coach at a siding near Pachuga.[20]

Edwards quickly got to know several of the refugees. As was her style, she immersed herself in their life stories, particularly their experiences during the war against Franco's forces. As the train chugged along and the stories flowed, Fortanet's personal canteen, filled with Bacardi rum, passed from mouth to mouth in the coach. Edwards happily took a swig and passed the canteen along to others. At times the refugees broke into singing songs of the brigades. Whenever any of the riders wanted to know what time it was, they asked Edwards, who sported the only watch on the expedition. She learned that during the evacuation from Barcelona, French border guards had confiscated money, watches, fountain pens, Kodak cameras—anything of value—from the refugees.[21]

At Pachuga, when the refugee train from Vera Cruz was coupled onto the coach, some of the men walked through the newly added cars to see if friends and relatives were among the 450 men, women, and small children on the refugee train. A few were reunited with loved ones for the first time since the fall of Barcelona. In conversations, Edwards listened to bitter, wrenching tales about France's treatment of the refugees. "The brutal shock of harsh treatment at the hands of the French whom they had considered friends seemed to have overshadowed much of the mad drama of the War," she observed. "Certainly it had engendered more bitterness and disillusionment."[22]

Sleep did not come easily in the train's crowded seats. The three men who shared the seat section with Edwards took turns sleeping in the aisle to free up more space for her as she tried desperately to get comfortable. Cramped and cold, Edwards shifted her body at restless moments to put pressure on a different set of muscles. "I remember shivering and trying to keep warm by rolling into a ball," she recalled, "only to have El Jefe slip half his fur lined leather trench coat over me."[23]

Spending a couple of such nights and days with the refugees gave Edwards a special empathy for their plight. She saw the looks of exhaustion on the faces of women with their children still suffering from infections, their pallid skin afflicted with crusted sores. Having been in Spain and witnessed some of the fighting, she now was observing the further trials and tribulations of those who had lost the battle against fascism. Men on the train washing and shaving each morning in icy water and women redoing their hair and adjusting their earrings seemed to Edwards "a valiant resistance to the rapidly disappearing niceties of life threatened by war, concentration camps, crowded ocean transport, more camps, more crowded transport, and now a desert hacienda—340,000 acres of it, behind dry, Mexican mountains."[24]

When the train rolled into the Chihuahua station, Edwards and the refugees learned that England had declared war against Germany. Some of the men began to talk about going back to rejoin the war, lamenting that they were now isolated in the desert of a foreign country. Three Mexican officials met the train, and in about an hour the refugees were distributed into buses, automobiles, and trucks. Families were taken to special housing, single men to barracks and small, crude hotels. The architects sketched blueprints for additional barracks while they waited for tents to arrive from the United States.[25]

Eager to get to the desert site of Colonia Santa Clara with the refugees, still about ninety miles away, Edwards finally found a way. She jumped into "a dissolute Ford touring car" with an engineer ("a handsome, mature one"), a veterinarian, and an army tank conductor. The bumpy ride, mostly through "deep, wild canyons over very primitive roads," heightened Edwards's sense of adventure: "It was thrilling, with the car stopping every few miles, sputtering and overheated. We chased rabbits while she cooled down enough to go on another mile stretch."[26]

Late that night the travelers stopped at the mud hut of a rancher, who got out of bed to kindle a fire and make coffee for them. The engineer made omelets, and Edwards pulled out some rum, wine, cheese, bread, sardines, and oranges she had brought with her. It was not until about one o'clock the next morning that the old Ford sputtered into Colonia Santa Clara.[27]

The site housed only barracks and a mud-brick shed. As the "first and only woman there to date," Edwards found herself in a socially awkward predicament with about fifteen men, but she seemed undaunted. "The men were a little anxious at first," she told her sister Anna Bell. "But you know I'm no stranger to sleeping with strange men unharmed and so I quickly reassured them, undressed and took a cot." As it turned out, Edwards and the men enjoyed "a wonderful visit" in the crude setting. "They were even more lonely than I so I think we all made each other very happy," she wrote. "Sunday I cooked them a good old fried chicken dinner and was overwhelmed by their enjoyment of it. A woman seldom gets the opportunity to win that amount of adulation. I should really have liked to remain with them for a month but it was a delicate matter and I could not manouever it quite."[28]

Edwards and the men bunked down in the mud shed, which had a dirt floor and no windows, but they had clean cots and sheets. They washed in cold water in basins set on boards outside the shed. The men "evacuated" behind the shed, but Edwards "found a semi-private corner in the cow pen." With a radio, chess set, and "men of charm and wit," Edwards found the rugged conditions of her adventure much to her liking.[29]

While on the trip, Edwards set up interviews with a couple of prominent government officials. In Chihuahua City, she interviewed the pro-labor Governor Gustavo Talamantes, who was "big [and] darker than I," she wrote. Edwards noted that Talamantes "rides horseback to the State House on one of those excitingly beautiful tooled leather saddles which Mexican horsemen sit with all the sure vanity of a beautiful woman in a becoming evening dress." On the way back to Mexico City on a Pullman car, she stopped to investigate collective farming in the Laguna district. With a letter of introduction, she sought out the state secretary of agriculture to view and discuss the collective *ejidos* (communally farmed plots of land) that were the showpiece of President Cárdenas's agricultural reforms.[30]

Upon reaching Torreón, Coahuila, on October 12, 1939, Edwards fell into bed exhausted after checking into a hotel, "a grubby little 3rd class dump." Health problems continued to plague her. "I'm still feeling rotten and have been in bed ever since I got here," she confided to Anna Bell the next day. Frightened by inexplicable pain that racked her body, she told Anna Bell she was going to write Dr. H. H. Clay, back in Gary, for his advice. "My head still seems the centre of the disturbance," she complained to her sister. "If I could figure out the base for it I probably wouldn't worry about it." Nevertheless, Edwards tried to put the best spin on her condition: "I'm sure there's nothing serious. I probably haven't comprehended how exhausted I am."[31]

Despite Edwards's halfhearted attempt to downplay her condition, she was scared enough to tell Anna Bell where her bank accounts and personal effects were located in the event of her death. She communicated her wishes in regard to what should be done with her possessions. "If I take a perverse notion and kick off take whatever you want first & give the rest to Mama and Thelma." Edwards wished her jewelry to go to Jack and Pat, daughters of her sister Marian; her diamond to be sold for their education; and her two watches and miscellaneous jewelry to be given to them when they reached the age of sixteen or seventeen. "Give [nephew] Billie [Marshall] anything you want," she said. In storage was her fur cap and a bust of *La Pasionaria* (communist icon Dolores Ibárurri Gómez), she reminded Anna Bell. "Most likely I'll be back to take care of everything myself," she wrote, "but just in case—immediate cremation, regardless of what Mama says."[32]

Thyra assured Anna Bell that after she got enough energy to present her credentials to the state agriculture secretary, she would go back to Mexico City and then to the Pacific Coast for some badly needed rest. After doing nothing but sleep for a couple of days, she called on the secretary. She described him to her sister as "tall, thin, handsome, young, . . . dark [and] so good looking."[33]

Since it was Saturday when Edwards met the secretary, he told her to outline the material she sought and come back on Tuesday for a lengthy interview. As it turned out, however, he surprised her by picking her up on Monday evening at the modest hotel where she was staying. Accompanied by two Mexican engineers educated in the United States and two high officials from the Philippines who were seeking similar information as Edwards, the secretary gave them a joint conference there at the hotel. Afterward, they drove to a few neighboring villages and then dined together. The next day, the secretary took Edwards to see the *ejidos*.[34]

Thyra confessed to Anna Bell that she needed a sexual liaison at this point in the trip to satisfy her physical and emotional needs: "You can see I'm out hunting for trouble. So far, however, it has eluded me."[35] A couple of weeks later, however, Thyra confided to her that she "'overtook trouble'—the trouble I'd been hunting" on the night before leaving Torreón. After getting off the train for a stay in Aguascalientes, Edwards was walking across the town square at midnight when "I ran face to face with it—in mighty handsome form." Without her knowing it, the young man had been on the same train, although he was riding in first class and Edwards was in second class. As it turned out, they were also staying at the same hotel in Aguascalientes that night. "Well, with all my proud boasts about wanting trouble," she confessed to her sister, "I was terrified when I met it in such pleasing form." Edwards and her "companion of the highway" enjoyed a "very beautiful holiday"—*El Dia de los Muertos*—in the area. Much to Edwards's chagrin, the romantic encounter did not last long, for her companion soon left to see his family in Mexico City while Edwards went to Guadalajara, Jalisco, for a week or two.[36]

In regard to her health problems, Edwards received a letter from Dr. Clay, who recommended that she give up all of her activities for at least sixty days.

On October 31, she told Anna Bell that after getting Clay's letter, she had loafed all week, thanks to her new but transient lover. "I'm obeying orders," she wrote. "It hasn't been hard with companionship. I shall miss this chap terribly."[37]

Thyra became very reflective about her life in letters from Mexico to her sisters Thelma, who apparently had become frustrated with her at times because of her vagabond lifestyle, and Anna Bell. Thyra, writing from her hotel room in Torreón while listening to a new radio she had purchased, told Anna Bell, "I can't see why I never had one before. When I get home and settled I want a combination radio and victrola. I am going to lead a quieter life in the future."[38] In another letter to Anna Bell, she dreamed about settling down and getting her own place in a year or so. She quickly added, however, that for the moment she was going to enjoy a few more extra days with her new lover. Then, she would work on getting some articles published, and then "get well."[39]

As Edwards reflected on her life, she took a critical look at her long-standing relationship with A. Philip Randolph. "And when I return," she confided to Anna Bell, "I've got to demonstrate myself out of the Philip situation. It is too completely unsatisfactory to justify continuance." The affair nagged at Edwards, but her experiences in Mexico helped to give her a new perspective on ending that relationship. "Mexico is helping me to see things more clearly," she wrote. "With that cleared I ought *demonstrate* a really wholesome and satisfactory relationship." She added humorously, "By that time I'll start a cult of my own that will be an eyeopener to the Christian Scientists and Unity followers."[40]

Thyra also wrote to her sister Thelma in an introspective mood during this period. Updating Thelma on the state of her health, she mentioned that she was following Dr. Clay's orders to rest: "For the last two weeks I've done nothing— save tramp the market places mornings, spend the afternoons in bed and perhaps write about 1 letter a day." She assured Thelma that she was feeling better, but said she did not know if it was the result of rest "or to a very satisfactory love affair I've been having. A transient one—but highly comfortable in its brief span."[41]

Although Edwards at times dreamed of a marital relationship and a quieter, sedentary lifestyle, the pull of international political activism was too great for her to give up. Thelma pointed to Thyra's past relationship with Claude Barnett as proof that she did not want to get married and settle down. "I think you're right," Thyra partly conceded. "I didn't want to marry Claude and I never wanted to be married in the routine way most of my friends are." She disputed Thelma's assumption, though, that she preferred to live by herself. "But I think you're wrong in thinking I want to live alone," she insisted. "I don't. In fact I find it increasingly unbearable. And when one reaches that stage about a condition something usually has to happen. I'm at that stage. Something positive has got to happen."[42]

While Edwards was in Mexico that fall, financial differences strained her friendship and professional relationship with Barnett. About five years earlier, before Barnett married Etta Moten, he and Edwards had entered a joint deal to buy real estate lots on Broadway Street in Gary. Both Edwards and Barnett invested money in the deal, but the status of the lots remained uncertain. For two years, Edwards had been waiting for Barnett to clarify where things stood in regard to the title on the property. She had loaned him $250 initially, and she pressed him for an explanation of the status of the property, the taxes on which remained unpaid for the previous year. She told him that her lawyer and friend, Judge E. Miles Norton, of Gary, would look into the matter, but she made clear she did not intend to sue for collection of the money he owed her. She wanted an amicable settlement. To clear up the matter, she proposed that she take title to one of the lots and return his notes.[43]

Barnett insisted that he had spent a lot more money on the property than she had. Until the previous year, he had paid the property taxes and made two or three payments on the note. He claimed to have spent about $2,500 at that point, whereas Edwards had spent only about $800 on the property. He proposed that Edwards pay him $250 by November 15, 1939, and cancel his notes. In turn, he would send her the deed and a quit claim: "The thing is a headache to me and I am as anxious to be rid of it as you are," he wrote on October 1, 1939.[44]

In a letter to Thelma, Thyra admitted she had made an error in mathematical calculations, but emphasized that she would have Judge Norton get in touch with Barnett about the matter. She downplayed the issue, however, playfully dismissing Barnett's anger at her: "I wrote Claude about it and have an amusing letter from him asking that I pay him $250.00 and return his notes and take the whole thing but giving me no statement of how things stand. Also included a little personal dig. I'm afraid the past has left a little nasty taste in his mouth."[45]

The financial dispute did not end the friendship and professional relationship between Barnett and Edwards. In the same letter in which she told him to expect a letter from Judge Norton, she told him she expected to stay in Mexico until January. "Mostly resting," she said. "I am so tired. I can't believe it." She noted that upon her return to the United States, she would "like to get on the Speakers Bureau for the 1940 campaign—New Deal Democrat. If you hear of anything let me know won't you?"[46]

Back in 1931 when Thyra had moved to Chicago and Thelma had replaced her as director of the children's home in Gary, they had agreed to review their lives in ten years in regard to their achievements. Noting that eight of those ten years had now passed, Thyra told Thelma that the success of those years had exceeded her wildest imagination. She conceded that "I've missed a few things I'd planned and I've accomplished a lot I didn't plan so it cancels." On the one hand, she had not yet finished her college degree, but "if I can swing these magazine articles and get started on a writing career I'll check that degree off." Thyra made clear, however, that she did not regret putting political travels ahead of finishing her education: "I've gotten a richer association with the world and with people than I could possibly have gotten had I stuck away in college. I still expect to study. But right now it's writing I want to do."[47]

Edwards planned to write a number of articles on her experiences in Mexico. When she got back to Mexico City, she intended to write one on the planned refugee resettlement in Santa Clara. Then it would be on to Acapulco to "do nothing for a month or two . . . stretch out on the beach all day." While there, she would catch up on reading and polish material for two more articles, one on the interview with the governor of Chihuahua and another on the Laguna district collective farms. "When I've 2 months of idleness to my credit and some articles accepted by the magazines," she told Anna Bell, "I'll start a weekly series to the Negro papers looking toward building interest for a tour next summer."[48]

As a writer, Edwards's interests in Mexico's culture went far beyond the resettlement of Spanish refugees. She wrote pieces on a number of political topics, including agricultural reform and the movement of right-wing students at the National University. She also wrote on cultural topics such as the tradition of Christmas *posadas,* celebrations of the Day of the Dead, bullfighting, and racial mores in Mexican society. After seeing her first bullfight, Edwards confessed to a friend who worked at the *Chicago Defender,* "I went to a bull fight yesterday and am ashamed to admit that I was thrilled."[49]

Based on her observations and experiences, Edwards praised what she believed was the absence of racism in Mexico. "I know of no country in the world with the exception of Russia and the Scandinavian countries," she wrote to black readers in the United States, "where one may move with such freedom and unrestraint in hotels, restaurants, smart night clubs, as here." The presence of brown people in government offices and the Cárdenas administration's approach to the "Indian question" as an economic and cultural, rather than a racial, one further encouraged Edwards to underestimate the depth of racism in Mexican society. Besides, she was trying to promote her own upcoming educational tour there in the summer of 1940. From the perspective of black Americans, Mexico *was* a noticeable improvement over the United States in terms of access to public accommodations and facilities. Edwards encouraged African Americans to use Mexico for medical, dental, church, and teachers' conventions: "No hunting ground for dingy halls and grimy hotels—the accommodation that makes the life of a Negro traveller such a hard one in the U.S.A."[50]

Edwards acknowledged that for several years, beginning under the presidency of Plutarco Elías Calles in the mid-1920s, Mexico had enforced border restrictions to keep out blacks, Arabs, and Jews. When she hosted her first educational seminar in Mexico in 1938, however, she had called on the Mexican consul in Chicago, who then arranged to waive the restriction on black tourists. Later that year, Eugene Holmes, an assistant professor of philosophy at Howard University, brought the matter to the attention of a writers' congress he attended in Mexico City. With the approval of the congress, he took up the matter directly with President Cárdenas, who then issued an executive order revoking the discriminatory racial restriction. The restriction continued in practice, however, for in July 1940, American attorney Sidney R. Redmond, president of the National Bar Association, filed a protest with the Mexican government because of its discriminatory treatment of blacks who visited the country.[51]

A couple of Edwards's friends did encounter the color bar at one or two hotels in Mexico City, and Edwards, in a meeting with an officer of the state tourist bureau, notified the officer of the incidents. The officer, whom she knew very well and who was very receptive to closer ties between African Americans and the people of Mexico, quickly contacted the hotels and threatened to revoke their licenses in the event of similar incidents in the future.[52]

Ultimately, of course, it was Edwards's plan to write her autobiography in Mexico, but between frenetic travel, health problems, diversions, and other freelance writing commitments, she stuck the book project on the back burner for the time being. "The book can rest in my system a little longer," she told Anna Bell, saying, "6 months is only 6 months and I want to get a toehold with magazines (non-Negro) first. I find the broader my experience becomes the more objective I can approach the Negro question—which will of course be the underlying theme of my book." Thyra planned to return to the United States in January or February, work for six months to get some money, and then come back to Mexico to "tackle that book." She called Anna Bell's attention to the impact of experiences in Mexico on her growth: "I feel that I am growing and developing here—and letting down gradually from the tension of a life time."[53]

Thyra invited Thelma to Mexico City for a visit with her and a mutual friend, Stella Phillips, who was going to spend the month of December with her in Mexico. Thyra expressed frustration over her health and personal problems but remained optimistic about her plans. "I'm disappointed that my health has slipped at just this point when I'd taken the 6 months to write. But after all what is 6 months. If I can finally relax, get myself in hand, take a good squint at these years I may be able to get my personal life straightened out. That's number 1 on my agenda now."[54]

At this point in her life, Edwards did not want a routine job when she returned to the United States. She wanted to be a writer without a rigid work schedule. Writing from Torreón on October 12, 1939, she told her friend Bill Pickens that she would like to earn some money as a lecturer on the Studebaker, Lyceum, or Adult Education series during the lecture season (October to April). She asked him to help her get placed on the speaker series, pointing out that if she did get on the speaker circuit, she could earn as much as on a "conventional job" and have time to enjoy about five months of the year for reading and writing. "That's what I want," she said. "I have a couple of books in my system that I'd like to try my hand at."[55]

As Edwards explained to Pickens, among her options were to go back to the Department of Public Welfare in Chicago for a job or to accept an offer in Washington, DC. "But those jobs mean tying up for at least 2 or more years, and are high pressure routine," she pointed out. "I want a little time to write." Telling him she had been traveling with the Spanish Refugee expedition, she confided, "At present I find I'm too tired and worn out to do anything very much just now in Mexico." She optimistically noted that she would soon be on Mexico's Pacific Coast, though, for "a complete rest and relaxation. I'll be back in February in New York and should be feeling fine."[56]

Edwards, who joined a hiking club to get involved in more group activities, celebrated Christmas and her forty-second birthday in Mexico City. On December 11, the beginning of Christmas celebrations in Mexico, she observed the mass pilgrimage of thousands of Indians to the Shrine of the Virgin of Guadalupe. She watched poor Indian families sleep out on the hard, cold pavement and then get up at daybreak and bring their offerings to the "painted Virgin, which, it is insisted was left there by the miraculous apparition of the Virgin and was not painted by any human hand (tho' it looks just ordinary human to me—perhaps because I lack divine faith)." For Edwards, the entire ritual was depressing: "The priests fight Cardenas because he insists upon educating the Indians which would mean freeing them from the domination of this superstition."[57]

The Christmas *posadas* did impress Edwards, though. The parties, which took place every night from December 16th through the 24th, featured a pageant of Joseph and Mary seeking a room at the inn and the breaking of a *piñata*. On one of the nights, Edwards went up into the mountain forests about ninety miles from Mexico City for a *posada*. As she described it, "A whole grove of pines hung with lanterns etc. We slept out that night, 80 of us, and made an exciting week end of it, coming back after a fruitful hunt for orchids."[58]

Despite persistent health problems, Edwards soon found herself on yet another rugged trip, this time into the tropical rain forest of Oaxaca. In the city of Oaxaca, one of Edwards's favorite places in Mexico, she enjoyed the sidewalk cafes and "the more interesting and sophisticated type of foreigner visiting there." Among the community of anthropologists, archaeologists, painters, artists, museum collectors, and sculptors, she "picked up with" a young couple commissioned by a New York museum and joined an expedition to the remote, "fascinating" tropical village of Chinantla. After taking a train as far as they could, they then took a boat and finally reached Chinantla by horseback.[59]

"Utterly primitive," was how Edwards described the experience. For a month, she and her new friends integrated themselves into the daily life of villagers in their palm-thatched bamboo huts. Each day, Edwards bathed and scrubbed her clothes in the river with the native women and their children. The women invited Edwards into their huts for visits, "where we grew to gossip of everything from children's toys to child bearing." As Edwards later reflected, "It was one of the most interesting experiences I've had in all my journeys and I still look back upon the Chinantla . . . [as] a tropical dream that never really happened—but by the evidence of half dozen beautiful *huipiles,* the dress of the native women of the Chinantla."[60]

Running low on money, Edwards began the long trip back to Mexico City. "I seem never to have the moral fortitude to bring a journey to a close," she admitted, "until the exchecquer [*sic*] is completely exhausted." She then headed to Vera Cruz, and by April 1940 she was in Houston to rest and recuperate from the exhausting, jam-packed six months of freelancing in Mexico.[61]

While in Houston, Edwards granted an interview with a newspaper reporter from the conservative *Negro Labor News.* When the reporter asked if she was a Communist or had ever worked for the Communist Party, she laughingly but emphatically denied the allegation. She acknowledged, however, that because of travels in her capacity as a social worker, many groups had tried to stop her activities. She told the reporter that allegations that she was a Communist had begun when she toured the country to raise money and support for the Spanish Loyalists and refugees in Mexico.[62]

In a discussion with the reporter about labor, Edwards firmly but tactfully disagreed with the anti-union philosophy of the *Negro Labor News.* She emphasized that a civil-rights movement needed alliances with other racial minorities, and she complained that many black leaders, too uninformed, supported outdated solutions to racial problems. She also predicted that in light of Germany's invasion of Denmark and Norway, the United States would enter the world war within two years.[63]

Scheduled to give a lecture to an interracial youth conference in Houston, Edwards announced that she would vote for President Roosevelt's reelection, even though she did not agree with him on many issues. The reporter, pointing out that Edwards knew many of the most prominent, distinguished sociologists, psychologists, and social reformers of the last decade, put her "at the top of the list of well-informed Negro leaders in world affairs."[64]

Not until 1946 would a specialist in New York City correctly diagnose the source of Edwards's physical problems. In the meantime, she would suffer recurring attacks, go through several doctors, and spend considerable time and money in a number of hospitals and clinics, desperate for answers.[65]

9

The Double V Years and
Marriage in New York City

In broken health, out of money, and politically depressed over the state of
world affairs, Edwards virtually withdrew from public life after returning from
Mexico in early 1940, but the United States' entry into World War II would
soon give her renewed energy for the Double V campaign—the fight for victory against fascism abroad and victory in the war against Jim Crow at home.
After harassment by the Federal Bureau of Investigation in Chicago, marriage
and a move to New York City would take her life in a new direction and open
new outlets for her political activism. She renewed left-liberal coalitions with
Communists, facilitated by the wartime alliance between Britain, the United States, and the Soviet Union. Unfortunately, though, FBI surveillance and
health problems would follow her to New York.

As soon as Edwards got back from Mexico in early 1940, she changed doctors but still failed to find the source of the severe health problems that often
crippled and confined her to home. She attended an annual meeting of the National Association of Housing in Pittsburgh in mid-May, but suffered a great
deal and limited her activities. On July 15, 1940, in a letter to Mary McLeod Bethune, of the National Youth Administration, she apologized for not yet having

written an article on Bethune Cookman College, like she had promised in a meeting with her the previous summer. "Unfortunately I have been ill almost continuously since our conference and have been unable to write even sufficient to keep abreast of my current correspondence," she explained. "I have recently changed Doctors and begin to hope for some real recovery."[1]

At the time of Edwards's return from Mexico, the National Negro Congress was in turmoil as a result of fallout from the Nazi-Soviet Pact. The NNC had not held a national conference since 1937. At the third conference, in April 1940, the organization imploded. A. Philip Randolph resigned the presidency to protest the NNC's subservience to the foreign-policy directives of the Soviet Union and at that time isolationist views of CIO leader John L. Lewis. In Randolph's view, the NNC had become the financial captive of the Communist Party and the white CIO unions closely tied to Communists who had maneuvered behind the scenes to oust him as president and replace him with Max Yergan.[2]

It is not clear how Edwards reacted to Randolph's resignation and the breakup of the Popular Front coalition. Although she was back in the United States at the time, she did not attend the NNC conference in 1940. Other than her role in the founding conference in Chicago in 1936 and her efforts to build bridges to the NAACP in early 1937, she had not played a significant role in the national organization. She had been elected one of the vice presidents at the 1937 conference in Philadelphia, but she was in Spain at the time and so did not attend. In fact, she did not go to any of the NNC's national conferences after the first one. Despite her friendship with Executive Secretary John P. Davis, tensions existed between them over policy issues. She had resigned as head of the Women's Committee in the fall of 1937. Her only contribution to the NNC after that was to give a talk on Mexico to the Cultural Committee of the NNC's Chicago Council on June 30, 1940.[3]

In Edwards's speech to the Cultural Committee, she sketched out Mexico's economic history, particularly its domination by foreign capital. She called attention especially to the role of Edward L. Doheny in the oil industry south of the border. She pointed out nationalist resentments against the domination of Mexico's resources by American and British capitalists. After praising the reforms of President Cárdenas, especially his successful literacy campaign in rural areas, Edwards noted that Mexico would soon elect a new president. American oil interests were backing the candidacy of General Juan Andreu Almazán, she argued, while the masses and President Cárdenas were supporting Manuel Ávila Camacho.[4]

Despite tensions with James Ford, Louise Thompson, and other top Communists over the 1939 conference of the American League for Peace and Democracy in Washington, DC, the evidence suggests that Edwards kept her pro-Soviet position even after the Nazi-Soviet Pact and Randolph's exit from the NNC. From Chicago in mid-September 1940, a year after the Nazis and Soviets had invaded Poland and three months after France's surrender to the Nazis, she cabled greetings to a meeting of the International Ladies' Auxiliary of the Brotherhood of Sleeping Car Porters in New York City, expressing hope of movement in a "concrete direction toward peace or preventing entry into war."[5] A month earlier in Chicago, she had spoken to the Second Peace Conference of the People's Federation for Peace.[6] The conference, organized by a coalition of peace advocates, soon led to the founding of the American Peace Mobilization. Prominent black novelists Richard Wright and Langston Hughes were members of the new organization. Unlike their recommendations during the Popular Front years, Communists in the organization now urged nonintervention in the war against fascism. The new organization, which took a firm pro-labor and pro-civil-rights stance, changed its name to American People's Mobilization in another about-face on the day Hitler invaded the USSR on June 22, 1941.

How Edwards rationalized and reconciled the tortured twists and turns in the Communist Party's foreign-policy positions is not clear, but because of health problems, demoralization, and apparently the end of her relationship with Randolph, her activities, writings, and public appearances dropped off sharply in this period. She did cohost a reception for Langston Hughes at the Lincoln Centre in Chicago on October 6, 1940, but generally kept a low profile. "Right now is tough sledding for us, I know," she conceded to Hughes on January 31, 1941. Describing herself as "tired and broke," she confided that "the insecurity is disturbing. But so is the world."[7]

Although Edwards was feeling better when she wrote to Hughes, she had not made any public appearances in months. Letter writing had become easier in the last month, she told him, but "I still have no yen for activity." She did manage to publish a recollection of her Christmas experiences in Denmark in 1933. Her article appeared in the chain of black newspapers owned by the *Atlanta Daily World.* She was very proud of the accomplishment because, as she explained to Hughes, "I've hardly been able to put pen to paper these past two years." Physically exhausted and politically depressed, she said she hoped to begin seeing people again in a month or so, but stressed that she did not plan to resume activities for another year. She complained that she "was simply burned out."[8]

At the time Edwards wrote to Hughes, public controversy was swirling around his poem "Goodbye, Christ," which had been published ten years earlier. When Hughes had given a scheduled reading at a hotel luncheon in Pasadena, California, followers of religious fundamentalist Aimee Semple McPherson, who was lampooned in the poem, protested outside the hotel. The protest brought negative publicity to the poem and to Hughes as an alleged communist. A few black ministers joined in the denunciations of Hughes and his writings and prompted the removal of his works from a number of libraries around the country.[9]

Edwards consoled Hughes by pointing out that a black minister in Cleveland had defended the poem and accepted it "as a challenge to honest ministers to make a reality of the Christian tenets." She reminded Hughes that "2000 years of Christianity have not effected a better life. Not because Christian principles are in error. But Christianity was misconstrued as you effectively pointed out in your poem and prostituted to crasser ends." She urged Hughes not to get demoralized: "Don't let the present state of the world discourage you, Lang. You have already given too much to the struggle of the people of the world to feel the slightest tremor of doubt now. It is your defiant defense of social decency that has translated your songs into the languages of the world and carried them to the remotest hideaway of those to whom the struggle for liberty is life's dominant motif."[10]

One of the ways in which Edwards had always earned money was through writing—her real passion at this stage of her life—but because it was now hard for her to grip a pen or type, she hit a dry spell as a writer. To make matters worse, health problems and wartime conditions put an end to her travel seminars. As a result, she fell back on social work to help sustain her during this time of personal and financial duress. Although she continued to live at the Lincoln Centre and work for the Chicago Relief Administration in 1940–1941, illness sometimes confined her to her studio apartment for long periods of time. She complained to Milton Webster in 1941 that she had suffered "another attack of low blood pressure which simply knocks me out and down."[11] She was on public relief from July 23 to August 7, 1941, but then went to work as an assistant project technician for the WPA on August 22, 1941. By now, after Hitler had invaded the Soviet Union, she had come to support a more interventionist position in the war. She accepted a role as acting secretary for the Victory Over Hitler conference held at the Wabash Avenue YMCA in Chicago on September 4, 1941.[12]

With improved health in 1942, Edwards took additional courses at the University of Chicago and accepted a position with the United States Public Health Service as Director of Personnel Training in a program to combat venereal disease in Chicago. Her interest in public campaigns to treat venereal disease dated back at least to her 1934 visit to a syphilis clinic in Denmark. In the Chicago campaign, Edwards trained field investigators to find victims of venereal disease, provide treatment, and educate the public in regard to the disease and medical treatment.[13] With a sense of physical and political rejuvenation, she told Langston Hughes that "my health is quite good once more and I feel fit and ready for action once more."[14]

Edwards saw that World War II opened new possibilities for a civil-rights coalition similar to the Popular Front. She spoke to Max Yergan, Paul Robeson, and Robeson's accompanist and arranger, Lawrence Brown, about how to create a new coalition when they came to see her in late 1942. The three men had recently performed and spoken to a crowd of 5,000 in Gary, Indiana. She also talked to Chicago's black congressman Bill Dawson about a new, coordinated push for civil rights. "The war has brought many warring elements together for the nonce," she wrote to Hughes. "Our job is to exploit this unity thro' a stronger cohesive and coherent Negro unity around an articulate program. I've been tugging at coat tails (the few encountered in semi-retirement) for 2 years now plugging for some coordinating activity *right now!*"[15]

Just as Edwards was starting to feel better with a renewed sense of political purpose, a threat emerged from a different direction. "While this year is certainly a marked improvement over the past two or three," she told Hughes on November 24, 1942, "it has not been without overt event. I've been on the pan with the F.B.I. since May."[16] The Chicago office of the FBI had summoned her on June 24, 1942, for questioning under oath about her alleged Communist activities.

The FBI's investigation of Edwards dated back to March 1938, when an anonymous source had mailed a one-sentence letter, dated March 12 and postmarked from Chicago, to the FBI in Washington, DC: "One Thyra Edwards of Chicago is a spy in employ of Soviet Russia."[17] At that time she was on a speaking tour on behalf of Loyalist Spain. Director J. Edgar Hoover had contacted the special agent in charge in Chicago and requested an investigation of Edwards and her activities. After an investigation failed to establish even that she lived in Chicago, the special agent in charge, citing lack of personnel, notified Hoover on November 28, 1941, that for administrative purposes he was putting the case in a deferred status until more personnel became available.

The investigation then languished until the Industrial "Red" Squad of the Chicago Police Department submitted a report to the FBI on Edwards. The Red Squad classified her as a Communist who had sent a letter requesting a permit for a demonstration on May 15, 1935. The Chicago Police Department also listed her as a sponsor of a conference of the American League against War and Fascism (which was later renamed the American League for Peace and Democracy) in the city on December 7–8, 1935. According to information provided by the Red Squad, Edwards had denied, though, that she was a Communist, and she had signed oaths of loyalty to the United States on three separate dates— June 30, October 6, and December 2, 1941.

As a federal employee, first with the WPA and then with the United States Public Health Service, Edwards faced increased scrutiny by the FBI on account of her political activities. In 1939, the Hatch Act had prohibited federal employment of an individual who belonged to an organization that advocated overthrow of the United States government. To enforce the Hatch Act, Attorney General Francis Biddle had created an interdepartmental committee to weed out alleged subversives on the federal payroll. In 1942, Biddle created a committee headed by Special Assistant Edwin Dickinson to investigate federal employees who were alleged subversives. The committee came up with a list of nearly fifty organizations deemed a threat to the security of the United States.

The classification of Edwards's case changed from espionage to internal security as the FBI and the Dickinson Committee investigated her. J. Edgar Hoover sent Paul V. McNutt, administrator of the Federal Security Agency, a copy of an investigative report on Edwards by a Chicago special agent on June 27, 1942. The report noted that she was a member of the CIO's State County and Municipal Workers of America, and the report alleged the existence of a Thyra Edwards Unit Number 10 of the Communist Party, consisting mostly of state, county, and municipal employees. The report, which also cited information obtained by the House Un-American Activities Committee, chaired by east Texas congressman Martin Dies, called attention to her role as an officer in the National Negro Congress, as well as her membership in other Popular Front organizations such as the American League against War and Fascism and the North American Committee to Aid Spanish Democracy.[18]

On June 24, just three days before the report was prepared, Edwards reported to the Chicago office of the FBI to sign under oath an affidavit responding to the allegations. In the affidavit, she denied she had ever been a member of the Communist Party or attended any of its meetings. When questioned about her role in the NNC, she pointed out that she had helped to arrange the 1936 founding conference in Chicago, but that she had not attended any conferences since then. She did acknowledge attending a meeting of the American League against War and Fascism in 1935 as a representative of the Women's International League for Peace and Freedom. She also attended the 1939 conference after the organization had changed its name to the American League for Peace and Democracy.[19]

The FBI forwarded a report highlighting the results of its investigation to the Dickinson Committee and the Federal Security Agency. Since the FBI had called attention to alleged Communist activities at the Abraham Lincoln Centre, where Edwards lived, Dickinson sent a memorandum to Hoover on November 2, 1942, asking about the credibility and reliability of one of its confidential informants who supposedly was closely connected to the settlement house. Hoover insisted that the informant was a highly reliable person who spent a great deal of time at the Lincoln Centre and who in the past had provided other information on alleged Communist activities there.[20]

On December 8, 1942, Edwards received a letter from Perrin E. Lowrey, executive secretary of the Federal Security Agency's Subversive Personnel Committee. Lowrey sent a list of questions for her to answer. On December 19, she submitted a written response to the committee's questions. Again, she denied any affiliation with the Communist Party or knowledge of a so-called Thyra Edwards Unit or any other unit of the party that held meetings at the Lincoln Centre. Edwards said she specifically asked Dr. Curtis Reese, director of the settlement house, whether any Communist meetings were held there, and he said they were not. She emphasized that Reese was president of the Western Unitarian Conference and regional vice president of the American Unitarian Association. She compared the activities of the Lincoln Centre to those at other settlement houses such as Hull House, the University of Chicago Settlement, and others. At that time, she pointed out, the director of the Cook County Selective Service and the Chicago Board of Education were sponsoring classes there three nights a week for eligible military draftees who were deferred because of illiteracy.[21]

Lowrey's questions solicited information on Edwards's travels in the Soviet Union, her education at Brookwood Labor College, and her membership on the Editorial Council of the magazine *Soviet Russia Today*. In addition, Lowrey questioned her affiliation with the so-called Drama Union of Chicago. Edwards disavowed knowledge of any group by this name, but did say that in the fall of 1935 she had delivered a talk to a conference of the New Theatre Group called "The Negro in the Theatre." Later that winter, after Chicago mayor Edward J. Kelley banned the production of *Tobacco Road* in the city, she had spoken at a meeting to protest the ban. Along the same lines, Lowrey asked if the Communist Party sponsored the "Drama Union's" production of the play *Stevedores* in January 1935. Edwards pointed out that the play was a commercial production with professional actors, many of whom were her friends and acquaintances, including Georgette Harvey, Abbie Mitchell, Leigh Whipper, Canada Lee, and Rex Ingram. Edwards said she had attended performances of the play in New York and Chicago, but stressed that to her knowledge none of the actors had political ties of any kind.[22]

It is not clear from the FBI's files who alerted the agency to Edwards's activities, but a few years later, she would claim it was Jenny Lawrence, a black shop supervisor whom she had publicly criticized during the 1935 Sopkins strike in Chicago. As Edwards explained toward the end of World War II, Lawrence wrote a letter to the Dickinson Committee claiming "I was a 'red.'" In a more triumphant mood near the end of the war, Edwards proclaimed: "Jenny Lawrence is dead and in time a lot of other old handkerchief heads will follow. Progress advances over the bodies of these."[23]

Just when her health had improved markedly, Edwards now faced the possibility of losing her job. In a letter to Langston Hughes, she said that she was notified on November 24, 1942, that she would receive a final hearing in early December. "That will determine whether I have a job or not," she told him.[24]

As Edwards awaited news of her fate, she considered moving back to Houston, but a new job offer came her way. In mid-January 1943, the Federal Security Agency notified J. Edgar Hoover that she was exonerated, that the agency found "no showing that this employee has engaged in activities which may properly be characterized as subversive or disloyal to the Government."[25] By this time, however, Edwards had packed her bags, waved good-bye to Chicago after eleven years, and boarded a train to New York City to become managing editor of *The People's Voice,* a leftist newspaper created in 1942 by Rev. Adam Clayton Powell Jr. On January 30, 1943, the newspaper announced that about three weeks earlier, Edwards, "a handsome self-confident brown-skinned, well proportioned woman," had come into the office and begun her new duties. "Since her high school days in Houston, Texas," the article noted, "she has been associated with efforts whose basic philosophy has been the improvement of the common man. Writing about and working with these efforts has sent her on a crazy itinerary that has run a course from Texas to Chicago, to Mexico, to Denmark, to Loyalist Spain, to Gary, and now the Big Town."[26]

In 1943, Powell was a politically ambitious member of the New York City Council whose newspaper adopted a working-class orientation and a strong commitment to civil rights. Although a non-Communist, he courted black Communists on his rise to power, including Benjamin Davis, a dynamic lawyer and editor of the Communist Party's *Harlem Liberator.* When Powell ran for the U.S. Congress in 1943, Davis won Powell's seat on the city council with his endorsement. Edwards also supported Davis. In fact, she was one of the sponsors of his campaign. Powell recruited a number of Communist writers, such as Max Yergan, Marvel Cooke, Doxey Wilkerson, and others, as well as left-leaning staff members to publish *The People's Voice* with a Popular Front focus on race and class. On the one hand, the newspaper reached out to Communists, who in a revisionist trend toward "Browderism" (referring to Earl Browder, general secretary of the Communist Party USA from 1934 to 1945) had toned down their criticisms of racial inequality in the United States for the sake of winning the war. On the other hand, the newspaper ran articles focusing on the Double V campaign with an emphasis on fighting racial segregation, too. The focus was consistent with Edwards's call for black unity to promote an aggressive class-based civil-rights agenda at home as well as support for the war overseas.[27]

After accepting her new position at *The People's Voice,* Edwards got an apartment at 1945 Seventh Avenue, near West 118th Street, in the heart of Harlem's cultural district. Even before assuming her new duties, she was well known in Harlem, in part because of her previous work in Popular Front organizations. Her cultural pursuits, political activities, and relationship with Randolph had often drawn her to New York City over the past decade. She had many friends in the arts and literary world, as well as on Broadway. A number of New York intellectuals, teachers, politicians, labor leaders, social workers, and political activists were in her circle of friends.

On April 10 and 11, 1943, Edwards spoke at the Eastern Seaboard Conference of the National Negro Congress. Held in the Abyssinian Baptist Church of her new employer, Rev. Adam Clayton Powell Jr., the conference condemned racial discrimination and called for full support for trade unions and unity among all oppressed people of color. In Edwards's speech, "A People's Victory— A People's Peace," she called for the full utilization of resources to win the war and condemned racial discrimination in various aspects of the military effort. She extended that critique overseas, criticizing South Africa's refusal to allow the use of black fighting troops. Calling for the immediate opening of a second military front in Europe, she likewise condemned British colonialism in India, urging the United Nations to recognize India's independence. The Atlantic Charter, she argued, should be extended to Puerto Ricans and other West Indians struggling for their freedom. Finally, she praised the Soviet Union for the way it had integrated its nationalities.[28]

Edwards maintained a high profile as a speaker/activist in Harlem. At a rally in March to celebrate the launch of a new Communist Party–supported weekly newspaper, *Pueblos Hispanos,* which called for Puerto Rican independence, she linked the common struggles of Puerto Ricans and African Americans. On July 13, 1943, she addressed a meeting held by the Harlem Committee of the Soviet-American Friendship Society in the Abyssinian Baptist Church. She called for friendship between African Americans and the Soviet Union through a better mutual understanding of their respective problems. She emphasized that the savage attacks on racial minorities that had characterized Czarist Russia were a thing of the past.[29]

On June 19, 1943, five months after moving to New York, Edwards married Murray Gitlin, a recently divorced radical Jewish writer and activist. They had met through a mutual friend at a dinner party in Chicago, where Gitlin had once been the assistant director of the Jewish People's Institute (JPI), a North Lawndale community center at 3500 West Douglas Boulevard. He had also headed the Writers Circle at the JPI. Gitlin, the son of Samuel and Sarah (Cooperstuck) Gitlin, of Colchester, Connecticut, was an official for the United Jewish Appeal. His parents were Russian immigrants from the province of Minsk in Byelorussia. According to FBI reports, Gitlin, too, was a Communist who at one time had been a magazine managing editor. In September 1943, Edwards and Gitlin moved into an apartment at 77 Washington Place, just around the corner from Washington Square Park in Greenwich Village. The FBI kept their apartment under surveillance.[30]

For Edwards, the choice of June 19, or "Juneteenth," as a wedding date had special significance. It was a holiday that had originated in 1865 in Galveston, Texas, to celebrate the abolition of slavery. Choosing a Juneteenth wedding was a political statement and reaffirmation of Edwards's identity and Texas cultural roots as she married into a Jewish family. Edwards, who had been divorced for eighteen years, now had a partner with similar political views and writing interests. The marriage symbolically linked the historical struggles of African Americans and Jews against racial oppression in the era of Jim Crow and the Holocaust.

For Edwards and Gitlin, of course, the problem of an interracial marriage went far beyond how their friends and family would respond. They expected some to oppose their marriage altogether. Beforehand they had spent endless nights considering the full range of implications should they marry. "The problem is," they explained, "have we the inner strength to take it? Strength for the discrimination which one of us had never known, for the Jim Crowing should we travel South, for the Jim Crowing in the North's restaurants and houses and hotels, for the present and future difficulties in employment."[31]

Many of their friends were supportive but had reservations, fearing that the depth of racism in the United States would sink them economically. Edwards and Gitlin, both of whom had been married before, disregarded those fears: "Certainly we ought to know what we want out of life by this time, and something about what life is, is not and can be. . . . We are not enamored of fine clothes and show. Our needs are modest." Summing up why they decided to marry, they posed the question, "Really now, what do we aspire to be? Isn't it just to be plain people—happy in each other, free of ignorance, hoping that we can do a little now and then toward making this world what potentially it can be and must some day become?"[32]

Edwards's tenure as managing editor of *The People's Voice* did not last long—less than a year, in fact. A clash with a member of the staff soon led to her dismissal. On May 28, 1943, a confidential FBI informant reported that he was present when Max Yergan and Ferdinand Smith, a Jamaican-born black Communist leader of the CIO's National Maritime Union, discussed a dispute between Edwards and the staff member in question. It is not clear what the dispute was about, but according to the informant, Smith sided with Edwards and believed the other staff member should be fired for inefficiency. On November 27, 1943, however, the informant advised that Adam Clayton Powell Jr. told him that he had fired Edwards instead, for creating disunity on the staff. Powell stressed, however, that he had thrown a farewell party to honor Edwards when she left the newspaper.[33]

By this time, Edwards's chronic health problems had put her in the hospital again anyway. She now found it hard to work at a desk for any length of time.

In fact, the progressive deterioration of her condition, still undiagnosed at this point, confined her to an armchair for extended periods. She went through major surgery in November 1943, but in March 1944, complications still had her restricted to home, unable to walk.[34]

The death of Edwards's father in Phoenix, Arizona, in early March 1944 was a devastating blow, especially at a time when she, too, was sick and incapacitated. Although she had rebelled against his explosive temper, harshness, and authoritarianism, he had instilled many lasting values in her. In fact, she was like him in many ways. Over the years, she had come to understand his volatility as a manifestation of frustrations over living in a Jim Crow society. Her civil-rights militancy, feelings of class democracy, and impatience with black, middle-class, "go slow" leaders had come from him.[35]

Soon Edwards felt well enough to assume a more active role as a writer in the political arena. After months of hospitalization and confinement to home, she was thrilled to be back on the beat. She jumped on a train to Philadelphia as a journalist to cover the twenty-sixth conference of the International Labor Organization (ILO). "This morning I packed my bag with glee," she wrote on April 29, 1944. "I've packed and unpacked it a half dozen times in as many months. But this time I was boarding a train instead of continuing the trek back and forth to hospitals."[36]

Edwards was determined to educate African American readers about why the ILO's proceedings were so important to them. The mission of the ILO, created by the Treaty of Versailles in 1919 as a labor agency of the League of Nations, was to sponsor and oversee enforcement of legislation to uphold collective bargaining rights and improve wage standards and working conditions around the world. The ILO, based in Geneva, Switzerland, and inspired in part by fear of the spread of Bolshevism, was founded on the principle of labor, government, and business cooperation to promote a model of economic development that would raise workers' living standards and encourage social justice. Of course, the United States had rejected the Treaty of Versailles, and because of the socialist views of many European trade union leaders, American businessmen and even leaders of the American Federation of Labor (AFL) had often distanced themselves from the ILO's activities. In fact, the United States and the AFL did not join until 1934.[37]

Edwards, critical of the AFL's history of racism, complained that AFL president William Green had ignored President Roosevelt's request that the AFL share representation with the CIO at the ILO meeting. She criticized Green's appointment of Robert Watt to the conference. "We know too well the Jim Crow policies of William Green," she wrote, bemoaning that the AFL would be the sole voice representing the labor movement in postwar planning and policy to shape the wages and working conditions of colonial subjects and people of color in many parts of the world.[38]

Edwards tracked Watt down at the conference and asked why not a single black adviser accompanied the AFL's team of advisers to the conference. Watt replied that none of the AFL unions had recommended a black expert to serve as an adviser. In response, Edwards pointed out that Ashley Totten, of the Brotherhood of Sleeping Car Porters, was probably the best-informed leader on conditions in the Virgin Islands and would have contributed significantly to the discussions at the conference. She also noted that there were many highly qualified Puerto Rican trade unionists and economists in Spanish Harlem who would have served well in an advisory role.[39]

Edwards sided with efforts by Vicente Lombardo Toledano, head of the Mexican labor movement and Mexico's delegate to the conference, to challenge the seating of workers' delegates from Argentina. Lombardo Toledano was a Marxist who in 1938 had also created the Confederación de Trabajadores de América Latina, a regional labor federation, to act as a counterweight to the dominant influence of the now-defunct Pan-American Federation of Labor, an AFL creation funded secretly in 1918 by the Woodrow Wilson administration. Edwards supported Lombardo Toledano, who at that time enjoyed friendly relations with the CIO, but not with the AFL, as he opposed seating Argentina's ILO delegates because of the government's openly fascist sympathies and policies. Citing author John Guenther's book *Inside Latin America*, Edwards described Argentina as "the one lily-white country in Latin America."[40]

Edwards protested that the AFL's Watt had backed the seating of Argentina's workers' delegates to the conference. Angered by the AFL's position, she urged African Americans to deluge Watt and AFL president Green with letters of protest. She even suggested that they contact Secretary of Labor Frances Perkins, who had read President Roosevelt's message of greetings to the conference when it opened. Edwards praised Lombardo Toledano for "carrying the ball for the colonial peoples—the black man's burden."[41]

Although conference delegates discussed unemployment, social security policies in Nazi-occupied areas, and minimal living standards for blacks and Indians in dependent territories of Britain and France, the plight of people of color in the United States and its dependent territories was virtually ignored. For Edwards, it was hard to decide where to focus her outrage. Of course, she criticized the AFL, but she also reserved fire for African Americans who had shown no interest in the ILO conference. With the notable exception of Carter Wesley's chain of Texas newspapers, she stressed, not a single black newspaper had given more than superficial attention to the conference. "Negro leaders would have taken the fastest means of transportation to address some forum in Keokuk," she complained mockingly, "but here at one of the important world conferences they were strangely absent and silent."[42]

For the last ten to twelve years, Edwards had been trying to raise black awareness of international events and issues, but the lack of interest in the ILO conference embarrassed and angered her. Meeting almost within sight of the ILO sessions was a conference of 3,000 black delegates of the African Methodist Episcopal Church, and yet no delegation came to the ILO conference to deliver a message of any kind on behalf of black workers. AME leaders did send a message inviting ILO delegates to hear Eleanor Roosevelt speak at their conference. It was left to Bishop Francis J. Haas, an Irish-American pro-union Catholic, to call attention to the oppression of African Americans during a full session of the ILO conference. There were only two African Americans in the large audience.[43]

For Edwards, even though the three weeks of discussions at the ILO conference did not produce any concrete results for the "dark peoples" who attended, they did bring attention to the future of colonialism and its subjects. She called attention to initiatives taken by France and the Netherlands in the direction of decolonization, as well as criticisms of Britain's colonialism by the British Trade Union Congress (TUC). She noted the significant role of trade union committees established by the TUC to help organize African workers under British rule, establish collective-bargaining rights, and prepare the workers for self-government. The ILO conference highlighted the need for economic and social planning. In reporting on the conference, Edwards emphasized that workers would expect postwar governments to commit to full employment. In her view, trade unions should act as partners with employers and the government to end colonialism and to raise the living standards of colonial subjects in the transition to independence. Hopeful, Edwards saw signs "that out of the blood and tragedy new conceptions of social responsibility and equality are being burnt deeply into the souls of men."[44]

Carter Wesley, a friend of Edwards's and owner of the *Houston Informer* who at the time was also a CIO supporter, published Edwards's articles on the ILO conference and hired her to write a weekly labor column in his newspaper. Edwards used her column, "The Negro Worker—Today and Tomorrow," to explore a wide range of international and domestic issues important to black workers. With the presidential election approaching, she urged readers to re-elect Roosevelt and to support the CIO and its Political Action Committee in the Double V campaign against fascism abroad and racism at home. She assured readers that "the CIO's record on the Negro during the seven years of its existence is the strongest and the most consistent of any organization in American life for his full integration into political and job equality."[45]

In addition to her newspaper column, Edwards assumed a position as the assistant director of public relations for the National Maritime Union (NMU), one of the CIO's most militant, democratic, and Communist-led unions. Edwards worked closely with Ferdinand Smith, the Jamaican-born Communist leader and civil-rights activist in Harlem who, along with Joseph Curran, a non-Communist, had been one of the founding officials of the NMU. Edwards had worked with Smith and James Ford on an NNC committee to aid strikers during the seamen's strike of 1936. She and a friend, Lottie Biggs, had given speeches in Harlem, visited relief kitchens, and raised money to support the seamen. The strike's defeat had led to the creation of the NMU in 1937. Smith's unswerving commitment to racial equality made him popular with the NMU's black sailors, in particular.[46]

Edwards defended Smith, who recently had negotiated a union contract prohibiting the use of race as a factor in hiring seamen, against Republican newspaper attacks on his radicalism and Jamaican citizenship. The War Labor Board approved the contract that he negotiated, and the president of the U.S. Shipping Lines spoke to about 2,500 dinner guests gathered to honor Smith in New York. A number of CIO officials, congressmen, and black activists attended a cocktail party in his honor before the dinner. Among them was Carter Wesley, who, she wrote, "is getting to be a familiar figure in New York."[47]

When Charles de Gaulle, military commander of the Free French movement against France's Hitler-backed Vichy government, came to the United States and held a press conference in Washington, DC, on July 10, 1944, Edwards was determined to get a press invitation. Only reporters accredited by the White House were allowed to participate, but she did an end run around the White House by calling and sending a telegram to de Gaulle's press attaché. She requested press credentials, stressing the important role of the *Houston Informer* in educating southern black readers on labor and foreign affairs. The attaché waived the rules and personally invited her to attend. As a result, she enjoyed a "ringside seat" among approximately 150 reporters.[48]

At the press conference, Edwards asked de Gaulle about the future of sixty million French colonial subjects, including thirty-four million black Africans. He promised self-government to them and praised the role of African recruits in the war against the Axis powers. He emphasized that France would do more to provide better health and educational services and to safeguard native cultures, music, and handicrafts. When the press conference ended, he shook hands with Edwards as his press attaché introduced them. "When, in sincere humility, I clasped the hand of this leader of one of the world's great states," she wrote, "he said humbly: 'Thank you, thank you, Madame, very much,' as though it were I who did him honor."[49]

The combat role of native Africans in the Free French forces continued to attract Edwards's attention. On September 2, 1944, she wrote a newspaper story about the impact of Felix Eboue, a black French colonial administrator and former governor of Chad who had initially mobilized the native army for the Free French. She praised Eboue, who had died earlier that year, for his role in promoting education, preserving traditional customs, and overall improving

French colonial policies toward native Africans. In February, General de Gaulle had formally adopted his policies. Edwards pointed out that "native African camel-mounted troops" under the command of General Jacques-Phillipe LeClerc had trekked across the Sahara Desert and joined up with British troops under General Bernard Montgomery in the successful campaign to drive General Erwin Rommel's German forces out of North Africa.[50]

On de Gaulle's trip to the United States, he also went to New York, where he met Marian Anderson at one of her concerts. During intermission, he joined her in singing the French national anthem. Edwards reported that de Gaulle, in response to a telegram from Paul Robeson and a committee planning to honor Eboue, replied that he was "deeply moved," and paid further tribute to Eboue as an important symbol of resistance against fascism.[51]

Edwards continued to devote her journalistic attention to French colonial subjects in Africa. She and her husband coauthored an article, "25 Million Negroes Getting New Deal in French Africa," published a few months after de Gaulle's visit. Praising France's plans to grant native Africans greater political representation in the French Parliament, to improve the status of women, to build more hospitals and send more doctors, and to raise living standards in its African colonies, Edwards and Gitlin predicted that other colonial powers would be influenced by France's policies. "To France goes the honor of being the first major power to break with the old colonial philosophy of exploitation for the benefit of the mother country," they proclaimed jubilantly, if prematurely, "and to put into practice the theory that colonial administration is a senior-junior partnership."[52]

In matters of domestic policy, Edwards supported the CIO and reelection of President Roosevelt, but she did not ignore the New Deal's shortcomings or the limitations of the Democratic Party on civil-rights issues. "No honest man denies the glaring omission in the Democratic platform," she conceded. "No honest man justifies the administration's failures."[53] Nevertheless, she pointed to Roosevelt's flexibility, emphasizing that he had bent to pressure from A. Philip Randolph and Walter White to create the Fair Employment Practices Commission to make sure racial discrimination did not keep minority workers out of industries that received wartime federal contracts. She argued that FDR was accessible to black leaders and that it was the job of African Americans to press ahead and work with coalition groups such as the CIO.[54]

Edwards did not hesitate to criticize black newspapers and black civil-rights leaders who backed Republicans. She criticized the *Pittsburgh Courier* for endorsing Thomas Dewey in the election of 1944, and she blasted Crystal Bird Fauset, a Democrat who had switched support from FDR to Dewey in the campaign. Fauset, the first black woman elected to a state legislature (Pennsylvania, in 1938), had served as a race- relations adviser to the president as well as to

Eleanor Roosevelt, but became disenchanted with the administration's record on race relations. She and Edwards knew each other from previous civil-rights and social-reform activities in organizations such as the NNC, but that did not keep Edwards from criticizing her for switching party allegiances.[55]

Despite Edwards's support for the New Deal, she complained that the federal government's use of "race specialists" and "race consultants" for advice on how to handle black problems had created a brain drain in the black community. As a result, black business enterprises, newspapers, and to a certain extent educational institutions suffered. Edwards interviewed a number of consultants and advisers who acknowledged that their service to the federal government had not led to the full integration of African Americans into American life. A couple of days after FDR's death in 1945, she concluded with pessimism that the New Deal would "be important in the history of the American Negro mainly because it created a new professional outlet for college-trained colored men and women, providing an avenue for lucrative careers in the business of 'advising' white people in high places what to do when Negroes demand too much or show sign of exploding from to [sic] much economic and social pressure." For Edwards, these advisers provided mere window dressing for the New Deal. According to her, they had been co-opted and seduced by careerism: "Representing no organized group in Negro life, responsible to no organized group, without defined authority or official status, these 'federal advisors' crystallized, it seems, into an artificial hierarchy of petty government officials divorced from the economic and social forces of Negro life and on the periphery of the technical stream of government administration."[56]

Edwards also used her weekly column in the *Houston Informer* to praise the interracial summer labor institutes sponsored by the AFL and the CIO. She fondly recalled her days at Brookwood Labor College and acknowledged Randolph for helping her to get a scholarship there. Writing in the summer of 1944, she called attention to an upcoming institute sponsored by the CIO's United Cannery, Agricultural, Packing and Allied Workers of America in Winston-Salem, North Carolina. She pointed out that half of the enrolled students at the institute were black.[57]

In October 1944, Edwards joined a presidential campaign tour with Ferdinand Smith and Hugh Mulzac, the distinguished Caribbean-born black captain of the Merchant Marine's SS *Booker T. Washington,* to support Roosevelt's reelection. Mulzac, when offered command of a Jim Crow ship in 1942, had insisted on a racially integrated crew, and the Merchant Marine had relented and granted his request. In two years, his ship had transported a dozen cargoes to ports in England, Africa, and the Mediterranean, and brought hundreds of German prisoners to American prison camps. The ship was cited for courage under heavy fire. Like Smith, Mulzac was a Communist member of the CIO's

National Maritime Union, but he also belonged to the AFL's Master Mates and Pilots Union. For Edwards, he and Smith, as black Communists, symbolized the progressive promise of the Merchant Marine.[58]

The campaign tour, which lasted about six weeks, took them to seventeen cities, including New York, Boston, Seattle, San Francisco, Los Angeles, Cincinnati, Louisville, Chicago, and others. They spoke to workers at factory gates between shifts, and to audiences in churches, auditoriums, high schools, cabarets, and hotel dining rooms. They met with mayors and other local officials. At a Negro Freedom Rally in Calvary Baptist Church in Milwaukee, Mulzac praised President Roosevelt and Edwards gave a speech titled "The Role of Negro Women in the Election." She reported encouraging signs as white and black crowds gave Smith and Mulzac warm receptions around the country. "The love and honor heaped on these two men everywhere by Negro and white alike, indicates that organized labor has achieved a place of leadership," she proclaimed. "Their representatives enjoy respect and confidence. The old rigid race lines are breaking up."[59]

The tour confirmed to Edwards that important wartime changes were taking place in the racial attitudes of many white people, especially in CIO unions. In San Francisco, Jim Drury, a white organizer for the NMU, introduced Mulzac to a cheering audience. Drury was a poor white from Georgia who had been a port agent in Baltimore, "the queen city of Jim Crow," when World War II broke out. Edwards pointed out that he had worked to persuade other white seamen that Jim Crow arrangements on ships should be a thing of the past.[60]

As Edwards and her traveling party entered a hall to speak in San Francisco, they received news of the death of Wendell Willkie, the Republican presidential candidate in the 1940 election. Although Edwards supported the New Deal, she had great respect for Willkie, a liberal Republican who in 1943 had published his best-selling *One World,* based on a trip he took around the world in 1942 as a special envoy of FDR's. She agreed with the ideals Willkie expressed in the book—the rights of all peoples to freedom and self-determination, regardless of racial differences. *One World* called for the end of colonialism overseas and the end of racial exploitation at home. According to Edwards, she, Smith, Mulzac, and the others in her group, inspired by the ideals in the book, gave the best speech of the whole tour in San Francisco after they learned of Willkie's death: "We spoke in behalf of common men and women, black and white, ordinary people; the people Wilkie [*sic*] spoke for so simply and effectively in 'One World.' Ourselves, the Negro people of whom he wrote and spoke constantly and fearlessly. We didn't speak of him there in the hall. The hurt and loss were too sharp and new to trust ourselves."[61]

When Edwards was in Los Angeles, an old sweetheart tried to look her up when he learned she was in town, but he had just missed her. She had already left for San Francisco, but a bouquet of long-stemmed red roses soon reached her there. "They were a soft note to a strenuous town," she beamed. On the stop in San Francisco, she visited her sister Marian and her two daughters, who admired the roses: "My young nieces, 17 and 16, found them reassuring. Men still send roses to girls past 40. . . . Then there's hope at 17."[62]

In Cincinnati, Edwards shared with her newspaper reading audience what it was like to stay in a Jim Crow hotel on the tour. She complained about being "parked in a 'cullud' hotel—if you know what I mean. And just in case you don't, it means I've been chasing roaches by day so's to take my clothes away vermin free." Unable to sleep because a porter was tacking down carpet outside her door in the middle of the night, she asked him to stop but to no avail. "The customer be damned," she wrote, "is the general policy in Negro hotels—Oh well."[63]

Despite her experience in Cincinnati, Edwards expressed optimism over breakthroughs in southern race relations. She called attention to the 1944 landmark Supreme Court case of *Smith v. Allright,* which abolished the Democratic Party's white primary in her home state of Texas. She praised the role of Carter Wesley in the long-standing legal battle against one of the chief tools of racial disfranchisement in the state.[64]

On the campaign tour in Louisville, Edwards was thrilled when she saw streamers supporting the candidacy of Hortense (Houston) Young for the local school board. She stayed at the home of Dr. Coleman Milton Young and his wife, a black civil-rights activist, librarian at the Louisville Municipal College, and writer for the *Louisville Defender* whose roots were in Houston, Texas. The CIO's Political Action Committee and a number of unions supported her school-board candidacy. At a mass meeting in Louisville presided over by Mayor Wilson Watkins Wyatt, a New Deal Democrat, the mayor introduced Captain Mulzac as a "great American" and handed him keys to the city. Blacks and whites sat side by side in the huge audience as Mulzac spoke. When Edwards asked a judge seated with them on the speaker's platform about the sources of racial unity in the city, the judge praised the tone set by President Roosevelt and bragged that white folks in Louisville had undergone a lot of changes as a result.[65]

Edwards criticized African Americans for not responding more favorably to the more liberal attitudes of many white southerners. An editorial in the *Houston Informer* defended her: "Now nobody can ever accuse Thyra Edwards of ever taking sides with the South or any other section of the nation against the rights and opportunities of her people." The editorial asked the newspaper's readers not to ignore her words but to dig deeper into them to understand the basis for her criticism and accept her remarks as a challenge.[66]

After Edwards finished the successful campaign tour and returned to New York, her husband shipped out with the Merchant Marine, and she decided to go to Houston to celebrate her birthday and the Christmas holiday season with her family. All of her sisters, as well as her brother, would be there. En route with her typewriter on a train to Texas, she was in a reflective mood as she approached her forty-seventh birthday. She stared out the window at the drab shacks that dotted the southern countryside. "No where except in Mexico and the Latin Americans [sic]," she observed, "are a hard-working farming people so ill housed." Sitting in the seat facing her was a Danish woman on the way to visit her son stationed in Corpus Christi. She, too, looked out at the shacks and asked Edwards, "How do the people live? It looks so poor, so poor."[67]

For a brief moment, Edwards became defensive. She insisted that Texas was a rich state, noting that cotton-picking time was now over and that it was hog-killing time. Lifted back in time, Edwards suddenly was a kid again at hog-killing time. Christmas memories swept over her. There was her father making a fire in the big heater, cutting a pine tree and putting it into a cedar water bucket in the sitting room of her childhood home. She was a little girl once again, cutting gifts from the tree's branches at four o'clock on Christmas/birthday morning, hurrying across the cross ties and tap track with her family taking Christmas boxes to Aunt Ellen and Uncle Si and Aunt Lou "before we sat down at home to the big turkey gobbler. And the end of the day, gathered around my mother at the piano, the music book opened to my father's favorite 'Far Away.'"[68]

The Danish woman on the train snapped Edwards back to reality by questioning her assertion that Texas was rich. On one level, of course, Edwards agreed with the woman's detached observations of southern rural poverty, but the people inside those shacks were not mere objects to be pitied. No, they were much more than that. Edwards knew their faces, their dreams, their laughter and tears, their scars, and their daily struggles to eke out a living and bring dignity to a harsh life: "Inside those lean gray cabins I was seeing Uncle Si and Aunt Lou and Aunt Ellen—a whole good brave company."[69]

Only eleven years earlier, Edwards had traveled through Denmark's countryside on her way to spend Christmas with the family of Forstander Rasmussen on the island of Fyn. Now, en route to Houston, she reflected on the small plots of land with modern whitewashed houses she had seen on that trip to Fyn: "I learned that the poorest Danish farmer was not poor in the way that Aunt Ellen and Uncle Si and that noble company were." Thanks to the Danish government's break-up of huge feudal estates and sale of small holdings to the people who worked them, rural conditions in Denmark were far more modern than in the American South. Edwards wondered what might have been if the radical Republicans' calls for confiscation of large slaveholding plantations and redistribution of land had been carried out during Reconstruction in the South. If only "forty acres and a mule" would have become a reality! she thought.[70]

Edwards spent ten days with her family in Houston in what she called "the happiest, most flawless of all the many Christmases I have known." For the first time in twenty-three and a half years, she and her three sisters were together again. "There were my sister Marian's two lovely daughters," she wrote, "grown-up young ladies, with parties and beau; and my brother's adorable little sons." Her mother, who had since married S. H. Dodson, cooked all the favorite dishes that she had prepared when Edwards and her sisters were young. Edwards praised Dodson for the quiet, graceful way in which he had become such an affectionate part of their household.[71]

In Houston, Edwards got a chance to talk to a few people she had known from her childhood. She and her sisters reminisced a bit with Dr. R. J. Ferrell, their childhood physician, who paid them a visit. Edwards could not find transportation out to family friend Charlie Brock's hog killing, but he called her while she was home for Christmas. He talked to her about his plans to develop his farm over the next twenty years. At age eighty, he was a source of inspiration for anyone "who is feeling beat out from world-weary."[72]

Edwards also chatted with a couple of activists in the black community of Houston who complained about "self-appointed Negro leaders who sell us down the bayou." T. A. Scott, of the Third Ward Civic League, criticized the mayor's interracial committees and teachers, in particular. Rev. L. V. Bolton told her that the Fifth Ward Civic League and the Colored Baptist Ministers Association were pushing for street improvements. Edwards applauded the activist role of the Civic League, but had little patience with complainers who did nothing to put pressure on city officials. She especially complained about the lack of spunk among Houston's black teachers: "I heard some lurid talks of Uncle Tomism among the teachers. I don't know any place where I've found teachers held in such mistrust and suspicion for abasing servility to whites and contemptuous arrogance to the parents who are their patrons, and as tax payers really their employers."[73]

When Edwards left Houston, she stopped in New Orleans to visit further with her sister Anna Bell Douglas, a civil-rights activist. At the end of the visit, when Anna Bell took Thyra to the railroad station to put her on the L & N for New York, a Pullman porter approached Anna Bell and said, "I've got another $100 for you." Anna Bell replied, "That pulls us up to $3,100 . . . and $1,900 to go." "To go where?" asked Thyra, and Anna Bell explained: "To the $5,000 New Orleans has pledged in the drive for a permanent FEPC [Fair Employment Practices Committee]."[74]

Anna Bell, a teacher who shortly before Christmas had participated in a community-action program to control venereal disease in New Orleans, was a member of a local council of the national movement to create a permanent Fair Employment Practices Committee to ensure continued access by racial minorities to jobs after the war. After Milton Webster and A. Philip Randolph, of the Brotherhood of Sleeping Car Porters, had visited New Orleans on November 25, 1944, a local council (the first in the South) was quickly set up. By Christmas, the New Orleans council had raised $2,000 in the black community to support an office and staff for the National Council, cochaired by Randolph, in Washington, DC.[75]

When Thyra learned about the efforts to raise $5,000 in New Orleans, she warned Anna Bell, "That's a big chew." Undaunted, Anna Bell replied, "That's what Philip Randolph and Milton Webster thought too. But you don't know New Orleans. We haven't been done to death by the Race Relations Committees and we've kept our souls free of Rosenwald Fund Domination." She added: "Negroes in New Orleans want freedom and they still believe in Negro leadership which means they know they've got to pay for what they want."[76]

Edwards, impressed by the response of black activists in New Orleans, endorsed the campaign for a permanent FEPC, which received initial contributions from the BSCP ($7,000), the International Ladies' Garment Workers Union ($5,000), and the NAACP ($5,000). "There's going to be a mad scramble for jobs after the war," she wrote, "and Negro workers will be lapped off wholesale without protection." She called the FEPC "the Magna Carta of foreign born and minority workers." She praised the donations from the black community and mocked white philanthropic foundations: "Not a drive from Father Rosenwald's fund (tho' I understand he can put his in if he's willing to just throw it in the common pot like everybody else)."[77]

In the political aftermath of Roosevelt's reelection, Edwards warned about the machinations of the defeated Republicans and conservative anti–New Deal Democrats. She condemned the House of Representatives' decision to extend the Dies Committee into the postwar period. She pointed out that most of the committee's energy had gone into harassing not only Communists but even moderate liberals such as William Pickens and Mary McLeod Bethune. In the meantime, fascist and racist organizations such as the German Bund and the Ku Klux Klan, as well as individuals such as Father Charles Coughlin, had received scant attention from the committee. Edwards urged the committee to go after these groups, more numerous and powerful, instead of the few thousand Communists in the United States. "The American Communists have their conspicuous faults," she conceded, "but race hatred is not one of them."[78]

As the world war neared its end, Edwards recalled what had happened to black workers—"the last to be hired and first to be fired"—at the end of the First World War. To her, planning for the post–World War II economy would be critical. The government, employers, and organized labor were planning, she noted, "but what are Negro leaders doing or thinking of doing?" She warned black leaders not to pin all of their hopes on the FEPC and not to congratulate themselves too much for the gains in the armed forces: "Freedom from the fear of unemployment! That is the star at which we're shooting. The gains we've made in the armed forces—Army and Navy officers, aviators, nurses, Red Cross workers—excellent as they are—do not touch peacetime economy. Employment is the crux of our lives, jobs and politics."[79]

Edwards called for full employment and a national health-care system. In response to the alarming disclosure that millions of military draftees were physically unfit, she pointed out that the United States was fifteenth on the list of nations in adult death rates. "We have dispensed health as we have dispensed so much else here—for those who can purchase it," she wrote, "and on a Jim Crow basis to boot."[80]

In February 1945, Edwards urged political action to support former vice president Henry Wallace, who had been dropped from President Roosevelt's ticket in 1944. President Roosevelt had since nominated Wallace, who expressed a commitment to full employment, to head the Department of Commerce. Wallace would soon become secretary of commerce, but at the time of Edwards's call for support, the Senate had tabled his confirmation as conservative opposition to his candidacy mounted. "For us, the Little People, a race of laborers, tenant farmers, with a margin of professional and businessmen, and all Negro business is small business, Wallace is unmistakenly our man. It's up to us to act."[81]

At age forty-seven, Edwards could look back on the wartime years with mixed emotions. On the one hand, she had taken great strides. The years had brought new romance, marriage, and personal excitement, a move to New York, and notable gains on the labor and civil-rights front. Her new husband, Murray Gitlin, was a political activist who seemingly did not feel threatened by her independent, activist lifestyle. Their marriage brought together common interests in the shared global struggles against fascism, racism, colonialism, and anti-Semitism. On the other hand, ongoing health problems continued to cripple her at times, and she had suffered the painful loss of her father. To make matters worse, the FBI continued to shadow her and Gitlin.

When it came to civil rights, Edwards knew that racist politicians and their constituents were biding their time until they could roll back some of the wartime advances in civil rights. She recognized the need to consolidate gains made by black workers and to pressure the government to dismantle Jim Crow institutions. In short, the Double V campaign, about to achieve success in the military fight against fascism abroad, was only partly successful in the struggle for civil rights at home. She acknowledged the wartime gains, but stressed that "the inequalities still persist, sanctioned by law, by custom, by inertia; sanctioned in the North as well as in the South." As she summed it up, "Jim Crow still rides in the army, the Negro ghettos rob youth of life, liberty and happiness; the Negro is still an outsider handed the leavings; the Jew is still maligned, beaten and discriminated against; the minorities—which have made and are America—have not been integrated into our life as equals, as Americans."[82]

10

The Final Years in Italy

As Edwards looked to the postwar period to continue her efforts on behalf of civil rights, labor, and women's rights, she at long last received a correct diagnosis of the health problems that had plagued her for nearly ten years. In 1946, a specialist in New York diagnosed her condition as *arthritis deformans,* or rheumatoid arthritis. When told by the doctor that there was no cure for the illness, Edwards asked how to treat it. The doctor replied: "If you have money you go to thermal baths every year or two; you get some relief. That way you keep going as long as you can . . . 10, 15 years."[1]

Shaken by the diagnosis, Edwards recalled the stunning change that had overcome her when the condition first reared its ugly head. One winter about a year before the condition hit her, she was returning from an assignment on the icy, snowy streets of Chicago. A companion who was about eight years younger than her had exclaimed with envy as Edwards was half-skipping, half-walking along the frozen street, "God you're alive." Reflecting on the crippling symptoms of her subsequent illness and the vast difference then in her vitality compared to that winter day, Edwards described it: "A year later my feet were weights, my legs collapsible, my head crowned the spinal column in pain and unease."[2]

After the diagnosis, Edwards spent a few months getting chiropractic treatments. This therapy gave her enough relief that she was able to work at a desk again. At first, she focused on writing light fare for a popular audience. In the 1946 premier edition of John P. Davis's magazine *Our World,* which featured singer and actress Lena Horne on the cover, Edwards wrote a very brief article in which she gave tips on hairstyling. "Coarse kinky hair is no handicap at all," she argued. "Beauty experts insist that coarse hair stands up better than softer textures. It lends itself to fuller, richer styling. You can make your own hair just as lovely as you choose." Edwards urged readers to "avoid the unskilled operator who scorches hair, the poorly manufactured gummy oils and hair setting fluids that eat through hair like lye." For women who do their own hair, she recommended brushing it dry rather than using hot-air dryers. "Simpler styles—the page boy or for shorter hair, the feather bob—can be achieved with kid curlers," she advised. "But the croquinole and finger wave are skilled operations which should not be attempted at home."[3]

As Edwards regained strength, she continued her publicity work for the National Maritime Union, and she worked with a coalition of peace and women's-rights activists to lay the groundwork for an American branch of the Women's International Democratic Federation (WIDF). The WIDF, created in late 1945, was explicitly antifascist. Its founding leaders were Eugenie Cotton and Marie-Claude Vaillant Couturier, both of whom had been Communist members of the French Resistance. The organization, which banned women who had belonged to fascist organizations, aimed to promote world peace and defend the economic, social, legal, and political rights of all women.[4]

On March 8, 1946 (International Women's Day), the founding conference of the WIDF-affiliated Congress of American Women (CAW) took place in New York City. Edwards was elected recording secretary of the new organization. Other officers included Dr. Gene Weltfish, a Columbia University anthropologist, president; Muriel Draper, vice president; Josephine Tims, secretary; and Helen Phillips, treasurer. Several other black women joined the new organization, including Dr. Charlotte Hawkins Brown, president of the Palmer Institute; Thelma Dale, field secretary of the National Negro Congress; and Vivian Carter Mason, of the National Council of Negro Women. "Whatever we may have suffered as a group here in the United States," Brown emphasized, "is nothing compared to what the women and children of Europe have suffered under fascism. . . . We must speak out, reach the hearts of the American people, and with their help wipe out fascist types from public office in the U.S.A., if our children are to be secure."[5]

In the Cold War political atmosphere, the interracial CAW quickly came under fire for its pro-labor, pro-Soviet sympathies. Edwards was one of the members singled out by the House Un-American Activities Committee (HUAC) as an alleged Communist. HUAC blasted the CAW as a Communist "front" organization, and under this pressure, the short-lived CAW began to splinter internally. The CAW dissolved in 1950, when the U.S. Justice Department ordered it to register as a foreign agent.[6]

Edwards continued to attract FBI surveillance. On November 26, 1946, she and fellow CAW officer Muriel Draper were among those who spoke at a dinner in New York City sponsored by the National Committee to Win the Peace and the Action Committee to Free Spain. Both of these groups appeared on the attorney general's list of subversive organizations.[7]

Edwards had also drawn FBI attention earlier that year, when she wrote articles on Ilya Ehrenburg, an internationally renowned Jewish novelist and war correspondent from the Soviet Union. Ehrenburg and writers Konstantin Simonov and Mikhail Galaktionov toured the United States as guests of the State Department in the summer of 1946. Ehrenburg, whose 1942 book *The Fall of Paris* described the Nazi occupation of France, had written for *Pravda* during the war. Born in Czarist Russia during the waves of pogroms, he praised the racial policies that had prevailed since the Bolshevik Revolution in 1917. During the war he had also organized the Soviet Anti-Fascist Committee to publicize Nazi atrocities. Under his leadership, the committee had compiled a Black Book to provide documentary evidence of Nazi war crimes.[8]

Ehrenburg, given a choice of which section of the United States he would like to visit, chose the "poll tax belt." Before leaving New York on a tour through the South, he met with Harlem students, educators, and journalists, Edwards among them. After touring the South, Ehrenburg returned to New York, where he spoke to about 20,000 people in Madison Square Garden. He and a number of other speakers, including Andrei Gromyko, the Soviet delegate to the United Nations; Joseph Davies, former ambassador to the Soviet Union; and W. E. B. DuBois called for good Soviet-American relations. Speakers also called attention to the fact that racial prejudice and anti-Semitism were a capital crime in the Soviet Union.[9]

Edwards and her husband, as soon as they heard he had returned to New York from his tour of the South, telephoned Ehrenburg and set up an interview at the Waldorf-Astoria Hotel, where he was staying. They had met him several times in New York, but they wanted to do the interview for a newspaper article. In the article, published in the *Chicago Defender,* they summarized some of Ehrenburg's experiences on the tour, including his discussions in meetings with a number of African American students, faculty, and newspaper editors. He had also visited with sharecroppers and workers. Edwards and Gitlin gave him an opportunity to combat anti-Soviet perceptions in the press and to highlight the special relationship between Russians and African Americans. Ehrenburg, when asked what experience on the southern tour impressed him the most, mentioned that he had met a female student at Fisk University whose mother was Russian and whose father was black. "Can you imagine what it meant to me, a Soviet citizen," he told Edwards and Gitlin, "to find a half Russian—she looked entirely Russian—living under the conditions imposed upon a Negro community in the South."[10]

Not long after the interview with Ehrenburg, Murray Gitlin's job took the couple overseas. The United Jewish Appeal appointed him as deputy director of a branch of the American Jewish Joint Distribution Committee to work with Jewish refugees in postwar Italy. Gitlin left their Long Island residence for the new job in Italy ahead of Edwards, who in early February 1947 applied for a passport to "join my husband." On February 11, 1947, the State Department issued her a passport for travel to France and Italy, but the War Department rejected a request from Carter Wesley, of the *Houston Informer*, that Edwards be granted credentials to cover political developments in Europe for his chain of newspapers. On July 5, 1947, Wesley wrote a letter to the War Department demanding an explanation, but to no avail.[11]

Before Edwards joined her husband in Italy, she visited Germany as a member of a WIDF commission "to study German women's activities in reeducating & democratizing their children." The commission compiled a report on its investigations, and Edwards wrote a couple of articles on German women and their attitudes toward Nazism and the war. Based on her observations, she found no remorse at all among Germans: "I'll simply say that the picture is pretty discouraging so far as any will to peace among the German people. 'Next time we'll win' is the general slogan."[12]

The loosely organized Combined Travel Board, which was under the Allied High Commission for Germany, oversaw travel policy at the time Edwards entered Germany. American passport officials barred her and any other members of the WIDF from entering Germany, but French authorities gave her an entry permit to the French zone of occupation there for a couple of days. The permit did not include the British and American zones. A U.S. official in Berlin sent a cable to the Passport Division of the State Department on May 23, 1947, complaining that Edwards's permit was a "serious breach" of regulations. From then on, any request for travel to the western sectors of Germany by anyone connected to the WIDF should be denied. Urging an investigation, the official cabled that the "most charitable explanation" for the breach was "French clerical error."[13]

After her quick visit to Germany, Edwards joined her husband in Galliano, a mountain village in the province of Como in northern Italy. At that time, they lived in "a sunny old house in the center of a garden that is really a royal park." Gitlin encouraged Edwards to take advantage of the leisure time and beautiful location to relax, paint, and devote herself to creative writing, but she did not make much progress on the writing front. On September 11, 1948, she briefed Langston Hughes on what she had been doing since reaching Italy, confessing her lack of progress on the book: "The first months I tried to set myself to creative writing, under Murray's encouraging aegis. After some months of hard work I emerged with one chapter that stood up under critical scrutiny. Somewhat discouraged—and a little uncertain by this time that there really is a book in me I've laid it aside."[14]

As Edwards reduced her political activities, she viewed the state of the postwar world with mixed emotions. On the one hand, she was impressed by Italy's economic recovery from the war, despite growing unemployment. She was also encouraged by the creation of Israel in May 1948, in keeping with a 1947 United Nations plan to partition Palestine. "I see and meet a good many Palestinians. And here is the real new man. As ardent as the new young Russians but more cosmopolitan since they are not confined but are free to travel at will outside the country."[15]

When it came to the civil-rights movement at home, however, Edwards was pessimistic. Like other African American activists, especially on the left, she had struggled to maintain a balance among her commitments to racial integration, interracial strategies, labor internationalism, and black nationalism. In the postwar atmosphere of growing political attacks against the left, she continued her public commitment to integration and interracial strategies, but privately bemoaned the weak state of black institutions and leadership. Disturbed by the lack of political mobilization by the black masses, in particular, she complained that African Americans as a result were forced to settle for a few political crumbs from the table of white paternalists. In a letter to Hughes, she looked back on Marcus Garvey's black nationalism in a favorable light:

> What basic, vital organization have we—vital, free and unhampered by our "good white friends." Garvey's idea of an independent country of our own is correct. Free of "our good white friends" of whatever stripe. Allies we must have but from our patrons and benefactors let us be delivered. And do let us have done with our piddling little victories—first Negro here, only Negro there, etc., etc. Not dramatic enough even to catch the world's attention—we don't even know what we want to be or not to be Jim Crowed—we, editorially, the cullud leaders as the average cullud man wants to be free—an undefined sort of freedom. But I'd like to see a general walk out of Negroes—from all Jim Crow schools, for example—that being the most dramatic point of focus.[16]

During her first year in Italy, Edwards generally kept a low public profile for a number of reasons, from her health to the fact that she was under surveillance by U.S. intelligence agents, of which she was well aware. She explained to Hughes, "I've read a lot, loafed a lot. . . . I live quietly at home, study Italian, know all my Italian neighbors and try to avoid any involvement in serious affairs."[17]

According to a confidential FBI informant in New York, however, Edwards did not keep an entirely low profile during this time. She wrote articles for an Italian feminist magazine, *Noi-Donne,* and complained about meddling by the United States on behalf of the triumphant Christian Democrats in the 1948 elections in Italy. According to the informant, Edwards requested that her observations on the elections be published anonymously, given the fact that FBI agents and U.S. State Department officials in Italy were on her tail. Edwards purportedly feared being forced to surrender her passport on account of political activities.[18]

The same FBI informant claimed that the State Department had approved Edwards for a newspaper assignment in Trieste and in the American sector of Germany, but U.S. Army officials had intervened against her on the grounds that she belonged to a Communist "front organization." Edwards assumed the officials must have been referring to her membership in the CAW, since it was the only organization she had belonged to in years. According to the informant, Edwards interpreted the army's rejection as a warning to avoid getting singled out for relatively unimportant issues so she could carefully continue her more important activities.

Edwards also criticized the decision by the United States Congress to include General Franco's Spain in the Marshall Plan. She pointed out that many formerly Popular Front Europeans were confused by the decision. She praised Paul Robeson's role in backing the third-party presidential candidacy of Henry Wallace in the 1948 election in the United States, expressing her own support for Wallace, too.[19]

During that first winter in Italy, it was more than political considerations, however, that made Edwards keep a low profile. Her rheumatoid arthritis kept her confined. She was racked with pain much of the time. Earlier, in Rome, she had searched for relief as the condition attacked her fingers, ankles, toes, and knees. Upon the recommendation of doctors whom she had consulted in Milan, she planned to go for treatment in the spring to the thermal baths at Abano.[20]

Edwards endured "the most excruciating days of my long odyssey" as she waited for the spring mud baths of Abano. "I recall the week I couldn't raise my head to be fed," she later noted, "our good Julia [servant] encouraging me—'but you are young, Signora. You will be well one day'—neither of us believing it." For Edwards, the pain and despair were overwhelming: "I remember looking from the increasing distortion of my feet to our window view of steep green mountain slopes and thinking, 'Once upon a time I would have climbed those slopes. Now for the rest of my life I can only gaze from far off.'"[21]

From time to time, though, hope returned as Edwards got through an occasional pain-free day. She would go for a walk in the park, maybe go down to the village, or resume painting. Her husband, lifted by those good days, encouraged her to have faith that her health might yet be restored.

One day in March 1948, the gardener who worked for Gitlin and Edwards introduced her to Angelo, a beekeeper who tended the apiaries for many villas in the area. When Angelo sang the praises of bee venom as a medicinal treatment, Edwards urged him to come back that Saturday afternoon, when Gitlin would be home. On Saturday, Angelo came back and regaled the couple with stories of how bee stings had been known to cure diseases. He cited the example of his priest, a diabetic who was stung by a stirred-up swarm of bees. According to Angelo, the mass stings put the priest in bed for a week with fever, but once the fever subsided, he no longer had diabetes. When Angelo, eagerly encouraged by Edwards and Gitlin to talk more about the healing power of bee venom, mentioned arthritis, they took him by the arm and led him down the path to the apiary. "Here, make one sting me," Edwards insisted, and Angelo arranged for a bee to sting her.[22]

Edwards was elated when she woke up Monday morning feeling great. Not since that frozen winter day in Chicago several years earlier had she felt so strong. As she walked outside to the gatekeeper's lodge, the gardener, the gatekeeper, and Julia all remarked how good she looked. "Indeed I had changed," Edwards recalled. "The deep lines which pain had cut in my face were gone. Three days later I canceled my reservation at the thermal bath. I pleaded with the beekeeper to take my case in hand." Angelo protested, "But I am not a doctor. I make many experiments. But I don't treat people." Edwards pressed him anyway: "Then describe the experiments to us, and stand by so we won't make mistakes."[23]

With Angelo in a consulting role, Edwards underwent a second bee sting and then another on each of three consecutive Saturdays. Her hand swelled from the stings, but the pain was a mere irritation, and each successive sting produced less swelling. Then Edwards increased the dose of venom gradually to four stings every other day. The stings did make her blood rush and created strange sensations, and at times she had trouble sleeping because of the intense itching caused by the stings. She still had minor pain in her ankle joints in late August, five months after her first bee sting, but she felt good enough to go out and climb the nearby mountains. Sharing the good news with Langston Hughes in September, she told him that she had "undergone a rigid health program (pretty primitive one, too, with live bees stinging the daylights out of me). And for the first time in 8 years I've felt like a normal human being, free for 6 whole months from pretty devastating pain. . . . I feel like a prisoner let out on parole."[24]

Upon learning from Angelo that bees stop producing venom as soon as the first frost comes, Edwards decided to rush the treatment without telling anyone. She doubled the dose every day, but "suddenly all the pains returned with their original ferocity." When Gitlin got home, she told him in despair that her hopes of being cured had been dashed. She dismissed the bee-venom therapy and concluded that her physician had been right when he warned her that the peasant remedy was no cure, but rather that the venom was a mere habit-forming drug.[25]

Angelo disagreed. He argued that bee venom was strong enough to break up calcified deposits without damaging a person's organic system. When Edwards confessed to him that she had rushed the treatment, he exclaimed, "Your blood is suffocated, overworking your heart. Your blood is not strong enough to absorb that dosage. Rest now for a couple of weeks, then begin again, gradually. But don't be in a hurry. Bees have their rhythm. Synchronize with it."[26]

Desperate, Edwards went through the treatment again. She suffered over a thousand bee stings in a number of spots on her body over the course of the treatment. She began with stings between the left thumb and forefinger, then on the wrist, elbow, and ankle, and then the base of the neck, then the lower spine. She also ate a quarter pound of pure honey every day, got at least a half hour of daily sunshine, and hiked through the mountains for exercise. When Angelo then told her to go back to her physician for X-rays, she prepared herself for the worst. "Possibly you were right, Doctor," she confessed. "It may be only a dope. In which case I am now a dope fiend." Much to her surprise, though, the X-rays showed a normal spine. "'Well,' the Doctor volunteered, 'these peasants have some things that elude the profession.'"[27]

With a new lease on a pain-free life, Edwards wrote an article on the bee-venom treatment that was published in March 1953. At that time, she admitted that she did not know if the treatment had cured her or not, but to skeptics, she emphasized that she had been living a normal life ever since. "I do not know if I am permanently cured any more than does a patient discharged from a tuberculosis sanatorium. But, permanent or transitory, four years free of pain are already something!"[28]

After Edwards and Gitlin moved back to Rome in late October 1948, she drew on her background in social work to do volunteer work with the local Jewish community. She evaluated the structure of "their existing (antiquated) social services institutions" and encouraged the modernization of their programs, particularly their children's institutions. She and Gitlin drove through most of Italy, "familiarizing ourselves with these nuclear communities and their institutions and recruiting trainees to be sent to the U.S.A. for social service training." As she observed to Langston Hughes, "It was also a very pleasant way to see Italy."[29]

While vacationing on the islands of Corsica and Sardinia, Edwards devoted time to writing. Gitlin, whose novel *The Embarkation* was published on February 15, 1949, began a new novel, and Edwards worked on a piece of fiction, "The Honey Arbor," or "The Life and Times of AnnaBella Bee." What she called "a little fantasy on the Life of the Bee" was an autobiography of a worker bee. At the time she wrote to Hughes on March 25, 1950, she told him that she had not yet found a publisher, but she expressed contentment with her new life in Italy: "I have passed three extraordinarily pleasant, tranquil years (in these troubled times) . . . and at the moment I'm only being a housewife which I find I don't mind."[30]

At Hughes's request, Edwards explored her contacts to see if an Italian opera company would put on a performance of *Troubled Island,* by black composer William Grant Still, with a libretto by Hughes and Verna Arvey, about the 1791 Haitian slave uprising. The Metropolitan Opera had turned down the opera a few years earlier, and when Hughes asked Edwards in 1948 to explore possibilities of staging a production in Italy, he and Still had not found an American opera company willing to put it on.[31]

At Edwards's request, Elizabeth Eyre de Lanux, an American artist she had met in Italy, talked to opera director Lucchino Visconti about *Troubled Island.* After getting the go-ahead from Lanux, Edwards urged Hughes in 1950 to write to Visconti and tell him that Lanux suggested the contact. Edwards also offered to talk to the Israeli consul in Rome about *Troubled Island.* She warned, however, that traditional opera still dominated in Italy, where companies showed reluctance to try anything new or experimental. She noted that "certainly in Rome the productions are a little hammy."[32]

In Edwards's correspondence with Hughes, she noted that she had received letters from a few mutual friends, including ship captain Hugh Mulzac, who had been blacklisted; in the postwar period, he could no longer get a ship to command because of racism and his radical political affiliations. "He has no ship and is facing the same thing he faced after World War I—but he has magnificent spirit," she said. Another letter to Edwards had come from Hermina Huiswoud, who had moved from New York to Amsterdam. Edwards told Hughes that she was glad to read about the successful run of *Lost in the Stars* on Broadway. She added that it was good to see that Todd Duncan, who played the leading role in both *Lost in the Stars* and *Porgy and Bess,* was doing well: "It's wonderful to get an occasional cheerful report as most of the news from the U.S.A. sounds pretty grim from this distance."[33]

Hughes tried to help Edwards find a publisher for her fiction piece "The Honey Arbor," which was delivered to him by houseguests of Edwards on their return to the United States in August 1950. On Edwards's behalf, Hughes sent the manuscript to literary agent Maxim Lieber, who sent it out to Random

House, Harcourt Brace, Doubleday, William Morrow & Co., and a number of other publishers in late 1950 and early 1951. On November 2, 1951, however, Hughes wrote Edwards that on account of a serious illness, Lieber was forced to close his business and go to Arizona. In reality, Lieber, a Communist who was subpoenaed to testify in the Alger Hiss case, had fled, or was preparing to flee, to Mexico as a political refugee. Lieber's wife returned the unsold manuscript to Hughes.[34]

Rather than have Hughes return the manuscript to her in Italy, Edwards instructed him to send it to their good friend Bernard Ades for safekeeping in New York City. By this time, she and Gitlin had moved back to the province of Como in the Lombardy region of northern Italy. They lived in the village of Crevenna in the municipality of Erba. She told Hughes that Ades was taking care of their stuff while they were abroad. "I'm afraid the manuscript won't go unless I get some recognized authority either in Child Education or in Bee culture to do a preface for it," she said. "I'm feeling around for some one in that field. Any suggestions?"[35]

Edwards thanked Hughes for his efforts and sent him the mailing address of Ades. "Now I am sorry to hear of Lieber's illness—or anybody's illness for that matter," she wrote on December 7, 1951, "having experienced so many years of it myself." She asked Hughes to extend her "warmest hopes for recovery" to him, and added, "I shall drop him a note myself, too."[36]

Despite Edwards's health problems and political semiretirement in Italy, U.S. intelligence surveillance of her increased as the Cold War deepened. In an interview with an FBI agent on June 30, 1950, Louis Budenz, former managing editor of the *Daily Worker* who had broken with the Communist Party in October 1945, named her as one of four hundred "concealed Communists" he knew. According to Budenz, who soon made a lot of money giving testimony against alleged Communists, it was James W. Ford and Eugene Dennis, general secretary of the Communist Party USA (CPUSA), who had told him that Edwards was a member of the Communist Party in the late 1930s and early 1940s. Budenz also claimed to have met her as a Communist at an enlarged national committee meeting or a national convention. Although he acknowledged that he did not have any information on her since about 1942–1943, he maintained that "she was one of the original infiltrators into the YWCA, if I remember correctly, and was of a quiet, pleasant personality."[37]

At the time Budenz named Edwards in 1950, of course, Cold War hysteria was sweeping the United States. After the expulsion of Earl Browder from the CPUSA in 1945 because of his view that communism and capitalism might coexist peacefully, the party had taken a much more confrontational position in keeping with changes in Soviet policy. As a result, the party became even more isolated as the U.S. government stepped up repressive measures to curb its influence. In 1947, the Taft-Hartley Act restricted the rights of trade unions, requiring officials to sign non-Communist affidavits with the government. Under pressure, the CIO purged Communist-led unions, and witch hunts for suspected Communists went on in government, schools, the NAACP, and other institutions. In 1949, with Budenz providing chief testimony for the prosecution, Eugene Dennis, Benjamin Davis, and a number of other top Communist leaders were tried, convicted, and sent to prison for violating the Smith Act, which made it a crime to belong to an organization allegedly devoted to the overthrow of the U.S. government. Furthermore, sections of the McCarran-Walter Act (1952) required Communists to register with the government and barred CP members from holding office or being granted passports.[38]

On September 20, 1950, the FBI's Washington Field Office asked the Passport Division of the United States Department of State to notify the agency in the event of any communications with Edwards about passport matters. The FBI also requested that the U.S. Customs Collectors on the eastern seaboard notify the New York FBI office in the event of her return to the United States. Her passport had been renewed on February 15, 1949, and the American Embassy in Rome notified the U.S. State Department on January 11, 1951, that she was expected to apply for an extension when her passport was to expire in February. A few months later, she was forced to surrender her passport at the embassy. Officials told her that she would get a new passport whenever she made arrangements to return to the United States.[39]

A medical crisis soon forced Edwards to get a new passport and return to the United States. She wrote to Langston Hughes to let him know that she and her husband would be leaving for New York March 29, 1952. "We have been nestled away in this, our favorite village [Galliano]," she wrote, "fighting a bout with a long and pernicious illness as a result of which we've had to relinquish an assignment to the Middle East." This time, the problem was not rheumatoid arthritis. As she confided to Hughes: "I turned up with a tumor in the left breast."[40]

Apparently, it had been sometime during a Rome visit from Edwards's friend Hermina Huiswoud in 1950 that Edwards had been diagnosed with breast cancer. She had concealed the diagnosis at that time. During Huiswoud's stay in Rome, she found Edwards very busy, taking an art course, voice lessons, and a physical education course. As Huiswoud later recalled, though, Edwards "failed to tell me the basic reason for her numerous visits to the doctor and the attendant tests."[41]

Edwards had refused to have her breast removed. "The struggle has been to unload the tumor and hold onto the breast—to which point of view doctors are little disposed," she explained to Hughes. No doubt encouraged by the way in which peasant folk remedies had relieved her of pain from rheumatoid arthritis, she opted instead for some kind of alternative treatment. She confessed to Hughes that she had been following "lowly peasant ways—painful and tedious—but the tumor is on the way out, and I still have the breast, a sick, tortured looking member at the moment, bearing only remote resemblance to its firmer companion."[42]

Edwards told Hughes that the cancer had kept her and Gitlin "cloistered" for four months, but she tried to be optimistic. She said that after arriving in New York, she would go to Houston to convalesce and visit her mother. Then she would be back in New York, where friends Shelby Rooks and Dorothy Maynor would be "trucking us away somewhere until the end of the summer by which time we should have pulled our stuff out of storage, dusted it off, and found an attic in which to resume house keeping."[43]

In that final letter to Hughes from Italy, Edwards noted that Maynor, a notable black soprano and music educator, and her husband, Rooks, pastor of the St. James Presbyterian Church in Harlem, had been visiting her and Gitlin for two weeks. From Maynor, Edwards had learned about the recent successful run of two of Hughes's shows on Broadway. Edwards congratulated Hughes and asked him to help her husband: "I think Murray's book would lend itself to staging. If you think so and have any producer contacts you could interest I'd say thank you the prettiest you ever heard."[44]

Edwards and Gitlin returned to New York on April 9, 1952, apparently staying for a while with Gitlin's family in West Hartford, Connecticut. They then went to Houston, apparently to help take care of her mother, according to what Edwards told Hermina Huiswoud. In none of Edwards's letters to Huiswoud at that time did she even mention her cancer.[45]

FBI agents soon followed Edwards right into the Lafayette Gardens Nursing Home in Brooklyn, where she was admitted as a patient on November 14, 1952. Her doctor told the investigating FBI agent that she had breast cancer, which had spread to her lungs. He emphasized that her condition was very serious and that if the FBI wanted to interview her, he would not allow it. When the FBI agent filed his report, he went out of his way to stress that, perhaps in a bit of sympathy for Edwards, he had not asked to interview her. He suggested, in fact, that, given her condition, the Bureau might wish to authorize her removal from its Security Index. Director J. Edgar Hoover insisted, however, that for the time being, at least, her file should remain open, just in case her condition improved.[46]

Edwards's condition did not improve. Murray Gitlin later told Hermina Huiswoud that "she had become unrecognizable, having wasted away to skin and bones but she swore that she was satisfied that she had lived a full life."[47] Edwards died on July 9, 1953, at the age of fifty-five in New York City's Lexington Hospital. With the exception of her father, all of her immediate family members survived her. Bernard Ades, a longtime friend, veteran of the Abraham Lincoln Brigade, and Communist civil-rights lawyer, gave her eulogy at a memorial service held at St. Philips Episcopal Church on July 12. He captured Edwards's essence when he described her as "a well-rounded, large soul, who knew how to combine all the softer virtues with the hard struggle for the rights of humanity. She not only knew how to do it, she did it. In her last days she said that she was satisfied that she had led a full, rich life and had no regrets. We agree."[48]

Epilogue

From crawfish ponds in Wharton, Texas, to the bright lights of European capitals and the Kremlin, Edwards's rebellion against "man's inhumanity to man" was the driving force behind her global quest for freedom. As a black woman and left-wing activist who negotiated in a white man's world, she spoke truth to power and contributed significantly to the radical roots of the post-1945 civil-rights movement. A popular interpreter of international events to African American audiences, she articulated an anti-imperialist, antifascist, Pan-African critique of world affairs from the perspectives of race, class, and gender. Her labor-based civil-rights activism anticipated the later deepening emphasis by Martin Luther King Jr. on the modern civil-rights movement's need to address the economic exploitation of black workers in the United States. Her commitments to peace and women's rights, too, were grounded in an analysis of class relations.[1]

Edwards had a reputation for doing things her own way. She was fiercely independent and a romantic with an enormous zest for life, intellectual curiosity, and bold sense of adventure. She found warmth in and drew inspiration from the daily struggles of people with whom she shared a sense of camaraderie and purpose. Her political sympathies were with the masses of people struggling against multilayered forms of exploitation. Unlike most of her activist contemporaries, she put her faith in the Communist Party and trade unions as the political instruments of mass mobilization to tear down the walls of racial segregation. For her, though, the struggle went beyond race. The war against Jim Crow and bigotry in the United States was part of a much broader campaign for democracy, human rights, and a world free of poverty and exploitation.

After investing so much of her energy in left-liberal coalitions before and during World War II, Edwards died during one of the darkest periods in American politics. The promise of the Double V campaign turned to bitter disappointment in the late 1940s and early 1950s, when the Cold War shredded leftist coalitions. Many white liberals in the CIO, for example, sought shelter from reactionary political forces by turning their backs on civil rights and their former Communist allies. The CIO purged its left-wing unions—the most racially progressive ones, laying the foundation for a reunification of the AFL and CIO under conservative leadership in 1955. Likewise, the NAACP cracked down on political radicals in its ranks, even expelling W. E. B. DuBois.

Many of Edwards's good friends and political allies were jailed, deported, hauled before HUAC, and/or forced to surrender their passports. Because of their Communist affiliations, for example, Ferdinand Smith was deported and Benjamin Davis was sent to prison. A number of other top CPUSA officials spent time in prison for violating the Smith Act. The revocation of blacklisted Captain Hugh Mulzac's master's license on account of his pro-labor, pro-Communist activities in the National Maritime Union kept him from finding a ship to command after the war. In 1953, the year of Edwards's death, the McCarthy Committee summoned Langston Hughes to testify about his Communist connections. The State Department revoked the passport of Paul Robeson to bar him from performing overseas. The chill of McCarthyism extended to Italy, too, where U.S. intelligence officials monitored and restricted Edwards's activities. Officials revoked her passport to prevent her from traveling anywhere outside Italy except back to the United States. Only fifteen years earlier, fascists had thrown some of her European friends into jail. In the final years of her life, she learned in despair that once again some of her friends were jailed for their radical political views, but this time, American authorities held the keys to their prison cells.[2]

Whether or not Edwards was a Communist is not entirely clear. Unlike Claudia Jones, a Caribbean-born Communist theoretician and fellow leader in the Congress of American Women who was jailed and deported from the United States in 1955,[3] for example, Edwards never laid out a clear articulation of her political philosophy. On the one hand, Edwards denied in sworn testimony to the FBI that she was a Communist. It is possible, then, that she simply may have been drawn to cooperation with the CPUSA because of its robust stance and leadership on civil-rights matters. Considering her travel experiences and field investigations in the Soviet Union in the mid- to late 1930s, and given how impressed she was with Soviet efforts against racism, her decision to work with Communist allies to wage war against Jim Crow in the United States might well have been a purely tactical one.

Thanks to the mentorship of A. Philip Randolph, a Socialist but staunch anticommunist, Edwards sharpened her critical skills and moved beyond her limited activism in interracial initiatives in Gary, Indiana, to develop a more penetrating anticapitalist critique. In the context of the Great Depression, she was transformed by her studies and experiences at Brookwood Labor College and the International People's College in Denmark, and by her labor activism with the International Ladies' Garment Workers Union and the Brotherhood of Sleeping Car Porters in Chicago. A labor education changed her understanding of the world and opened her eyes to new intellectual horizons. Her exposure to Marxist thought, Randolph's philosophy, and European Social Democracy favorably disposed her to class analysis, cooperative institutions, social insurance, public housing, and a greater role for the state in social and economic reforms. Armed with a better understanding of the role of the Labour Party in British politics, she saw the need for an independent party of some kind to represent the American working class. She emphasized, however, that such a political party as well as trade unions must be free of racist practices.

The evidence suggests, though, that Edwards moved beyond Randolph's socialist philosophy. Their relationship more or less followed the general evolution of her political consciousness. Until the late 1930s, they worked closely together in a number of coalitions, but apparently when the Popular Front ended, so, too, did their relationship. By then, Randolph's fierce anticommunism had become more prominent. For all intents and purposes, their relationship ended sometime after the shocking Nazi-Soviet Pact in 1939 and Randolph's subsequent angry departure from the National Negro Congress. Randolph blasted the NNC for its subservience to Soviet foreign policy and to the isolationist views of CIO leader John L. Lewis, who surprisingly had broken with President Roosevelt to support his Republican opponent, Wendell L. Willkie, in the election of 1940. In regard to Edwards's position during the fallout from the Nazi-Soviet Pact, the evidence, sketchy as it is, points to her ongoing support for the CPUSA, despite its sudden about-face and newborn characterization of the war in Europe as "imperialist." At a time when she was sidelined by poor health and suffered from political burnout, the decision to stick with the CPUSA through this period further isolated her.

After Hitler invaded the Soviet Union, Edwards resumed her work in left-liberal coalitions to fight the war against fascism and support the reelection of President Roosevelt. She backed Harlem Communist Benjamin Davis in his successful bid to win a seat on the city council to replace Adam Clayton Powell Jr., and she worked as a publicist for Ferdinand Smith, the Jamaican-born Harlem Communist leader of the militant National Maritime Union. For her, the CIO's left-wing unions held the most promise for the future of the civil-rights movement. Although the CPUSA tended to soften its attacks on racial segregation and inequality during the war, Edwards did not. She pushed the Double V campaign with vigor, using her pen to promote civil rights, an Allied victory, and decolonization.

Edwards was an internationalist, but her philosophy balanced racial and class consciousness. She viewed African Americans and other racial minorities in the United States as victims of internal colonialism. On the one hand, she shared the CPUSA's position during the Third Period (1928–1935) that African Americans in the South constituted an oppressed nation within a nation, with rights of self-determination. On the other hand, she had been active in building left-liberal coalitions and interracial unions long before the CPUSA adopted the Popular Front strategy and turned away from rigid sectarianism in 1935. With her labor education and background and training in social work, she had moved quickly to marry civil rights to trade unions and coalition politics on the left. She remained highly critical of middle-class black leaders who urged black workers to remain loyal to white employers. For her, the CPUSA was the most forceful political organization in its commitment to labor and civil rights. The preponderance of evidence suggests that she likely embraced a nonsectarian communist philosophy—broadly defined—while maintaining intellectual independence and keeping the civil-rights struggle at the forefront of her political activism.

This does not mean, of course, that at times racial frustrations and political setbacks did not complicate the way she integrated class and internationalism into her political outlook. Near the end of her life, for example, at a time of political despair and failing health, she expressed in a private letter to Langston Hughes her frustrations over the meager returns from political coalitions with white liberals and radicals alike. She complained that Marcus Garvey had been right to call for black separatist institutions, including a separate nation. At the time, the kind of mass mobilization she had envisioned on the part of African Americans had not occurred, and the Cold War had stuck a dagger in the heart of left-liberal coalitions, both inside and outside the labor movement. Nevertheless, her sense of political pessimism in the early 1950s should not obscure her long-standing activism on behalf of civil rights and international peace through alliances with progressive/radical labor unions that were committed to racial, economic, and social justice.

Edwards died a year before the landmark Supreme Court decision in the case of *Brown v. Board of Education.* Neither did she live to see the grassroots activism of African Americans spearheaded by Rosa Parks in the Montgomery Bus Boycott a couple of years later. Had Edwards, who worked so hard to bring about mass activism and mobilization from the bottom up, lived even a decade longer, she might well have served as an important bridge between the labor and civil-rights struggles of the 1930s and the social movements of the 1960s.

It is hard to gauge how Edwards's radical politics and marriage across the color line into a Jewish family affected her relationships with other members of her family. In the 1945 article that she and her husband published about their recent marriage, they hinted that family tensions did exist but provided no specifics. Apparently, Edwards did not stay in close touch with her family during the years with Gitlin. Her sister Thelma Marshall, who traveled to New York for her memorial service, confided to Claude Barnett that Edwards's "last ten years were hazy to all of us." Her mother, who opposed cremation and had religious differences with Edwards, also attended the memorial service, but by the time she and Marshall got there, Edwards's body had already been cremated.[4]

Edwards's radical politics may have created a few tensions in the family, but likely not between her and Marshall, with whom she had left Houston for Gary in 1920. Marshall forged an impressive career of her own as a pioneer social worker and civil-rights and peace activist in Gary. Like Edwards, she worked in the National Negro Congress and the Women's International League for Peace and Freedom (WILPF). As a community and union activist in Gary, where a children's home now bears her name, Marshall spearheaded a drive to attract federally subsidized low-rent housing. She also fought against discrimination in housing and hiring, working with A. Philip Randolph in the nation's capital on behalf of the National Council for a Permanent Fair Employment Practices Commission. In 1945, she helped to pressure the U.S. State Department for black representation at the founding conference of the United Nations in San Francisco. Like Edwards, she hoped to promote decolonization after World War II. In 1974, less than four years before Marshall died, she and a number of WILPF activists attended a seminar in Moscow.[5]

Neither is it likely that Edwards's political radicalism alienated her from other members of the family. In fact, the tradition of labor and civil-rights activism that she embodied can be seen in other of her siblings, most notably Anna Bell, who also enjoyed a career as a teacher, social worker, and civil-rights activist in New Orleans. Edwards had no children, but Marshall's son, William Horace Marshall, a political radical and critically acclaimed Broadway and Hollywood actor who was educated at New York University, carried on the family tradition as he battled racism and blacklisting in Hollywood in the McCarthy era. It was Edwards who had taken him backstage as a child after a Broadway production of *The Green Pastures*. The experience inspired Marshall to become an actor, and years later he played the leading role as "De Lawd" in a 1951 production of the play. Noted especially for his stage portrayals of Frederick Douglass, Paul Robeson, and Othello, Marshall perhaps received wider fame because of his Hollywood role as a vampire in *Blacula* and its sequel. His long-standing partner was Sylvia Gussin Jarrico, who was formerly married to blacklisted screenwriter Paul Jarrico.[6]

Marshall died in 2003, but his daughter, Gina Loring, an internationally acclaimed slam poet, hip hop performer, singer-songwriter, actor, and political activist, was able to use her talents in the "Barack the Vote" campaign to elect Barack Obama president. A graduate of Spelman College, Loring also attended Columbia University and studied with hip hop historian Michael Eric Dyson. For her, Edwards's political radicalism serves as an inspiration rather than a stain on the family's history. In fact, Loring's father told her that he had wanted to name her Thyra, but her mother had overruled him.[7]

What is particularly amazing about Edwards's life of international activism is that for about the last fifteen of her fifty-five years, she suffered from and at times was completely sidelined by rheumatoid arthritis and cancer. Not to be deterred, however, she continued her political activism, often rejecting conventional wisdom, treatments, and mores as well as family advice. After Edwards was cremated, her ashes were scattered over the Atlantic Ocean, a fitting tribute to her lifelong search crossing oceans for solutions to the system of racial and class exploitation that marginalized African Americans at home and held other peoples of color in subjugation overseas.

Notes

Introduction

1. For a collection of essays on black history and culture in Houston, see Howard Beeth and Cary D. Wintz, eds., *Black Dixie: Afro-Texan History and Culture in Houston.*

2. *Houston Informer,* Nov. 12, 1938.

3. Helen Chappell, "Chatter and Some News," *Chicago Defender,* Feb. 3, 1940.

4. Elmer P. Martin and Joanne M. Martin, "Thyra J. Edwards: Internationalist Social Worker"; Gwynne Gertz, "Thyra J. Edwards." For other studies that devote significant attention to Edwards, see especially Beth Tompkins Bates, *Pullman Car Porters and the Rise of Protest Politics in Black America, 1925–1945;* Melinda Chateauvert, *Marching Together: Women of the Brotherhood of Sleeping Car Porters;* Bruce A. Glasrud and Gregg Andrews, "Confronting White Supremacy: The African American Left in Texas, 1874–1974"; Kathleen A. Brown and Elizabeth Faue, "Revolutionary Desire: Redefining the Politics of Sexuality of American Radicals, 1919–1945"; and Kathleen A. Brown and Elizabeth Faue, "Social Bonds, Sexual Politics, and Political Community on the U.S. Left, 1920s-1940s." In early April 2009, the Southern Oral History Program at the University of North Carolina hosted the conference "The Long Civil Rights Movement: Histories, Politics, Memories." For a discussion, see especially Jacquelyn Dowd Hall, "The Long Civil Rights Movement and the Political Uses of the Past"; Eric Arnesen, "Reconsidering the 'Long Civil Rights Movement'"; David L. Chappell, "The Lost Decade of Civil Rights"; Kevin Boyle, "Labour, the Left, and the Long Civil Rights Movement"; Sundiata Keita Cha-Jua and Clarence Lang, "The 'Long Movement' as Vampire: Temporal and Spatial Fallacies in Recent Black Freedom Studies"; Thomas J. Sugrue, *Sweet Land of Liberty: The Forgotten Struggle for Civil Rights in the North;* and Glenda Elizabeth Gilmore, *Defying Dixie: The Radical Roots of Civil Rights, 1919–1950,* which is a collective biography of black and white southern radical activists who were Edwards's contemporaries, but does not include Edwards.

5. For recent studies of radical black women who were Edwards's contemporaries, see especially Carole Boyce Davies, *Left of Karl Marx: The Political Life of Black Communist Claudia Jones;* Gerald Horne, *Race Woman: The Lives of Shirley Graham DuBois;*

Claire Nee Nelson, "Louise Thompson Patterson and the Southern Roots of the Popular Front"; Sara Elizabeth Rzeszutek, "Love and Activism: James and Esther Cooper Jackson and the Black Freedom Movement in the United States, 1914–1968"; David Levering Lewis, Michael H. Nash, and Daniel J. Leab, eds., *Red Activists and Black Freedom: James and Esther Jackson and the Long Civil Rights Revolution;* Dayo Falayon Gore, "'To Hold a Candle in the Wind': Black Women Radicals and Post World War II U.S. Politics"; Dayo F. Gore, Jeanne Theoharis, and Komozi Woodard, eds., *Want to Start a Revolution? Radical Women in the Black Freedom Struggle;* Barbara Ransby, *Ella Baker and the Black Freedom Movement: A Radical Democratic Vision;* Erik S. McDuffie, "Long Journeys: Four Black Women and the Communist Party, USA, 1930–1956"; Erik S. McDuffie, "A New Freedom Movement of Negro Women: Sojourning for Truth, Justice, and Human Rights during the Early Cold War"; and Erik S. McDuffie, "The March of Young Southern Black Women: Esther Cooper Jackson, Black Left Feminism, and the Personal and Political Costs of Cold War Repression."

    6. "Brown Gal, or a Brown Gal in Seven League Boots," undated notes, box 1, folder 5, Thyra J. Edwards Papers, Chicago History Museum, Chicago.

    7. *Negro Labor News,* Apr. 13, 1940.

Chapter 1

    1. Thyra Edwards, "Thyra Edwards Sees and Likes Green Pastures." The images of Wharton County are in Thyra J. Edwards, "A Thread from Every Man in the Village," 1–2, box 1, folder 5, Edwards Papers. For a sketch of the history of Wharton County, see Merle R. Hudgins, "Wharton County," in *Handbook of Texas Online,* http://www.tshaonline.org/handbook/online/articles/WW/hcw6.html (accessed Mar. 1, 2009).

    2. U.S. Census, 1900, Enumeration District 54, p. 24A, Justice Precinct 1, Wharton, TX.

    3. Online alphabetical list of 1863–1898 Galesburg High School graduates and the 1899 Galesburg High School attendees (transcribed by Bob Miller from the book *History of the Galesburg High School,* comp. and pub. by Roy Livingston Piatt, May 1899), Knox County, Illinois, Genealogy & History, The IL GenWeb Project; Winifred Hiles Sackey Memoir, typed manuscript of tape-recorded interviews by Margaret Klusmeyer for the Oral History Office, 1974, 46, Archives/Special Collections, Norris L. Brookens Library, University of Illinois at Springfield; "Washington the Man and His Plan of Salvation," *Galesburg Mail,* Feb. 1, 1900, copy in Special Collections and Archives, Seymour Library, Knox College, Galesburg, IL; Louis R. Harlan, Raymond W. Smock, and Barbara S. Kraft, eds., *The Booker T. Washington Papers,* vol. 5, *1899–1900* (Urbana: University of Illinois Press, 1976), 132. Walker later became a teacher at Tuskegee, working as Booker T. Washington's secretary, and traveled around the United States as a lecturer.

    4. Gertz, "Thyra J. Edwards," 244; Martin and Martin, "Thyra J. Edwards," 163–64; Thelma Marshall, "The Ancestors of William Marshall," 1. I would like to thank Gina Loring, of Atlanta/Los Angeles, for giving me a copy of the latter document in the family's possession. I would also like to thank Vee Edwards, of Pasadena, CA, for providing internet access to the Edwards family's history. On the importance of Galesburg to the Underground Railroad, see Wilbur Henry Siebert, *The Underground Railroad: From Slavery to Freedom* (New York: MacMillan, 1899), 96–97.

    5. Marshall, "The Ancestors of William Marshall," 1. On slavery in the Hannibal area, see Terrell Dempsey, *Searching for Jim: Slavery in Sam Clemens's World.*

6. Edwards, "A Thread from Every Man," 1, box 1, folder 5, Edwards Papers.

7. Ibid.

8. Ibid., 1–2.

9. Marshall, "The Ancestors of William Marshall," 1; Edwards, "A Thread from Every Man," 3, box 1, folder 5, Edwards Papers.

10. Edwards, "A Thread from Every Man," 4, box 1, folder 5, Edwards Papers; Marshall, "The Ancestors of William Marshall," 1.

11. Marshall, "The Ancestors of William Marshall," 1–2. See Dempsey, *Searching for Jim,* chap. 4, for a discussion of organized abolitionist activities in the area.

12. Edwards, "A Thread from Every Man," 5, box 1, folder 5, Edwards Papers.

13. Ibid., 5; Marshall, "The Ancestors of William Marshall," 2.

14. Edwards, "A Thread from Every Man," 5–7, box 1, folder 5, Edwards Papers.

15. Ibid., 7–8. Liza's mother lived in Hannibal until she died around 1902 or 1903 at the age of 104.

16. Marshall, "The Ancestors of William Marshall," 1; Edwards, "A Thread from Every Man," 1, box 1, folder 5, Edwards Papers. Anna Johnson was the only child in her family to graduate from high school. She was a contemporary of Carl Sandburg. For a while, in fact, they attended the same school in Galesburg.

17. Edwards, "A Thread from Every Man," 9, box 1, folder 5, Edwards Papers.

18. Ibid., 1; Marshall, "The Ancestors of William Marshall," 2; Robert Lowry and William H. McCardle, *A History of Mississippi* (Jackson, MS: R. H. Henry, 1891), 316. On McWillie's plantation in Arkansas, see James Monaghan and R. Jones Monaghan, reporters, *The Chester County Reports: Reports of Cases Decided by the Supreme Court of Pennsylvania and the Several County Courts of the Commonwealth, Being Chiefly Cases Decided by or Arising in the Court of Chester County* (Philadelphia: Rees Welsh, 1888), 1:473–74.

19. U.S. Census, 1880, Woolfolk & Gibbs, Enumeration District 132, Yazoo County, MS.

20. Marshall, "The Ancestors of William Marshall," 2.

21. Ibid.; U.S. Census, 1880, Woolfolk & Gibbs, Enumeration District 132, Yazoo County, MS.

22. Marshall, "The Ancestors of William Marshall," 2; Edwards, Outline, "A Thread from Every Man," 1, box 1, folder 5, Edwards Papers; U.S. Census, 1910, Justice Precinct 2, Hardin County, TX; U.S. Census, 1920, Independence Heights, Harris County, TX.

23. James M. Sorelle, "The Darker Side of 'Heaven': The Black Community in Houston, Texas, 1917–1945."

24. Edwards, untitled, undated handwritten notes, 3, box 1, folder 5, Edwards Papers.

25. Ibid., 3–4.

26. Ibid.

27. Ibid., 5.

28. Ibid.

29. Edwards, Outline, "A Thread from Every Man," 1, box 1, folder 5, Edwards Papers.

30. Edwards, "Deep in the Heart of Texas," 50.

31. Edwards, "The Negro Worker—Today and Tomorrow," Nov. 4, 1944. On the Edwards family's neighborhood in Houston, see U.S. Census, 1910, Enumeration District 97, p. 3B, Houston Ward 3, Harris County, TX.

32. Edwards, "Deep in the Heart of Texas," 50. Subsequent page references from this work in the following paragraphs will be given parenthetically in the text. On the street

location of the Lurie family, see U.S. Census, 1910, Enumeration District 97, p. 25B, Houston Ward 3, Harris County, TX.

33. For an excellent study of the broader context in which black and white children learned the rules of racial etiquette in the segregated South, see Jennifer Ritterhouse, *Growing Up Jim Crow: How Black and White Southern Children Learned Race.*

34. On Edwards's teaching career in Houston, see Gertz, "Thyra J. Edwards," 244.

35. Untitled, undated handwritten notes, 1, box 1, folder 5, Edwards Papers.

36. Ibid., 1–2.

37. Ibid., 3.

38. Edwards, "A Thread from Every Man," 11, box 1, folder 5, Edwards Papers.

39. Ibid., 12.

40. Ibid., 11.

41. Ibid., 13.

42. Cheryl Knott Malone, "Quiet Pioneers: Black Women Public Librarians in the Segregated South," *Vitae Scholasticae* 19 (Spring 2000): 67; Cheryl Knott Malone, "Accommodating Access: 'Colored' Carnegie Libraries, 1905–1925" (PhD diss., University of Texas at Austin, 1996), 103–4.

43. Gertz, "Thyra J. Edwards," 244.

44. Charles J. Hill, "A Brief History of I.L.A. Local 872: From the Files of Freemas [*sic*] Everett" (Houston: International Longshoreman's Association, 1960), 1. On Everett's address, see U.S. Census, 1920, Enumeration District 59, p. 8A, Houston Ward 3, Harris County, TX.

45. On the Camp Logan Riot, see especially Robert V. Haynes, *A Night of Violence: The Houston Riot of 1917,* and Edgar A. Schuler, "The Houston Race Riot, 1917."

46. Quoted in Sorelle, "The Darker Side of 'Heaven,'" 81.

47. Ibid., 78–89; William Henry Kellar, *Make Haste Slowly: Moderates, Conservatives, and School Desegregation in Houston,* 28–31.

48. *Houston Informer,* Feb. 7, 1920.

49. Sorelle, "The Darker Side of 'Heaven,'" 361–62.

50. Ibid., 362; "Application for Charter," May 31, 1918, and C. F. Richardson to Board of Directors, National Association for the Advancement of Colored People, June 1, 1918, both in reel 19, NAACP Papers, pt. 12, Selected Branch Files, 1913–1939, ser. A, The South; Merline Pitre, *In Struggle against Jim Crow: Lulu B. White and the NAACP, 1900–1957,* 27.

51. Henry L. Mims to John R. Shillady, July 5, 1918, and "Civic Betterment League Withdraws from Contest for N.A.A.C.P. Charter," *Houston Observer,* Aug. 10, 1918, both in reel 19, NAACP Papers, pt. 12, Selected Branch Files, 1913–1939, ser. A.

52. Mims to Shillady, July 5, 1918, reel 19, NAACP Papers, pt. 12, Selected Branch Files, 1913–1939, ser. A; Mark Robert Schneider, *"We Return Fighting": The Civil Rights Movement in the Jazz Age,* 224.

53. G. N. T. Gray to Walter White, June 26, 1918, reel 19, NAACP Papers, pt. 12, Selected Branch Files, 1913–1939, ser. A.

54. E. O. Smith to Walter White, Asst. Sec. of NAACP, July 1918, and H. [Horace] F. Edwards and C. A. Paillet to Sec., NAACP, June 28, 1919, both in reel 19, NAACP Papers, pt. 12, Selected Branch Files, 1913–1939, ser. A. On Horace Edwards's business interest in the Informer Publishing Company, see Douglas Hales, "Nickerson, William N., Jr.," in *Handbook of Texas Online,* http://www.tsha.utexas.edu/handbook/online/articles (accessed Nov. 17, 2007).

55. On black activism and repression in the era of the First World War in Texas, see especially Steven A. Reich, "Soldiers of Democracy: Black Texans and the Fight for Citizenship, 1917–1921," 1478–1504, and Gregg Andrews, "Black Working-Class Political Activism and Biracial Unionism: Galveston Longshoremen in Jim Crow Texas, 1919–1921," 627–68.

56. Thomas Yenser, ed., *Who's Who in Colored America,* 173.

Chapter 2

1. Thyra Edwards, "Professional History," box 1, folder 5, Edwards Papers; "Indiana," *Chicago Defender,* Nov. 6, 1920; U.S. Census, 1920, Enumeration District 110, p. 4B, Ward 5, Gary, Lake County, Indiana.

2. See Commission of Inquiry, Interchurch World Movement, *Report on the Steel Strike of 1919* (New York: Harcourt, Brace and Howe, 1920), for a detailed report on the strike. Ruth Needleman, *Black Freedom Fighters in Steel: The Struggle for Democratic Unionism,* 22–24. Needleman also points out that local sources claimed that a preponderance of black workers supported the strike.

3. Cohen, Ronald D., *Children of the Mill: Schooling and Society in Gary, Indiana, 1906–1960,* 68.

4. Ibid., 71; U.S. Census, 1920, Enumeration District 110, p. 4B, Ward 5, Gary, Lake County, Indiana. On Strickland's teaching experience in Houston and friendship with the Edwards sisters, see "Texas Notes," *Houston Informer,* Apr. 6, 1938.

5. In 1916, Randolph S. Bourne, a well-known student of Dewey's, had written a favorable book on the Gary schools after he visited there. See Randolph S. Bourne, with an Introduction by William Wirt, *The Gary Schools* (Boston: Houghton Mifflin, 1916).

6. Cohen, *Children of the Mill,* 68–71; Neil Betten and Raymond A. Mohl, "The Evolution of Racism in an Industrial City, 1906–1940: A Case Study of Gary, Indiana," 54–55.

7. Thyra J. Edwards, "The Gary Interracial Program," 551.

8. Ibid., 545.

9. Ibid., 546.

10. Ibid.

11. James B. Lane, *"City of the Century": A History of Gary, Indiana,* 93.

12. Ibid., 93–95; Leonard Joseph Moore, *Citizen Klansmen: The Ku Klux Klan in Indiana, 1921–1928,* 176–78; Emma Lou Thornbrough, *Indiana Blacks in the Twentieth Century,* 49–50.

13. Edwards, "The Gary Interracial Program," 546–48.

14. Ibid., 548–49.

15. Ibid., 549–50; Yenser, ed., *Who's Who in Colored America,* 173.

16. Edwards, "The Gary Interracial Program," 550.

17. Ibid., 552; Dharathula Millender, *Gary's Central Business Community,* 58. On the Stewart House, see Ruth Hutchinson Crocker, *Social Work and Social Order: The Settlement Movement in Two Industrial Cities, 1889–1930,* 183–210.

18. Edwards, "The Gary Interracial Program," 550–54 (quote on 554).

19. "One Hundred Million Dollars Represented at Business League," *Pittsburgh Courier,* Aug. 20, 1927.

20. Obiagele Lake, *Blue Veins and Kinky Hair: Naming and Color Consciousness in African America,* 60–61. On Malone and the rise of St. Louis as a center for black beauty culture, see DeAnna J. Reese, "Domestic Drudges to Dazzling Divas." For a study of the

wider context in which black beauty culture evolved, see Susannah Walker, *Style and Status: Selling Beauty to African American Women, 1920–1975.*

21. Thyra J. Edwards to Marian Anderson, Dec. 9, 1933, Marian Anderson Papers, folder 1598, MS collection 200, Annenberg Rare Book and Manuscript Library, University of Pennsylvania, Philadelphia.

22. Jane Addams's eulogy at Helen Mead's funeral is in Alfred L. Castle, *A Century of Philanthropy: A History of the Samuel N. and Mary Castle Foundation,* rev. ed. (Honolulu: University of Hawaii Press, 2004), 11–13. On George Herbert Mead, see, for example, Gary A. Cook, *George Herbert Mead: The Making of a Social Pragmatist* (Urbana: University of Illinois Press, 1993).

23. "Thyra Edwards Is Honored at Dinner Party," *Pittsburgh Courier,* Oct. 20, 1934; Leslie Hudson, *Hyde Park* (New York: Arcadia, 2003), 94. For a symposium on McDowell shortly after her death, see Caroline M. Hill, comp., *Mary McDowell and Municipal Housekeeping: A Symposium* (Chicago: n.p., 1938).

24. For a brief sketch of Watson's career, see Ruth Winegarten, *Black Texas Women: 150 Years of Trial and Triumph,* 249–50.

25. Evangeline Roberts, "Social Group Gathers at Country Club," *Chicago Defender,* Oct. 8, 1927.

26. "Lake County Home to Be Opened Soon," *Gary Colored American,* Dec. 8, 1927; "Opening of Children's Home Draws Hundreds in Gary," *Gary Colored American,* Dec. 22, 1927; Margaret Rose Vendryes, *Barthé: A Life in Sculpture,* 131.

27. "250 Present at Unveiling Here," *Gary American,* Apr. 26, 1928.

28. "Kiddies' Home Wants a Santa," *Gary American,* Dec. 14, 1928; "Resigns," *Chicago Defender,* Nov. 28, 1931.

29. *Gary American,* Jan. 3, 1930.

30. "Society," *Gary American,* Nov. 22, 29, 1930.

31. Edwards, "Thyra Edwards Sees and Likes Green Pastures." In 1936, the play was turned into a black film classic. See Marc Connelly and Thomas Cripps, *The Green Pastures* (Madison: University of Wisconsin Press, 1979).

32. "Social Service Worker Elected Vice President," *Chicago Defender,* Nov. 10, 1928. On her attendance at the National Conference of Social Work, see, for example, "Many Race Delegates at Confab," *Pittsburgh Courier,* May 21, 1927.

33. "On Way to Europe," *Chicago Defender,* Aug. 31, 1929; Ivan H. Browning, "Across the Pond," *Chicago Defender,* Oct. 5, 1929.

34. Sheila Tully Boyle and Andrew Bunie, *Paul Robeson: The Years of Promise and Achievement,* 213–14, 226.

35. Quoted in *Gary American,* Nov. 29, 1929, 1.

36. Quoted in Frank L. Hayes, "Negro Workers Need Training, League Is Told," *Gary American,* May 2, 1931.

37. "Resigns," *Chicago Defender,* Nov. 28, 1931; Edwards, "Professional History," box 1, folder 5, Edwards Papers.

38. "Englishwoman Seeks Her Long Lost Black Lover," *Pittsburgh Courier,* Mar. 24, 1934.

39. Edwards, "A Thread from Every Man," 11, 13, box 1, folder 5, Edwards Papers; U.S. Census, 1930, Enumeration District 18, p. 3A, Caddo Parrish, Shreveport, LA; U.S. Census, 1930, Enumeration District 14, p. 22B, Phoenix, Maricopa County, AZ; U.S. Census, 1930, Houston, Harris County, TX. In 1923, Thyra, Thelma, and Bell visited

in Galesburg for the Thanksgiving holiday. This may have been the final time they saw their grandmother Johnson. See "Illinois State News," *Chicago Defender,* Dec. 8, 1923.

Chapter 3

1. Elisabeth Lasch-Quinn, *Black Neighbors: Race and the Limits of Reform in the American Settlement House Movement, 1890–1945,* 25–26.

2. Bates, *Pullman Car Porters,* 116–18. See also Bates, "Mobilizing Black Chicago: The Brotherhood of Sleeping Car Porters and Community Organizing, 1925–35"; Chateauvert, *Marching Together;* and Eric Arnesen, *Brotherhoods of Color: Black Railroad Workers and the Struggle for Equality,* especially chap. 4. For biographies of Randolph and Webster, see especially Jervis Anderson, *A. Philip Randolph: A Biographical Portrait,* and William H. Harris, *Keeping the Faith: A. Philip Randolph, Milton P. Webster, and the Brotherhood of the Sleeping Car Porters, 1925–1937.* See also Eric Arnesen, "A. Philip Randolph: Labor and the New Black Politics." Arnesen is currently writing a political biography of Randolph.

3. Thyra Edwards, "The Negro Worker—Today and Tomorrow," July 29, 1944. See Charles F. Howlett, *Brookwood Labor College and the Struggle for Peace and Social Justice in America,* for a history of Brookwood College. On the wider context of labor colleges in the United States, see Richard J. Altenbaugh, *Education for Struggle: The American Labor College of the 1920s and the 1930s.*

4. Edwards, "The Negro Worker—Today and Tomorrow," July 29, 1944; Richard J. Altenbaugh, "'The Children and the Instruments of a Militant Labor Progressivism': Brookwood Labor College and the American Labor College Movement of the 1920s and 1930s," 403; John Daniel, *Rogue River Journal: A Winter Alone* (Berkeley, CA: Shoemaker and Hoard, 2005), 28.

5. Edwards, "The Negro Worker—Today and Tomorrow," July 29, 1944. For Strong's career, see Tracey Strong and Helen Keyysar, *Right in Her Soul: The Life of Anna Louise Strong.*

6. Edwards, "The Negro Worker—Today and Tomorrow," July 29, 1944.

7. Altenbaugh, "'The Children and the Instruments of a Militant Labor Progressivism,'" 406.

8. Muste and several prominent radical intellectuals left the American Workers Party when it lost its identity as a result of its merger with the new Trotskyist party in late 1934. See Michael Denning, *The Cultural Front: The Laboring of American Culture in the Twentieth Century,* 430–32.

9. Ibid., 71; Archie Green, "Death of Mother Jones," *Labor History* 1 (1960): 6.

10. "Negro Students Quit Brookwood Labor College with Muste," *Gary American,* Mar. 24, 1933. On the Muste split with Brookwood, see the statements prepared by the opposing sides in the conflict in box 1, folder 4, Clarina Michelson Papers, 1926–1979, Tamiment Library/Robert F. Wagner Labor Archives, New York University, New York.

11. "Negro Students Quit Brookwood Labor College with Muste," *Gary American,* Mar. 24, 1933.

12. Ibid.

13. "Garyite Brookwood College Striker Makes Denial of 'On the Fence' Charge," *Gary American,* Apr. 7, 1933.

14. Ibid.

15. Edwards, "The Negro Worker—Today and Tomorrow," July 29, 1944.

16. David Thoreau Wieck, *Woman from Spillertown: A Memoir of Agnes Burns Wieck*, 162–63. For a brief discussion of Wieck's life, see Thomas Dublin's foreword to this book. On the Women's Auxiliary, see Caroline Waldron Merithew, "'We Were Not Ladies': Gender, Class, and a Woman's Auxiliary's Battle for Mining Unionism."

17. Wieck, *Woman from Spillertown*, 163.

18. Quoted in Thyra J. Edwards, "'Sister Katie.'" I would like to thank Greg Boozell for sending me a photocopy of this article. On De Rorre, see also Caroline Waldron Merithew, "Sister Katie: The Memory and Making of a 1.5 Generation Working-Class International."

19. Quoted in Thyra J. Edwards, "'Sister Katie.'"

20. Ibid.

21. Wieck, *Woman from Spillertown*, 163.

22. Ibid.; Edwards, "'Sister Katie,'" 3.

23. Frank Z. Glick, "The Illinois Emergency Relief Commission," *Social Service Review* 7 (Mar. 1933): 23–48; Randi Storch, *Red Chicago: American Communism at Its Grassroots, 1928–1935*, 166–67. On the BSCP in Chicago, see especially Bates, *Pullman Car Porters*.

24. "Chicago Scottsboro Committee Formed," *Pittsburgh Courier*, June 10, 1933.

25. Bates, *Pullman Car Porters*, 117–18. On the activities of the Urban League, see Touré F. Reed, *Not Alms but Opportunity: The Urban League and the Politics of Racial Uplift, 1910–1950*.

26. "Scholarship in Denmark," *Pittsburgh Courier*, July 15, 1933; "Former Gary Girl Gets Scholarship at College in Denmark," *Gary American*, July 14, 1933; Edwards, "Educational Background," box 1, folder 5, Edwards Papers. See Peter Manniche, *Denmark: A Social Laboratory* (London: Oxford University Press, 1939), for a discussion of the history of folk schools and cooperative traditions in Denmark. On the International People's College, see Jindra Kulich, "The Danish Folk High School: Can It Be Transplanted? The Success and Failure of the Danish Folk High School at Home and Abroad."

27. "Adventures of a Texas Girl in Europe Found Interesting," *San Antonio Register*, Jan. 12, 1934.

28. Ibid.

29. Ibid.

30. Thyra Edwards, untitled manuscript, [1934?], 1–2, box 1, folder 1, Edwards Papers. See also "Adventures of a Texas Girl in European Climes," *San Antonio Register*, Jan. 5, 1934. On Ghosh's role in the Progressive Writers Association, see Malik Hafeez, "The Marxist Literary Movement in India and Pakistan," 651.

31. Thyra Edwards, untitled manuscript, [1934?], 2–3, box 1, folder 1, Edwards Papers.

32. Ibid., 4.

33. Edwards to "My Dears," Nov. 4, 1933, box 1, folder 1, Edwards Papers.

34. Ibid.

35. Ibid.

36. Ibid.

37. Ibid.

38. Edwards to ?, n.d. [Nov. 10, 1933?], Edwards to "My Dears," Nov. 4, 1933, and Edwards to A. J. Muste (quote), Jan. 4, 1934, all in box 1, folder 1, Edwards Papers.

39. Thyra J. Edwards, "Negro Literature Comes to Denmark," 140.

40. Ibid.

41. Edwards to "My Dears," Nov. 4, 1933, box 1, folder 1, Edwards Papers.

42. Ibid.

43. Edwards to ?, n.d. [Nov. 10, 1933?], box 1, folder 1, Edwards Papers.

44. Thyra Edwards, notes for "The Town of Elsinore by Paul Christensen, Mayor of Elsinore," and Thyra Edwards to "Miss Josephensen," Feb. 12, 1934, both in box 1, folder 1, Edwards Papers.

45. Edwards to ?, n.d. [Nov. 10, 1933?], box 1, folder 1, Edwards Papers.

46. Ibid.

47. Ibid.

48. Thyra J. Edwards to William Pickens, Nov. 10, 1933, reel 10, William Pickens Papers (additions), 1909–1950, Schomburg Center for Research in Black Culture, New York Public Library, New York.

49. Pickens to Edwards, Nov. 22, 1933, reel 10, Pickens Papers.

50. Edwards to "My Dears," Nov. 4, 1933, box 1, folder 1, Edwards Papers.

51. Edwards to "Philip" [A. Philip Randolph?], Jan. 5, 1934, box 1, folder 1, Edwards Papers. On Thomas, see Ionie Benjamin, *The Black Press in Britain,* 31, and LaRay Denzer, "Women in Freetown Politics, 1914–61: A Preliminary Study," 439–56.

52. Edwards to Pickens, Nov. 10, 1933, reel 10, Pickens Papers.

53. Thyra J. Edwards to Georg Blickingberg, Dec. 1933, box 1, folder 1, Edwards Papers.

54. Edwards to Blickingberg, Jan. 5, 1934, box 1, folder 1, Edwards Papers.

55. Allan Keiler, *Marian Anderson: A Singer's Journey,* 126; Thyra J. Edwards to Marian Anderson, Dec. 9, 1933, folder 1598, Anderson Papers.

56. Quoted in Keiler, *Marian Anderson,* 127.

57. Thyra J. Edwards to "Mrs. Lewis," Jan. 4, 1934, box 1, folder 1, Edwards Papers.

58. Ibid.

59. Ibid.

60. Untitled, undated outline notes, box 1, folder 1, Edwards Papers.

61. Edwards to ? [Curtis Reese?], Jan. 6, 1934, box 1, folder 1, Edwards Papers.

62. Ibid.

63. Ibid.

64. Ibid.

65. Edwards to A. J. Muste, Jan. 4, 1934, box 1, folder 1, Edwards Papers.

66. Edwards to ? [Curtis Reese?], Jan. 6, 1934, box 1, folder 1, Edwards Papers.

67. Ibid.

68. Edwards to "Mrs. Lewis," Jan. 4, 1934, box 1, folder 1, Edwards Papers.

69. Edwards to A. J. Muste, Jan. 4, 1934, box 1, folder 1, Edwards Papers.

70. Ibid.

71. Ibid.

72. Ibid.

73. Ibid.; Robert Dallek, *Franklin D. Roosevelt and American Foreign Policy, 1932–1945,* 80–81.

74. Edwards to ? [Curtis Reese?], Jan. 6, 1934, box 1, folder 1, Edwards Papers.

75. Thyra Edwards, "WELANDERHJEMMENE," Feb. 3, 1934, box 1, folder 1, Edwards Papers.

76. Edwards, "Englishwoman Seeks Her Long Lost Black Lover."

77. Ibid.

78. Thyra Edwards, untitled, undated notes, box 1, folder 1, Edwards Papers.

79. Edwards to "Philip" [A. Philip Randolph?], Jan. 5, 1934, box 1, folder 1, Edwards Papers.

80. Ibid.

81. Ibid.

82. Ibid.; Thyra Edwards to Etha Bell, Apr. 14, 1934, box 1, folder 1, Edwards Papers.

83. Edwards, "Negro Literature Comes to Denmark," 141.

84. Ibid., 146.

Chapter 4

1. Thyra Edwards to Claude Barnett, May 15, 1934, box 1, folder 1, Edwards Papers.

2. Ibid.; Thyra J. Edwards to Herr Alf Ahlberg, Apr. 4, 1934, and Ahlberg to Edwards, Apr. 5, 1934, box 1, folder 1, Edwards Papers.

3. Thyra Edwards to Etha Bell Rogers, Apr. 14, 1934, box 1, folder 1, Edwards Papers.

4. Edwards to Barnett, May 15, 1934, box 1, folder 1, Edwards Papers.

5. Edwards to Rogers, Apr. 14, 1934, box 1, folder 1, Edwards Papers.

6. Ibid.

7. Ibid.

8. Ibid.

9. Ibid.

10. Ibid.

11. Edwards to Barnett, May 15, 1934, box 1, folder 1, Edwards Papers.

12. Edwards to Rogers, Apr. 14, 1934, box 1, folder 1, Edwards Papers.

13. Ibid.

14. John Barton to Knud Larsen, Apr. 5, 1934, box 1, folder 1, Edwards Papers.

15. Edwards to Barnett, May 15, 1934, box 1, folder 1, Edwards Papers; Dolores Hayden, *Redesigning the American Dream: Gender, Housing, and Family Life*, 111.

16. Edwards to Barnett, May 15, 1934, box 1, folder 1, Edwards Papers; "Thyra Edwards Calls Denmark Home of Adult Education," *Chicago Defender*, Oct. 27, 1934.

17. Edwards to Barnett, May 15, 1934, box 1, folder 1, Edwards Papers.

18. Thyra Edwards, "A Finnish Domestic Servant," 1, box 1, folder 1, Edwards Papers.

19. Ibid., 2; Jason Edward Lavery, *The History of Finland*, 96.

20. Edwards, "A Finnish Domestic Servant," 3, box 1, folder 1, Edwards Papers.

21. Edwards to Barnett, May 15, 1934, box 1, folder 1, Edwards Papers. Dr. Felix Iversen later played a role in the Communist-led Finnish Peace Committee after World War II. He was awarded the Stalin Peace Prize in 1954. See Lawrence S. Wittner, *The Struggle against the Bomb: A History of the World Nuclear Disarmament Movement through 1953*, 224.

22. Edwards to Barnett, May 15, 1934, box 1, folder 1, Edwards Papers.

23. Ibid.

24. "Thyra Edwards Calls Denmark Home of Adult Education," *Chicago Defender*, Oct. 27, 1934.

25. Thyra Edwards, "Germany—Not in the Baedaker," 1934, pt. 2, p. 4, box 1, folder 1, Edwards Papers.

26. Edwards to Barnett, May 15, 1934, box 1, folder 1, Edwards Papers.

27. Ibid.

28. Ibid.

29. Edwards to ?, June 2, 1934, box 1, folder 1, Edwards Papers.

30. Ibid.

31. Ibid.

32. Ibid.

33. David Clay Large, *Between Two Fires: Europe's Path in the 1930s*, 79–82; Stanley G. Payne, *A History of Fascism, 1914–1945*, 248–49; Michael Zalampas, *Adolph Hitler and the Third Reich in American Magazines, 1923–1939*, 53–54.

34. Thyra Edwards, "Wien . . . I Visit the Volksheim," 1, 1934, box 1, folder 1, Edwards Papers.

35. Ibid.

36. Ibid., 1–3.

37. Edwards, "Germany—Not in the Baedaker," 1934, pt. 1, 2, box 1, folder 1, Edwards Papers. Subsequent page references from this paper in the following paragraphs will be given parenthetically in the text.

38. Thyra Edwards, notes from the MS *Lafayette*, June 30, 1934, 1, box 1, folder 1, Edwards Papers.

39. Ibid.

40. Ibid.

41. Ibid., 2.

42. Ibid., 6.

Chapter 5

1. Edwards to Pickens, Oct. 10, 1934, reel 11, Pickens Papers.

2. "Women Must Stand By Men in Fight for Economic Rights," *Pittsburgh Courier*, Sept. 15, 1934. On the role of Wilson, see Bates, *Pullman Car Porters*, 115, 140. See Ann Meis Knupfer, *The Chicago Black Renaissance and Women's Activism*, for a discussion of women's activism in Chicago's black community at the time.

3. "Thyra Edwards Honored by Friends on U. of C. Campus," *Chicago Defender*, Oct. 13, 1934. The dinner was sponsored by a number of Chicago's educators, social workers, lawyers, ministers, and labor leaders: Mary E. McDowell, Ima Abernathy, Zonia Baker, Maudelle Bousfield, Dixie Brooks, Annette Dietman, Lorraine Green, Theodosia Hall, Mamie Mason Higgins, Lula E. Lawson, Dr. [Albert] Sidney Beckham, A. L. Foster, Judge Albert B. George, A. L. Jackson, Rev. Harold M. Kingsley, Chandler Owen, Dr. Curtis W. Reese, Attorney C. Francis Stradford, and Milton P. Webster.

4. Edwards to Wilkins, Aug. 21, 1934, box 1, folder 1, Edwards Papers.

5. Edwards to Pickens, Oct. 10, 1934, reel 11, Pickens Papers.

6. "'Stevedores' Will Go to Chicago for Month's Run," *Pittsburgh Courier*, Dec. 15, 1934. Bill Mullen, *Popular Fronts: Chicago and African-American Cultural Politics, 1935–46*, 100, 102–3.

7. Nettie George Speedy, "Chicago Town Topics," *Pittsburgh Courier*, Dec. 29, 1934.

8. "Labor Department in Big Job Campaign," *Chicago Defender*, Jan. 19, 1935.

9. Thyra J. Edwards, "Let Us Have More Like Mr. Sopkins"; Thyra J. Edwards, "Who Is Disinterested?"; Frank R. Crosswaith, "Trade Unionism—Our Only Hope," *Crisis* (June 1935): 166–67, 187; Bates, *Pullman Car Porters*, 120–21.

10. Edwards, "Let Us Have More Like Mr. Sopkins," 72; Edwards, "Professional History," box 1, folder 5, Edwards Papers; Crosswaith, "Trade Unionism," 166. According to Storch, *Red Chicago,* 167, the failure of the needle workers' strike helped to persuade Chicago Communists to adopt a more flexible, less sectarian approach to organizing black workers.

11. Edwards, "Let Us Have More Like Mr. Sopkins," 82.

12. J. Wellington Evans, "Thumbs Down on Unions!" *Crisis* (Apr. 1935): 103, 114; Edwards, "Who Is Disinterested?" 173.

13. Edwards, "Who Is Disinterested?" 173, 174.

14. Thyra J. Edwards, "An Open Letter to Ishmael P. Flory," Apr. 11, 1934, box 1, folder 1, Edwards Papers. On Flory's expulsion, see, for example, Joel Rosenthal, "Southern Black Student Activism: Assimilation vs. Nationalism," 116–17.

15. Newton Defense Committee, "Chicago's Dred Scott Case: *The Eviction of Herbert and Jane Emery Newton,*" 1935, 1–13, box 1, folder 1, Edwards Papers; Hazel Rowley, *Richard Wright: The Life and Times,* 94–95; Storch, *Red Chicago,* 76, 78.

16. Newton Defense Committee, "Chicago's Dred Scott Case," 6–7, 9, box 1, folder 1, Edwards Papers.

17. Ibid., 7, 9, 10.

18. Ibid., 12.

19. "Herndon Raises the Soviet Torch in Chicago," *Pittsburgh Courier,* Jan. 19, 1935.

20. "Will Demand Freedom for Scottsboro 9," *Chicago Defender,* June 29, 1935.

21. Bates, *Pullman Car Porters,* 118–21.

22. Thyra Edwards, "Jane Addams Loved All Races . . . She Was a Real Neighbor."

23. A copy of Edwards's tribute, dated May 24, 1935, is in box 1, folder 1, Edwards Papers. The quote is on p. 4. Compare the copy in her papers to the version published in the *Pittsburgh Courier,* June 1, 1935.

24. Thyra J. Edwards, "Attitudes of Negro Families on Relief—Another Opinion," 214.

25. Ibid., 215.

26. Ibid.

27. Ibid.

28. Ibid.

29. Thyra J. Edwards, "Chicago in the Rain (Relief for Homeless Negro Men on the South Side)," 282.

30. Ibid., 284.

31. "Swedish Senator a Guest," *Chicago Defender,* Nov. 2, 1935.

32. John P. Davis to Walter White, memorandum, n.d. [Mar. 1935?], reel 7, frame 199, NAACP Papers, pt. 10, Peonage, Labor, and the New Deal, 1913–1939. Edwards was on the seventh session of the conference program, May 20, 1935. See National Negro Congress Papers, pt. 1, Records and Correspondence, 1933–1942, reel 2, frame 679 (hereafter cited as NNC Papers).

33. John P. Davis to Thyra J. Edwards, July 6, 1935, frame 736, and "The Official Proceedings of the National Negro Congress," Feb. 14, 15, 16, 1936, frames 251, 267, both in reel 2, NNC Papers; Davis to Edwards, Jan. 29, 1936, reel 4, frame 700, NNC Papers.

34. A. Philip Randolph to John P. Davis, Dec. 28, 1935, reel 7, NNC Papers, pt. 1.

35. Davis to Edwards, July 6, 1935, frame 736, and "The Official Proceedings of the National Negro Congress," Feb. 14, 15, 16, 1936, frames 251, 267, both in reel 2, NNC Papers; Davis to Edwards, Jan. 29, 1936, reel 4, frame 700, NNC Papers.

36. Thyra Edwards, Morris Topchevsky, and John Greene, press release, Jan. 15, 1936, box 58, folder 1107, Langston Hughes Papers; John P. Davis to Langston Hughes, Jan. 29, 1936, reel 5, NNC Papers; Charles Wesley Burton, Chairman, Chicago Sponsoring Committee, to Thyra Edwards, Feb. 2, 1936, frame 681, and Edwards to Davis, Jan. 31, 1936, frame 735, and Davis to Edwards, Jan. 29, 1936, frame 689, all in reel 4, NNC Papers. On black cultural politics and the multidimensional thrust of the Popular Front in Chicago through World War II, see Mullen, *Popular Fronts.*

37. Roy Wilkins to the Board of Directors on the National Negro Congress, memorandum, p. 4, Mar. 9, 1936, reel 16, NAACP Papers, pt. 11, Special Subject Files, 1912–1929, ser. B, Warren G. Harding through YWCA.

38. Ibid.; Louise Thompson, "Toward a Brighter Dawn," *Woman Today* (Apr. 1936): 14, 30.

39. Wilkins to the Board of Directors, memorandum, p. 6, Mar. 9, 1936.

40. A. Philip Randolph to Walter White, Feb. 4, 1936, reel 16, NAACP Papers, pt. 11, Special Subject Files, 1912–1929, ser. B. On the controversy over Browder, see Charles Wesley Burton, "The Life and Work of A. Philip Randolph," 8–9, reel 33, A. Philip Randolph Papers.

41. Zulme McNeill to Walter White, Mar. 17, 1936, reel 16, NAACP Papers, pt. 11, Special Subject Files, 1912–1929, ser. B. For a discussion of the weaknesses of the NNC and tensions with the NAACP, see Bates, *Pullman Car Porters,* 135–38, 227n53.

42. Burton to Davis, May 18, 1936, reel 3, NNC Papers.

43. "Supplementary Memorandum to the Report on the *National Negro Congress* from Mr. Wilkins," Mar. 10, 1936, reel 3, NNC Papers.

44. Houston to White, Feb. 29, 1936, reel 3, NNC Papers.

45. Wilkins to Davis, Mar. 3, 1936, reel 3, NNC Papers.

46. Ibid.

47. "To Put Race Demands Up to Roosevelt," *Chicago Defender,* Mar. 7, 1936; Bates, *Pullman Car Porters,* 138.

48. "1st Race International Labor Unit Is Chartered," *Chicago Defender,* June 13, 1936.

49. "NNC To Give Cooperation to CIO Drive," *Chicago Defender,* Aug. 29, 1936. On Johnson, see Stephen Brier, "Labor, Politics, and Race: A Black Worker's Life," 416–21.

50. "NNC To Give Cooperation to CIO Drive," *Chicago Defender,* Aug. 29, 1936; Bates, *Pullman Car Porters,* 138–40.

51. Eleanor Rye to John P. Davis, May 13, 1936, reel 7, NNC Papers. See also Bates, *Pullman Car Porters,* 141.

52. John P. Davis to Henry Johnson, July 23, 1936, reel 6, NNC Papers.

53. Johnson to Davis, Sept. 10, 1936, reel 6, NNC Papers.

54. Ibid.

55. Edwards to Wilkins, Jan. 27, 1937, Edwards to Juanita E. Jackson, Jan. 27, 1937, and Special Counsel Charles H. Houston to Edwards, Jan. 28, 1937, all in reel 17, NAACP Papers, pt. 11, Special Subject Files, 1912–1939, ser. B.

56. Davis to White, Jan. 15, 1937, and "National Negro Congress Demands Government Investigation of Peonage and Forced Slavery in South," n.d., 3, both in reel 17, NAACP Papers, pt. 11, Special Subject Files, 1912–1939, ser. B.

57. James H. Baker Jr. to John P. Davis, Dec. 18, 1936, reel 3, NNC Papers; Baker to "NNCer," Feb. 1, 1937, and Max Yergan to Friends, Feb. 19, 1937, both in reel 17, NAACP Papers, pt. 11, Special Subject Files, 1912–1939, ser. B.

58. John P. Davis to Ishmael Flory, Apr. 22, 1938, reel 13, NNC Papers.

59. Burton to Davis, Oct. 18, 1938, reel 7, NNC Papers.

60. Flory to Davis, Dec. 27, 1938, reel 13, NNC Papers. On Jones and the WPA, see Lasch-Quinn, *Black Neighbors,* 24.

Chapter 6

1. Thyra Edwards, memorandum, Dec. 17, 1935, reel 4, frames 697–98, NNC Papers.

2. Ibid.

3. Ibid.; "Social Workers to Tour Europe This Summer," *Pittsburgh Courier,* Apr. 18, 1936, 9; A. L. Foster, "Experiences with an American Tourist Party Traveling in Europe," *Chicago Defender,* Aug. 8, 1936.

4. Thyra J. Edwards, "Seminar to Soviet Is Gotten Underway." On the new magazine, which was based in New York, see its editorial statement, *Woman Today* (Mar. 1936): 10.

5. Thyra J. Edwards, "Imperial Policy of Britain Is Analyzed"; "Negro Travel Tide Is Rising," *New York Times,* July 19, 1936.

6. Thyra Edwards, "Swedish Wives Show Us a Thing or Two"; "Ill. Housewives," *Chicago Defender,* Oct. 5, 1935.

7. Quoted in Edwards, "Swedish Wives Show Us a Thing or Two," 11.

8. Thyra Edwards, "The Moscow Theatre for Children."

9. Thyra Edwards to Claude Barnett, Oct. 30, 1936, reel 6, Claude A. Barnett Papers, pt. 2, Associated Negro Press Organizational Files, 1920–1966, microfilm.

10. Edwards to Barnett, June 19, Aug. 25, 1936, and Claude Barnett to Soviet Embassy and Soviet Consulate, June 17, 1936, both in reel 6, Barnett Papers, pt. 2.

11. Barnett to Edwards, Sept. 24, 1936, reel 6, Barnett Papers, pt. 2.

12. Edwards to Barnett, Oct. 20, 1936, reel 6, Barnett Papers, pt. 2.

13. Edwards to Barnett, Oct. 30, Oct. 20, 1936, reel 6, Barnett Papers, pt. 2.

14. Edwards to Barnett, Oct. 20, 1936, reel 6, Barnett Papers, pt. 2.

15. Ibid.

16. Ibid.

17. Edwards to Barnett, Oct. 26, 1936, reel 6, Barnett Papers, pt. 2.

18. "Thyra Edwards Writes Editor from Russia," *Chicago Defender,* Oct. 3, 1936. For recent studies on the relationship between African Americans and Russians in the Soviet Union, see especially Joy Gleason Carew, *Blacks, Reds, and Russians: Sojourners in Search of the Soviet Promise;* Kate A. Baldwin, *Beyond the Color Line and the Iron Curtain: Reading Encounters between Black and Red, 1922–1963;* and Allison Blakely, *Russia and the Negro: Blacks in Russian History and Thought.*

19. Edwards to Barnett, Oct. 30, 1936, reel 6, Barnett Papers, pt. 2.

20. Thyra Edwards to Fred Atkins Moore, Emergency Peace Campaign, Oct. 31, 1936, box 39, folder "Miss Thyra Edwards," Emergency Peace Campaign Records, 1936–1937, Document Group 012, Swarthmore College Peace Collection, Swarthmore College, Swarthmore, PA.

21. Edwards to Barnett, [?] 1936, reel 6, Barnett Papers, pt. 2.

22. Ibid.

23. Edwards to Barnett, Oct. 26, 1936, reel 6, Barnett Papers, pt. 2.

24. Ibid.

25. Ibid.

26. Ibid.

27. Edwards to Moore, Oct. 31, 1936, box 39, folder "Miss Thyra Edwards," Emergency Peace Campaign Records, 1936–1937, Swarthmore College Peace Collection.

28. Edwards to Barnett, Oct. 26, 1936, reel 6, Barnett Papers, pt. 2.

29. Barnett to Edwards, Nov. 14, 1936, and Edwards to Barnett, Dec. 7, 1936, both in reel 6, Barnett Papers, pt. 2.

30. Edwards to Moore, Oct. 31, 1936, box 39, folder "Miss Thyra Edwards," Emergency Peace Campaign Records, 1936–1937, Swarthmore College Peace Collection.

31. Ibid.

32. Ruth D. Ellington, "The Social Institute," *Pittsburgh Courier*, Jan. 2, 1937.

33. "Reds Give 10,000 Rubles to Ethiopia," *Chicago Defender*, Jan. 2, 1937.

34. Edwards to Barnett, Apr. 30, 1937, reel 6, Barnett Papers, pt. 2.

35. *Houston Informer*, May 8, 1937; "News from Wiley College, Marshall, Texas," *Chicago Defender*, Apr. 24, 1937; "Thyra Edwards to Speak at Prairie View This Week," *Chicago Defender*, May 8, 1937; Edwards to Barnett, Apr. 30, 1937, reel 6, Barnett Papers, pt. 2.

36. Edwards to Barnett, Apr. 30, 1937, reel 6, Barnett Papers, pt. 2.

37. Irene Roland, Associated Negro Press, to Thyra J. Edwards, May 8, 1937, reel 6, Barnett Papers, pt. 2.

38. Edwards to Barnett, May 31, 1937, reel 6, Barnett Papers, pt. 2.

39. Ibid.

40. Edwards to Barnett, June 16, 1937, reel 6, Barnett Papers, pt. 2.

41. "Thyra Edwards," 2, box 2, folder 7, Hermina Dumont Huiswoud Papers; Joyce Moore Turner, *Caribbean Crusaders and the Harlem Renaissance*, 222, 224; *Galveston Voice*, Mar. 27, 1937, 4, copy in folder "Thyra J. Edwards," Ruthe Winegarten Papers, Center for American History, University of Texas at Austin.

42. "Thyra Edwards and Seminar Group Tell of Trip Abroad," *Pittsburgh Courier*, Oct. 2, 1937.

43. Edwards to Barnett, Aug. 5, 1937, box 1, folder 3, Edwards Papers.

44. Edwards to Davis, Oct. 2, 1937, reel 13, NNC Papers; *Houston Informer*, Oct. 20, 1937.

Chapter 7

1. *Houston Informer*, Oct. 20, 1937; "Welfare Workers Aid Children of Loyalists," *Pittsburgh Courier*, Oct. 30, 1937; "2 Chicagoans in Spain to Make Survey," *Chicago Defender*, Oct. 30, 1937. On Kyle's relationship to the NNC, see John P. Davis, Executive Secretary, National Negro Congress, to Constance Kyle, Feb. 4, 1936, reel 6, NNC Papers.

2. For a discussion, see, for example, M. D. Gallagher, "Leon Blum and the Spanish Civil War"; Tom Buchanan, *Britain and the Spanish Civil War*; Robert Felix Bauer, *Leon Blum, the Popular Front, and the Spanish Civil War*; and Julian Jackson, *The Popular Front in France: Defending Democracy, 1934–38*.

3. "Thyra Edwards," 2, box 2, folder 7, Huiswoud Papers.

4. Edwards to Barnett, Oct. 15, 1937, reel 6, Barnett Papers, pt. 2.

5. Constance Kyle to Belle Taub, Oct. 19, 1937, box 2, folder 13, Frances Patai Papers, 1937–1998, Abraham Lincoln Brigade Archive, Tamiment Library/Robert F. Wagner Labor Archives, New York University, New York.

6. Constance Kyle to Herman Reissig, Oct. 18, 1937, box 2, folder 13, Patai Papers.

7. Kyle to Taub, Oct. 19, 1937, box 2, folder 13, Patai Papers.

8. See Edwards's story in the *Houston Informer,* Nov. 17, 1937. The *Pittsburgh Courier,* Dec. 18, 1937, published a photo of the two social workers at the Rosa Luxemburg colony under the caption "Americans Succor Spanish Refugee Children." In the photo, Edwards holds a child in her arms.

9. Quoted in "Native Houstonian Speaks in Spain," *Negro Labor News,* Jan. 1, 1938. On the meeting with foreign relief workers, see Kyle to Taub, Oct. 19, 1937, box 2, folder 13, Patai Papers.

10. Edwards to Barnett, Oct. 30, 1937, reel 6, Barnett Papers, pt. 2.

11. Robin D. G. Kelley, *Race Rebels: Culture, Politics, and the Black Working Class,* 124–25.

12. Thyra Edwards, "Social Worker Visits Spanish Loyalist Men," *Chicago Defender,* Feb. 12, 1938; *The Collected Works of Langston Hughes,* vol. 9, *Essays on Art, Race, Politics, and World Affairs,* 177–78. On Cueria, see also his biographical sketch in the Tamiment Library's Online Abraham Lincoln Brigade Archives, http://www.alba-valb. org/volunteers/basilio-cueria-y-obrit (accessed Dec. 2, 2008).

13. "Thyra Edwards," 4, box 2, folder 7, Huiswoud Papers.

14. Thyra J. Edwards, "Kill Kin of A. Herndon in Civil War." "Milton Herndon," Online Abraham Lincoln Brigade Archives, Tamiment Library, http://www.alba-valb.org/ volunteers/milton-herndon (accessed Dec. 2, 2008).

15. Thyra Edwards, "Moors in the Spanish War," 84, 85.

16. Ibid., 85.

17. Edwards to Barnett, dated Nov. 1936 [actually 1937], reel 6, Barnett Papers, pt. 2; "The Robert Weavers Fete Thyra Edwards," *Pittsburgh Courier,* Nov. 27, 1937. On Harris and Frazier, see Jonathan Scott Holloway, *Confronting the Veil: Abram Harris Jr., E. Franklin Frazier, and Ralph Bunche, 1919–1941.*

18. "Working for Children's Home in Spain," *Chicago Defender,* Feb. 12, 1938.

19. "Thyra Edwards Speaks to Shaw Univ. Students," *Chicago Defender,* Mar. 5, 1938; "Thyra Edwards Speaks at A. & T.," *Pittsburgh Courier,* Mar. 5, 1938; Thomas J. Darden, "Nashville, Tenn.," *Chicago Defender,* Mar. 12, 1938; "Nashville Deltas Present World-Wide Traveler," *Chicago Defender,* Apr. 2, 1938.

20. "Texas State," *Chicago Defender,* Apr. 2, 1938; *Houston Informer,* Mar. 30, 1938; "The National Religion and Labor Foundation Sponsors Thyra J. Edwards," n.d. [ca. 1934], reel 13, frames 31–33, NNC Papers. On her appearance at the Wesley Chapel, see *Houston Informer,* Apr. 27, 1938.

21. *Houston Informer,* Apr. 9, 1938; *Negro Labor News,* Apr. 9, 1938.

22. *Negro Labor News,* Apr. 23, 1938.

23. "Miss Thyra J. Edwards, World Traveler, Visits, Lectures in San Antonio," *San Antonio Register,* Apr. 22, 1938.

24. *Houston Informer,* Apr. 27, 1938.

25. "Two Seminars in Mexico: June 12 to July 2, 1938, July 3 to July 25, 1938," box 1, folder 1, Edwards Papers; Friedrich E. Schuler, *Mexico between Hitler and Roosevelt: Mexican Foreign Relations in the Age of Lázaro Cárdenas, 1934–1940,* 56–57, 58, 59, 203. The quote is in an untitled, undated advertisement of the seminar in Mexico in reel 13, frame 15, NNC Papers.

26. "Two Seminars in Mexico," box 1, folder 1, Edwards Papers.

27. Quoted in *Houston Informer,* June 4, 1938. See also *San Antonio Register,* Apr. 22, 1938.

28. "Salaria Kea Returns from Spanish Front," *Chicago Defender,* June 4, 1938; "Chicagoans Close Club Year's Work," *Chicago Defender,* July 2, 1938; *Houston Informer,* June 4, Aug. 13, 1938; Edwards to Barnett, May 24, 1938, reel 6, Barnett Papers, pt. 2. In 1938, the Negro People's Committee to Aid Spanish Democracy, along with the American Medical Bureau to Aid Spanish Democracy and the North American Committee to Aid Spanish Democracy, published a pamphlet, "Salaria Kea: A Negro Nurse in Republican Spain." For a copy of the pamphlet, see Online Abraham Lincoln Brigade Archives, Tamiment Library, http://www.alba-valb.org/resources/robeson-primary-resources/salaria-kea-a-negro-nurse-in-republican-spain (accessed Aug. 31, 2010). For a discussion of volunteer nurses in Republican Spain, see Frances Patai, "Heroines of the Good Fight: Testimonies of U.S. Volunteer Nurses in the Spanish Civil War, 1936–1939." Materials related to the ambulance tour are in "Tour of the Negro People's Ambulance for Loyalist Spain," Scrapbook, Edwards Papers.

29. Edwards to Davis, July 30, 1938, reel 13, frame 38, NNC Papers. An itinerary of the ambulance tour is in reel 6, Barnett Papers, pt. 2.

30. Ibid.; Edwards to Davis, Aug. 4, 1938, frame 42, and Davis to Edwards, Aug. 6, 1938, frames 40–41, both in reel 13, NNC Papers.

31. Thyra Edwards, Field Report, to John Sherman, American Medical Bureau to Aid Spanish Democracy, week ending 8/20/38, 1, box 1, folder 11, Patai Papers.

32. Ibid.

33. Ibid., 2.

34. Ibid., 3.

35. Ibid., 4; "Organize Spanish Aid Group at Hampton," *Chicago Defender,* Oct. 29, 1938.

36. Thyra Edwards, Field Report, to John Sherman, American Medical Bureau to Aid Spanish Democracy, 9/10/38–9/17/38, 6, box 1, folder 11, Patai Papers.

37. Ibid.

38. "Working to Help Loyalists," *Pittsburgh Courier,* Sept. 3, 1938; "Pickens to Visit Spain," *Pittsburgh Courier,* Aug. 27, 1938; Milton Beverly, "Springfield," *Chicago Defender,* Nov. 12, 1938.

39. "Proceedings of the First International Convention, International Auxiliary Order, Ladies' Auxiliaries to the Brotherhood of Sleeping Car Porters (an International Union) Affiliated with the American Federation of Labor," Chicago, Sept. 24–27, 1938, in reel 1, Records of the Brotherhood of Sleeping Car Porters, ser. A, pt. 2, Records of the Ladies' Auxiliaries of the BSCP, 1931–1968, frames 43–44, microfilm. See also Chateauvert, *Marching Together,* 87.

40. "Proceedings of the First International Convention, International Auxiliary Order, Ladies' Auxiliaries to the BSCP," reel 1, frame 44. See Mark Gallicchio, *The African-American Encounter with Japan and China: Black Internationalism in Asia, 1895–1945,* for a discussion of the history of African American perceptions of Japan and China.

41. "Proceedings of the First International Convention, International Auxiliary Order, Ladies' Auxiliaries to the BSCP," reel 1, frame 45.

42. Ibid., frame 44. See also Chateauvert, *Marching Together,* 71–72.

43. "Proceedings of the First International Convention, International Auxiliary Order, Ladies' Auxiliaries to the BSCP," reel 1, frame 67.

44. Thyra Edwards to Blanche Lowenthal, Dec. 15, 1938, and Davis to Edwards, Dec. 12, 1938, both in reel 13, NNC Papers. On Lowenthal, see also Storch, *Red Chicago,* 219.

45. Thyra Edwards to James W. Ford, dated Jan. 26, 1938 [actually 1939], box 15, folder 29, Louise Thompson Patterson Papers, 1909–1999; "Leaders of Race Endorse Peace Parley," *Chicago Defender,* Dec. 24, 1938.

46. Edwards to Davis, Dec. 15, 1938, reel 13, NNC Papers.

47. Davis to Edwards, Dec. 17, 1938, reel 13, NNC Papers; Edwards to Davis, Dec. 20, 1938, reel 13, NNC Papers.

48. Edwards to Ford, dated Jan. 26, 1938 [1939], box 15, folder 29, Patterson Papers.

49. Negro People's Committee to Aid Spain, "The Negro People Defend Democracy by Aid to Spain's People" (1939), 5, box 7, folder 23, Veterans of the Abraham Lincoln Brigade Records, 1933–2006, Tamiment Library/Robert F. Wagner Labor Archives, New York. On Donawa's services in Spain, see *The Collected Works of Langston Hughes,* vol. 14, *Autobiography: "I Wonder As I Wander,"* 366.

50. Edwards to Ford, dated Jan. 26, 1938 [actually 1939], box 15, folder 29, Patterson Papers.

51. Ibid.

52. Ibid.

53. Ibid.

54. Ibid.

55. Ibid.

56. Ibid.

57. Edwards to Davis, Oct. 2, 1937, reel 13, NNC Papers.

Chapter 8

1. Thyra Edwards, "Bee Stings Cured My Arthritis," 89.

2. Ibid., 89, 90.

3. Thyra Edwards Group, *Locust Farm Newsletter,* vol. 1, nos. 4, 5, July 27, 1939, Joseph P. Lash Papers.

4. Edwards to "Pat," Sept. 1, 1939, and "Eyes Refugees in Old Mexico," undated newspaper clipping, both in box 1, folder 3, Edwards Papers.

5. Edwards to "Pat," Sept. 1, 1939, box 1, folder 3, Edwards Papers.

6. Ibid.

7. Ibid.

8. Ibid. On Almazán and the election of 1940 in Mexico, see John W. Sherman, *The Mexican Right: The End of Revolutionary Reform, 1929–1940,* 117–32.

9. Pauli Murray to Thyra Edwards, Sept. 28, 1939, box 72, folder 1244, Pauli Murray Papers. Pauli Murray, *Song in a Weary Throat: An American Pilgrimage,* 133. On Murray, see especially her autobiography, *Pauli Murray: The Autobiography of a Black Activist, Feminist, Lawyer, Priest, and Poet;* and Anne Firor Scott, ed., *Pauli Murray and Caroline Ware: Forty Years of Letters in Black and White.*

10. Ibid.

11. Edwards to Murray, Oct. 3, 1939, box 72, folder 1245, Murray Papers.

12. Ibid.

13. Murray to Edwards, Nov. 8, 1939, box 72, folder 1245, Murray Papers.

14. Ibid. See also Murray, *Song in a Weary Throat,* 133–34, for a brief discussion of her tenure as acting executive secretary of the NPC.

15. Joseph North, *Men in the Ranks: The Story of 12 Americans in Spain,* with a foreword by Ernest Hemingway (New York: Friends of the Abraham Lincoln Brigade, 1939). On Constancia de la Mora in New York, see Soledad Fox, *Constancia de la Mora in War and Exile: International Voice for the Spanish Republic,* 84–105.

16. Edwards to "Jack," Sept. 8, 1939, box 1, folder 3, Edwards Papers. This twenty-page letter is titled "The Spanish Refugee Expedition to Santa Clara."

17. Ibid.

18. Edwards to "Pat," Sept. 1, 1939, box 1, folder 3, Edwards Papers.

19. Ibid.

20. Edwards to "Jack," Sept. 8, 1939, box 1, folder 3, Edwards Papers.

21. Ibid.

22. Ibid.

23. Ibid.

24. Ibid.

25. Ibid.

26. Edwards to Anna Bell Douglas, Oct. 16, 1939, box 1, folder 3, Edwards Papers.

27. Ibid.

28. Ibid.

29. Ibid.

30. Ibid. On Talamantes, see Mark Wasserman, *Persistent Oligarchs: Elites and Politics in Chihuahua, Mexico, 1910–1940* (Durham, NC: Duke University Press, 1993), 61–66.

31. Edwards to Douglas, Oct. 13, 1939, box 1, folder 3, Edwards Papers.

32. Ibid.

33. Edwards to Douglas, Oct. 16, 1939, box 1, folder 3, Edwards Papers.

34. Ibid.

35. Ibid.

36. Edwards to Douglas, Oct. 31, 1939, box 1, folder 3, Edwards Papers. Edwards wrote an article about the holiday, "The Day of the Dead," for the Associated Negro Press. The article appeared in *The Call* (Kansas City), Dec. 1, 1939.

37. Edwards to Douglas, Oct. 31, 1939, box 1, folder 3, Edwards Papers.

38. Edwards to Douglas, Oct. 16, 1939, box 1, folder 3, Edwards Papers.

39. Edwards to Douglas, Oct. 31, 1939, box 1, folder 3, Edwards Papers.

40. Ibid.

41. Edwards to Thelma Marshall, Nov. 3, 1939, box 1, folder 3, Edwards Papers.

42. Ibid.

43. Edwards to Barnett, Sept. 20, 1939, reel 6, Barnett Papers, pt. 2.

44. Barnett to Edwards, Oct. 1, 1939, reel 6, Barnett Papers, pt. 2. See also E. Miles Norton to Claude Barnett, Oct. 11, 1939, and Jan. 10, 1940, and Claude Barnett to Judge E. Miles Norton, n.d., all in reel 6, Barnett Papers, pt. 2.

45. Edwards to Marshall, Nov. 3, 1939, box 1, folder 3, Edwards Papers.

46. Edwards to Barnett, Sept. 20, 1939, reel 6, Barnett Papers, pt. 2.

47. Edwards to Marshall, Nov. 3, 1939, box 1, folder 3, Edwards Papers.

48. Edwards to Douglas, Oct. 16, 1939, box 1, folder 3, Edwards Papers.

49. Thyra J. Edwards to Consuelo Young McGhey, Apr. 1938, box 1, folder 3, Edwards Papers. A number of Edwards's articles written for the Associated Negro Press and other outlets are in her papers, box 1, folders 3 and 4.

50. Thyra J. Edwards, "Mexico Is Last North American Outpost in Liberal Unprejudical [*sic*] Attitude," *The Call* (Kansas City), Jan. 5, 1940.

51. Ibid.; "Mexico Places Ban against Colored Tourists," *Chicago Defender*, July 27, 1940.

52. Edwards, "Mexico Is Last North American Outpost," *The Call* (Kansas City), Jan. 5, 1940.

53. Edwards to Douglas, Oct. 16, 1939, box 1, folder 3, Edwards Papers.

54. Edwards to Marshall, Nov. 3, 1939, box 1, folder 3, Edwards Papers.

55. Edwards to Pickens, Oct. 12, 1939, reel 13, Pickens Papers.

56. Ibid.

57. Edwards to Clara Paul Paige, Apr. 10, 1940, box 1, folder 4, Edwards Papers.

58. Ibid.

59. Ibid.

60. Ibid.

61. Ibid.; Concepción Moller to Edwards, Feb. 8, 1940, box 1, folder 4, Edwards Papers.

62. *Negro Labor News,* Apr. 13, 1940.

63. Ibid.

64. Ibid.

65. Edwards, "Bee Stings Cured My Arthritis," 90.

Chapter 9

1. Edwards to Bethune, July 15, 1940, box 1, folder 4, Edwards Papers. On the housing conference, see "Hold Housing Meeting in Pittsburgh," *Chicago Defender,* May 25, 1940.

2. Anderson, *A. Philip Randolph,* 234–40. For a biography of Yergan, see David Henry Anthony III, *Max Yergan: Race Man, Internationalist, Cold Warrior.*

3. Murray, *Song in a Weary Throat,* 133–34; Report, June 27, 1942, 6–8, Federal Bureau of Investigation, U.S. Dept. of Justice, file no. 65–943. A copy of the brochure advertising Edwards's lecture to the Chicago Council's Cultural Committee is in box 1, folder 4, Edwards Papers.

4. Fanny Buford, "Miss Edwards Speaks before Congress Set," unidentified newspaper clipping, July 6, 1940, box 1, folder 4, Edwards Papers.

5. A copy of the telegram is in "Proceedings of the First International Convention, International Auxiliary Order, Ladies' Auxiliaries to the BSCP," Sept. 15–20, 1940, reel 1, Records of the Brotherhood of Sleeping Car Porters, ser. A, pt. 2, Records of the Ladies Auxiliaries of the BSCP, 1931–1968, 25.

6. Report, June 27, 1942, 2–3, FBI file no. 65–943.

7. Edwards to Hughes, Jan. 31, 1941, box 58, folder 1107, Hughes Papers. On the reception for Hughes, see "Will Honor Play-wright at Reception," *Chicago Defender,* Oct. 5, 1940.

8. Edwards to Hughes, Jan. 31, 1941, box 58, folder 1107, Hughes Papers.

9. Arnold Rampersad, *The Life of Langston Hughes,* vol. 1, *1902–1941, I, Too, Sing America,* 390–91.

10. Edwards to Hughes, Jan. 31, 1941, box 58, folder 1107, Hughes Papers.

11. Edwards to Webster, 1941, box 1, folder 4, Edwards Papers.

12. Report, June 27, 1942, 2, FBI file no. 65–943; Elizabeth Galbreath, "Typovision," *Chicago Defender,* Sept. 6, 1941.

13. Report, June 27, 1942, 2, FBI file no. 65–943. Materials on the venereal disease–control program in Chicago are in box 1, folder 6, and box 2, folders 1 and 2, Edwards Papers.

14. Edwards to Hughes, Nov. 24, 1942, box 58, folder 1107, Hughes Papers.

15. Ibid.

16. Ibid.

17. J. Edgar Hoover, Director, FBI, to Special Agent in Charge, Apr. 8, 1938, photocopy, FBI file no. 65–943–1.

18. Report, dated June 27, 1942, enclosed in J. Edgar Hoover, Director, FBI, to Paul V. McNutt, July 23, 1942, FBI file no. 65–943.

19. Ibid., 5–8.

20. Edwin D. Dickinson, memorandum for J. Edgar Hoover, Director, FBI, Nov. 2, 1942, and Hoover, memorandum for Dickinson, both in FBI file no. 65–943.

21. Thyra J. Edwards to Perrin E. Lowrey, Dec. 19, 1942, box 1, folder 4, Edwards Papers.

22. Ibid.

23. Thyra Edwards, "The Negro Worker—Today and Tomorrow," Nov. 18, 1944.

24. Edwards to Hughes, Nov. 24, 1942, box 58, folder 1107, Hughes Papers.

25. Assistant Administrator, Federal Security Agency, to J. Edgar Hoover, Jan. 16, 1943, FBI file no. 65–943.

26. *The People's Voice,* Jan. 30, 1943. See also "Thyra Edwards Now Manager of New York's P.V.," *Negro Labor News,* Feb. 13, 1943, and "Thyra Edwards," 4, box 2, folder 7, Huiswoud Papers.

27. Alan Wald, *Trinity of Passion: The Literary Left and the Antifascist Crusade,* 108–11; "5 Prominent Women Join Davis Sponsors," *Daily Worker,* Oct. 12, 1943, copy in box 1, folder 4, Edwards Papers. On Davis and tensions over "Browderism" in New York City, see Gerald Horne, *Black Liberation/Red Scare: Ben Davis and the Communist Party,* especially chap. 7. For a brief sketch of Cooke, see Rodger Streitmatter, *Raising Her Voice: African-American Women Journalists Who Changed History,* 84–94.

28. Report, May 26, 1943, FBI File on National Negro Congress, reel 1.

29. Report, May 3, 1945, 4, 6, FBI file no. 65–943. On the newspaper, see César J. Ayala and Rafael Bernabe, *Puerto Rico in the American Century: A History since 1898,* 147–48.

30. Report, May 3, 1945, 1, 12, FBI file no. 65–943. On Gitlin's connections to the Writers Circle in Chicago, see Bettina Drew, "Drifting into a Career," *The Missouri Review* 11 (Spring 1988). Edwards sometimes went by the name *Thyra Edwards Gitlin* after her marriage, but I refer to her throughout the book as *Edwards* for simplicity's sake, except in citations of any of her works where she used the name *Edwards Gitlin.*

31. Thyra Edwards Gitlin and Murray Gitlin, "Does Interracial Marriage Succeed?" 63.

32. Ibid., 64. For a broader contextualization, see Renee C. Romano, *Race Mixing: Black-White Marriage in Postwar America.*

33. Report, May 3, 1945, 6, 7, FBI file no. 65–943. For a biography of Smith, see Gerald Horne, *Red Seas: Ferdinand Smith and Radical Black Sailors in the United States and Jamaica.*

34. Edwards, "Bee Stings Cured My Arthritis," 90; Martin and Martin, "Thyra J. Edwards," 173.

35. "Father of Gary Social Worker Dies in Arizona," *Chicago Defender,* Mar. 11, 1944; Martin and Martin, "Thyra J. Edwards," 173.

36. Thyra Edwards, "ILO Will Play Role in Future of Negro."

37. For a concise history and discussion of the ILO, see Virginia A. Leary, "Labor," in Oscar Schachter and Christopher C. Joyner, eds., *United Nations Legal Order,* vol. 1 (Cambridge: Cambridge University Press, 1995), 473–502. On the decision of the United States to join the ILO in 1934, see Gary B. Ostrower, "The American Decision to Join the International Labor Organization."

38. Edwards, "ILO Will Play Role in Future of Negro."

39. Thyra Edwards, "The ILO and Postwar Planning for the African Colonies."

40. Thyra Edwards, "AFL Supports Lily-White Argentine Delegation at ILO Convention in Philly." On the CTAL, see Norman Caulfield, *Mexican Workers and the State: From the Porfiriato to NAFTA,* 72, and *NAFTA and Labor in North America,* 29. On the Pan-American Federation of Labor, see especially Sinclair Snow, *The Pan-American Federation of Labor;* Harvey A. Levenstein, *Labor Organizations in the United States and Mexico: A History of Their Relations,* 78–89; and Gregg Andrews, *Shoulder to Shoulder? The American Federation of Labor, the United States, and the Mexican Revolution, 1910–1924.*

41. Edwards, "AFL Supports Lily-White Argentine Delegation."

42. Thyra Edwards, "Bishop Tells ILO Meet of Negro's Plight"; Edwards, "The ILO and Postwar Planning for the African Colonies," 220.

43. Edwards, "Bishop Tells ILO Meet of Negro's Plight." For broader studies of African Americans and foreign affairs in this era, see especially Carol Elaine Anderson, *Eyes Off the Prize: The United Nations and the African American Struggle for Human Rights, 1944–1955;* Brenda Gayle Plummer, *Rising Wind: Black Americans and U.S. Foreign Affairs, 1935–1960;* and Brenda Gayle Plummer, ed., *Window on Freedom: Race, Civil Rights, and Foreign Affairs, 1945–1988.*

44. Edwards, "The ILO and Postwar Planning for the African Colonies," 220.

45. Thyra Edwards, "The Negro Worker—Today and Tomorrow," June 17, 1944.

46. Thyra Edwards, "The Negro Worker—Today and Tomorrow," June 3, 1944; Horne, *Red Seas,* 27.

47. Thyra Edwards, "The Negro Worker—Today and Tomorrow," Sept. 30, 1944.

48. Thyra Edwards, "African Freedom Promised."

49. Thyra Edwards, "De Gaulle Pledges French Colonies Self Government." See also ibid.

50. Thyra Edwards, "The Man Who Saved France."

51. Thyra Edwards, "De Gaulle Pledges French Colonies Self Government."

52. Thyra Edwards and Murray Gitlin, "25 Million Negroes Getting New Deal in French Africa."

53. Thyra Edwards, "Hastie's Letter to CIO's PAC Untimely."

54. Ibid.; Edwards, "The Negro Worker—Today and Tomorrow," Sept. 23, 1944.

55. Edwards, "The Negro Worker—Today and Tomorrow," Sept. 23, Oct. 14, 1944.

56. Thyra Edwards, "Are 'Race Relations Advisors' Helping or Hindering the Advance of the Negro?"

57. Edwards, "The Negro Worker—Today and Tomorrow," July 29, 1944. Edwards's enthusiasm about the promise of such interracial developments in CIO unions in the area was not unfounded. See Robert Rodgers Korstad, *Civil Rights Unionism: Tobacco Workers and the Struggle for Democracy in the Mid-Twentieth-Century South,* for an

excellent study of interracial unionism in the tobacco industry in Winston-Salem at the time. See also Robert Korstad and Nelson Lichtenstein, "Opportunities Found and Lost: Labor, Radicals, and the Early Civil Rights Movement," for a discussion of important strides made by organized labor in the area of interracial unionism as a result of World War II. The Cold War soon helped to reverse these strides. See also Vicki L. Ruiz, *Cannery Women, Cannery Lives: Mexican Women, Unionization, and the California Food Processing Industry, 1930–1950,* and Michael K. Honey, *Southern Labor and Black Civil Rights: Organizing Memphis Workers.*

58. Edwards, "The Negro Worker—Today and Tomorrow," Sept. 23, Oct. 14, 1944. On Mulzac, see Edwards's article "The Mulzac School of Seamanship." See also Mulzac's autobiography, *A Star to Steer By* (New York: International Publishers, 1963).

59. Edwards, "The Negro Worker—Today and Tomorrow," Nov. 18, 1944; "Milwaukee, Wisc.," *Chicago Defender,* Nov. 11, 1944. On their stop in Chicago, see "Chicago Mayor Greets Captain Mulzac," *Chicago Defender,* Oct. 28, 1944.

60. Edwards, "The Negro Worker—Today and Tomorrow," Nov. 4, 1944.

61. Edwards, "The Negro Worker—Today and Tomorrow," Oct. 28, 1944.

62. Ibid.

63. Edwards, "The Negro Worker—Today and Tomorrow," Oct. 14, 1944.

64. Edwards, "The Negro Worker—Today and Tomorrow," Sept. 30, 1944.

65. Edwards, "The Negro Worker—Today and Tomorrow," Nov. 11, 1944.

66. "Editorially Speaking," *Houston Informer,* Feb. 3, 1945.

67. Edwards, "The Negro Worker—Today and Tomorrow," Dec. 30, 1944.

68. Ibid.

69. Ibid.

70. Ibid.

71. Edwards, "The Negro Worker—Today and Tomorrow," Jan. 13, 1945.

72. Ibid.

73. Ibid.

74. Edwards, "The Negro Worker—Today and Tomorrow," Jan. 20, 1945.

75. Ibid.; "End Campaign to Effect Control of Social Disease," *Pittsburgh Courier,* Dec. 23, 1944.

76. Edwards, "The Negro Worker—Today and Tomorrow," Jan. 20, 1945.

77. Ibid.

78. Edwards, "The Negro Worker—Today and Tomorrow," Feb. 3, 1945.

79. Edwards, "The Negro Worker—Today and Tomorrow," July 1, 1944.

80. Edwards, "The Negro Worker—Today and Tomorrow," Oct. 7, 1944.

81. Edwards, "The Negro Worker—Today and Tomorrow," Feb. 10, 1945.

82. Edwards, "Deep in the Heart of Texas," 54.

Chapter 10

1. Edwards, "Bee Stings Cured My Arthritis," 89.

2. Ibid.

3. Thyra Edwards, "What Shall I Do about My Hair?"

4. Thyra Edwards, "Negro Heads NMU Picketers"; Kate Weigand, *Red Feminism: American Communism and the Making of Women's Liberation,* 48. According to FBI reports, Thyra was a member of the board of directors of the George Washington Carver

School in New York and was slated to teach there in the fall term of 1945. See Russell S. Garner, Report, June 21, 1946, FBI file no. 65–943.

5. Quoted in Thyra Edwards, "New U.S. Women's Group Outgrowth of Paris Meet." On the founding of the CAW, see also "Congress of Women Plans Wide Activity," *New York Times,* Mar. 9, 1946; "Women of America Organize Own 'PAC,'" *New York Times,* May 26, 1946; and Weigand, *Red Feminism,* 48. For a biography of Charlotte Hawkins Brown, see Charles W. Wadelington and Richard F. Knapp, *Charlotte Hawkins Brown and Palmer Memorial Institute: What One Young African American Woman Could Do* (Chapel Hill: University of North Carolina Press, 1999).

6. House Un-American Activities Committee, *Report on the Congress of American Women,* 1949. For a discussion of the CAW, see Amy Swerdlow, "The Congress of American Women: Left-Feminist Peace Politics in the Cold War."

7. Report, Apr. 25, 1949, 3, FBI file no. 65–943.

8. Thyra Edwards, "Famous Soviet Novelist Selects 'Poll Tax Belt' For U.S. Tour"; Thyra Edwards, "20,000 Hail Soviet Writers, Laud USSR Race Policy."

9. Ibid.

10. Thyra Edwards and Murray Gitlin, "Russian Author Shocked at Racism in Southern U.S."

11. Report, June 21, 1949, 2, FBI file no. 65–943.

12. Edwards to Hughes, Sept. 11, 1948, box 58, folder 1107, Hughes Papers.

13. Report, June 21, 1949, 2, FBI file no. 65–943.

14. Edwards to Hughes, Sept. 11, 1948, box 58, folder 1107, Hughes Papers.

15. Ibid.

16. Ibid.

17. Ibid.

18. Report, Apr. 25, 1949, 4–5, FBI file no. 65–943.

19. Ibid., 4–6.

20. Edwards, "Bee Stings Cured My Arthritis," 90.

21. Ibid.

22. Ibid., 91.

23. Ibid.

24. Edwards to Hughes, Sept. 11, 1948, box 58, folder 1107, Hughes Papers.

25. Edwards, "Bee Stings Cured My Arthritis," 91–92.

26. Ibid., 92.

27. Ibid.

28. Ibid.

29. Edwards to Hughes, Mar. 25, 1950, box 58, folder 1107, Hughes Papers.

30. Ibid.

31. Ibid. The New York City Opera Company put on the first performance of *Troubled Island* at City Center on Mar. 31, 1949. On the struggle to stage a production of the opera in New York, see Judith Anne Still and Lisa M. Headlee, eds., *Just Tell the Story—"Troubled Island": A Collection of Documents Previously Published and Unpublished, Pertaining to the First Significant Afro-American Grand Opera, "Troubled Island"* (Flagstaff, AZ: Master-Player Library, 2006).

32. Edwards to Hughes, Mar. 25, 1950, box 58, folder 1107, Hughes Papers.

33. Ibid.

34. Hughes to Thyra Edwards Gitlin, Sept. 1, 1950, Nov. 2, 1951, and Edwards to Hughes, Sept. 4, 1950, box 58, folder 1107, Hughes Papers.

35. Edwards to Hughes, Dec. 7, 1951, box 58, folder 1107, Hughes Papers.

36. Ibid.

37. A copy of a blind memorandum by Budenz is included in SAC, New York, to Director, FBI, Aug. 8, 1950, FBI file no. 65–943.

38. On how Browder's expulsion and the subsequent shift in the CPUSA's official line affected peace activism in the early postwar years, see Robbie Lieberman, *The Strangest Dream: Communism, Anticommunism, and the U.S. Peace Movement, 1945–1963,* especially 32–56. On the NAACP's internal purge, see Anderson, *Eyes Off the Prize,* 166–209. For a more critical assessment of the NAACP's ouster of W. E. B. Du Bois on account of his Communist affiliations, see Gerald Horne, *Black & Red: W.E.B. Du Bois and the Afro-American Response to the Cold War, 1944–1963,* 97–112. Steve Rosswurm, ed., *The CIO's Left-Led Unions,* is a collection of essays on the leftwing unions expelled from the CIO.

39. See the office memorandum in SAC, Washington Field Office, to Director, FBI, Jan. 19, June 19, 1951, and Report, Feb. 26, 1951, 4, all in FBI file no. 65–943.

40. Edwards to Hughes, dated Mar. 17, 1953 [actually 1952], box 58, folder 1107, Hughes Papers.

41. "Thyra Edwards," 5, box 2, folder 7, Huiswoud Papers.

42. Edwards to Hughes, dated Mar. 17, 1953 [actually 1952], box 58, folder 1107, Hughes Papers.

43. Ibid.

44. Ibid.

45. "Thyra Edwards," 5–6, box 2, folder 7, Huiswoud Papers.

46. SAC, New York, to Director, FBI, May 22, 1952; SAC, New Haven, to Director, FBI, July 31, 1952; SAC, New York, to Director, FBI, Jan. 6, 1953; Director, FBI, to SAC, New York, Feb. 2, 1953; all in FBI file no. 65–943.

47. "Thyra Edwards," 6, box 2, folder 7, Huiswoud Papers.

48. Bernard Ades, "Eulogy of Thyra Edwards Gitlin Delivered at Saint Philips Church, July 12, 1953," box 1, folder 5, Edwards Papers. For her obituary, see "Thyra Edwards Dead; Hold N.Y. Rites," *Chicago Defender,* July 25, 1953, and "Deaths," *New York Times,* July 11, 1953.

Epilogue

1. For an excellent treatment of the strike that brought King to Memphis in March 1968 to stand with striking sanitation workers in their struggle for economic justice and union recognition, see Michael K. Honey, *Going Down Jericho Road: The Memphis Strike, Martin Luther King's Last Campaign.*

2. Faith Berry, *Langston Hughes: Before and Beyond Harlem,* 317–20.

3. On Jones, see Davies, *Left of Karl Marx.* For a discussion of Jones's important intellectual role in the Congress of American Women, see Weigand, *Red Feminism,* 102–8.

4. Thelma Marshall to Claude Barnett, Aug. 13, 1953, reel 6, Barnett Papers, pt. 2.

5. For a brief biographical sketch of Thelma Marshall, see Joyce Blackwell, *No Peace without Freedom: Race and the Women's International League for Peace and Freedom, 1915–1975,* 46–48, 106, 136, 145, 147. See photo number 8 for a picture of Marshall and other WILPF activists in Moscow in 1974. In the fall of 1948, she accepted a position as one of two new assistant deans of women at Fisk University. See *Chicago Defender,* Oct. 2, 1948.

6. Paul Buhle and Dave Wagner, *Radical Hollywood: The Untold Story behind America's Favorite Movies,* 430n55.

7. Gina Loring, conversation with author, Apr. 1, 2009. For William Marshall's obituary, see, for example, *Independent,* July 3, 2003, and *New York Times,* June 21, 2003. A tradition of creativity in music, labor organizing, and the performance arts exists in the family. For example, Bruce Edwards (Thyra's uncle) was a musician who played in the Silas Green Band, and one of her cousins, Teddy Edwards Sr., was a legendary jazz tenor saxophonist. Thyra's cousin, Paul Winfield, became a noted television, film, and theater actor who won an Academy Award nomination for his role in the film *Sounder* (1972). The son of Lois Beatrice Edwards, a labor organizer in the Los Angeles garment industry, Winfield later won an Emmy Award.

Bibliography

Manuscript Collections and Archival Materials

Abraham Lincoln Brigade. Archives. Tamiment Library/Robert F. Wagner Labor Archives, New York University, New York.

Ades, Bernard. Papers. Tamiment Library/Robert F. Wagner Labor Archives, New York University, New York.

Anderson, Marian. Papers. Walter J. and Leonore Annenberg Rare Book and Manuscript Library, University of Pennsylvania, Philadelphia.

Barnett, Claude A. Papers. Microfilm. Frederick, MD: University Publications of America, 1985.

Bontemps, Arna Wendell. Papers. Special Collections Research Center, Syracuse University Library, Syracuse, NY.

Brotherhood of Sleeping Car Porters. Records. Ed. William H. Harris. Microfilm. Bethesda, MD: University Publications of America, 1990.

Communism Collection. Sophia Smith Collection. Smith College, Northampton, MA.

Edwards, Thyra J. Papers. Chicago History Museum, Chicago.

Emergency Peace Campaign. Records. Swarthmore College Peace Collection, Swarthmore College, Swarthmore, PA.

Highlander Research and Education Center Records. Wisconsin Historical Society, University of Wisconsin, Madison.

Hughes, Langston. Papers. Beinecke Rare Book and Manuscript Library, Yale University, New Haven, CT.

Huiswoud, Hermina Dumont. Papers. Tamiment Library/Robert F. Wagner Labor Archives, New York University, New York.

Lash, Joseph P. Papers. Franklin D. Roosevelt Library, Hyde Park, NY.

Michelson, Clarina. Papers. Tamiment Library/Robert F. Wagner Labor Archives, New York University, New York.

Murray, Pauli. Papers. Schlesinger Library, Radcliffe Institute for Advanced Study, Harvard University, Cambridge, MA.

National Association for the Advancement of Colored People. Papers. Microfilm. Part 10, Peonage, Labor, and the New Deal, 1913–1939, ed. John H. Bracey Jr. and August Meier. Bethesda, MD: University Publications of America, 1990.

———. Part 11, Special Subject Files, 1912–1939, Series B: Warren G. Harding through YWCA, ed. John H. Bracey Jr. and August Meier. Bethesda, MD: University Publications of America, 1991.

———. Part 12, Selected Branch Files, 1913–1939, Series A: The South, ed. John H. Bracey Jr. and August Meier. Bethesda, MD: University Publications of America, 1991.

National Negro Congress. Papers. Frederick, MD: University Publications of America, 1988.

Patai, Frances. Papers, 1937–1998. Abraham Lincoln Brigade Archive. Tamiment Library/Robert F. Wagner Labor Archives, New York University, New York.

Patterson, Louise Thompson. Papers, 1909–1999. Manuscript, Archives, and Rare Book Library, Emory University, Atlanta.

Pickens, William. Papers (additions), 1909–1950. Microfilm. Schomburg Center for Research in Black Culture, New York Public Library, New York.

Randolph, A. Philip. Papers. Ed. John H. Bracey Jr. and August Meier. Microfilm. Bethesda, MD: University Publications of America, 1990.

Winegarten, Ruth. Papers. Center for American History, University of Texas at Austin.

Selected Publications by Thyra J. Edwards

"AFL Supports Lily-White Argentine Delegation at ILO Convention in Philly." Houston Informer, Apr. 29, 1944.

"African Freedom Promised." Houston Informer, July 15, 1944.

"Are 'Race Relations Advisors' Helping or Hindering the Advance of the Negro?" Houston Informer, Apr. 14, 1945.

"Attitudes of Negro Families on Relief—Another Opinion." Opportunity 14 (July 1936): 214–15.

"Bee Stings Cured My Arthritis." Pageant (Mar. 1953): 88–92.

"Bishop Tells ILO Meet of Negro's Plight." Houston Informer, May 20, 1944.

"Chicago in the Rain (Relief for Negro Homeless Men on the South Side)." In Writing Red: An Anthology of American Women Writers, 1930–1940, ed.

Charlotte Nekola and Paula Rabinowitz, 282–84. New York: Feminist Press, 1987.

"Deep in the Heart of Texas." *Negro Digest* 2 (Apr. 1944): 50–54.

"De Gaulle Pledges French Colonies Self Government." *Chicago Defender,* July 22, 1944.

"English Woman Seeks Her Long Lost Black Lover." *Pittsburgh Courier,* Mar. 24, 1934.

"Famous Soviet Novelist Selects 'Poll Tax Belt' for U.S. Tour." *Chicago Defender,* June 1, 1946.

"The Gary Interracial Program." *Southern Workman* 54 (Dec. 1925): 546, 550, 552.

"Hastie's Letter to CIO's PAC Untimely." *Houston Informer,* Sept. 9, 1944.

"The ILO and Postwar Planning for the African Colonies." *Crisis* (July 1944): 218–220, 233.

"ILO Will Play Role in Future of Negro." *Houston Informer,* Apr. 29, 1944.

"Imperial Policy of Britain Is Analyzed." *Chicago Defender,* Dec. 26, 1936.

"Jane Addams Loved All Races . . . She Was a Real Neighbor." *Pittsburgh Courier,* June 1, 1935.

"Kill Kin of A. Herndon in Civil War." *Chicago Defender,* Nov. 20, 1937.

"Let Us Have More Like Mr. Sopkins." *Crisis* (Mar. 1935): 72, 82.

"The Man Who Saved France." *Houston Informer,* Sept. 2, 1944.

"Moors in the Spanish War." *Opportunity* 16 (Mar. 1938): 84–85.

"The Moscow Theatre for Children. *Woman Today* (Mar. 1937): 6–7.

"The Mulzac School of Seamanship." *Negro Digest* 3 (Feb. 1945): 73–75.

"Negro Heads NMU Picketers." *Chicago Defender,* Aug. 4, 1945.

"Negro Literature Comes to Denmark." *Crisis* (May 1936): 140–41, 146.

"The Negro Worker—Today and Tomorrow." *Houston Informer,* June 3, 17, 24, July 1, 29, Aug. 26, Sept. 23, 30, Oct. 7, 14, 28, Nov. 4, 11, 18, 25, Dec. 9, 30, 1944, Jan. 13, 20, 27, Feb. 3, 10, 17, 1945.

"New U.S. Women's Group Outgrowth of Paris Meet." *Chicago Defender,* Mar. 2, 1946.

"NMU Picket Lines Directed by Negro." *Houston Informer,* July 28, 1945.

"Seminar to Soviet Is Gotten Underway." *Chicago Defender,* Dec. 10, 1936.

"'Sister Katie.'" *Progressive Miner,* Apr. 21, 1933, 3.

"Swedish Wives Show Us a Thing or Two." *Woman Today* (Feb. 1937): 10–11.

"Thyra Edwards Sees and Likes Green Pastures." *Gary American,* Dec. 20, 1930.

"20,000 Hail Soviet Writers, Laud USSR Race Policy." *Chicago Defender,* June 8, 1946.

"What Shall I Do about My Hair?" *Our World* (Apr. 1946): 36.

"Who Is Disinterested?" *Crisis* (June 1935): 173–74.

"Women's Rights and the Coming Election." *Houston Informer,* Oct. 21, 1944.

Edwards, Thyra, and Murray Gitlin. "Russian Author Shocked at Racism in Southern U.S." *Chicago Defender,* July 13, 1946.

———. "A Surgeon of Democracy." *Coronet,* Apr. 1946, 118–20.

———. "25 Million Negroes Getting New Deal in French Africa." *Chicago Defender,* Jan. 13, 1945.

Edwards Gitlin, Thyra, and Murray Gitlin. "Does Interracial Marriage Succeed?" *Negro Digest* 3 (July 1945): 63–64.

Government Documents

Federal Bureau of Investigation. File on National Negro Congress. Wilmington, DE: Scholarly Resources, 1987. 2 reels.

Federal Bureau of Investigation. File on Thyra J. Edwards (Case file no. 65–943), obtained under the Freedom of Information/Privacy Acts. Archives, Federal Bureau of Investigation, Washington, DC.

House Un-American Activities Committee. Report on the Congress of American Women. Oct. 23, 1949. 81st Congress, 2d Session, House Report No. 1953.

U.S. State Department Central Files: Spain, Internal Affairs, 1930–1939, pt. 1, Political, Governmental and National Defense Affairs, Decimal Numbers 852.0–852.3. Frederick, MD: University Publications of America, 1986.

Books, Articles, and Dissertations

Albers, Patricia. *Shadows, Fire, Snow: The Life of Tina Modotti.* Berkeley: University of California Press, 1999.

Altenbaugh, Richard J. "'The Children and the Instruments of a Militant Labor Progressivism': Brookwood Labor College and the American Labor College Movement of the 1920s and 1930s." *History of Education Quarterly* 23 (Winter 1983): 395–411.

———. *Education for Struggle: The American Labor College of the 1920s and the 1930s.* Philadelphia: Temple University Press, 1990.

Anderson, Carol Elaine. *Eyes Off the Prize: The United Nations and the African American Struggle for Human Rights, 1944–1955.* Cambridge: Cambridge University Press, 2003.

Anderson, Jervis. *A. Philip Randolph: A Biographical Portrait.* Berkeley: University of California Press, pap. ed., 1986. Originally published in 1972.

Andrews, Gregg. "Black Working-Class Political Activism and Biracial Unionism: Galveston Longshoremen in Jim Crow Texas, 1919–1921." *Journal of Southern History* 74 (Aug. 2008): 627–68.

——. *Shoulder to Shoulder? The American Federation of Labor, the United States, and the Mexican Revolution, 1910–1924*. Berkeley: University of California Press, 1991.

Anthony, David Henry, III. *Max Yergan: Race Man, Internationalist, Cold Warrior.* New York: New York University Press, 2006.

Arnesen, Eric. "A. Philip Randolph: Labor and the New Black Politics." In *The Human Tradition in American Labor History,* ed Eric Arnesen, 173–92. Lanham, MD: Rowman and Littlefield, 2004.

——. *Brotherhoods of Color: Black Railroad Workers and the Struggle for Equality.* Cambridge, MA: Harvard University Press, 2001.

——. "No 'Graver Danger': Black Anticommunism, the Communist Party, and the Race Question." *Labor: Studies in Working- Class History of the Americas* 3 (Winter 2006): 13–52.

——. "Passion and Politics: Race and the Writing of Working- Class History." *Journal of the Historical Society* 6 (2006): 323–56.

——. "Reconsidering the 'Long Civil Rights Movement.'" *Historically Speaking* 10 (Apr. 2009): 31–34.

Arnesen, Eric, ed. *The Black Worker: A Reader.* Urbana: University of Illinois Press, 2007.

Ayala, César J., and Rafael Bernabe. *Puerto Rico in the American Century: A History since 1898.* Chapel Hill: University of North Carolina Press, 2007.

Baldwin, Kate A. *Beyond the Color Line and the Iron Curtain: Reading Encounters between Black and Red, 1922–1963.* Durham, NC: Duke University Press, 2002.

Bates, Beth Tompkins. "Mobilizing Black Chicago: The Brotherhood of Sleeping Car Porters and Community Organizing, 1925–35." In *The Black Worker: A Reader,* ed. Eric Arnesen, 195–221. Urbana: University of Illinois Press, 2007.

——. "A New Crowd Challenges the Agenda of the Old Guard in the NAACP, 1933–1941." *American Historical Review* 102 (Apr. 1997): 340–77.

——. *Pullman Car Porters and the Rise of Protest Politics in Black America, 1925–1945.* Chapel Hill: University of North Carolina Press, 2001.

Bauer, Robert Felix. *Leon Blum, the Popular Front, and the Spanish Civil War.* Cambridge, MA: Harvard University Press, 1973.

Beeth, Howard, and Cary D. Wintz, eds. *Black Dixie: Afro-Texan History and Culture in Houston.* College Station: Texas A&M University Press, 1992.

Belknap, Michal R. *Political Justice: The Smith Act, the Communist Party, and American Civil Liberties.* Westport, CT: Greenwood, 1977.

Benjamin, Ionie. *The Black Press in Britain.* Staffordshire: Trentham Press, 1995.

Bermack, Richard. *The Front Lines of Social Change: Veterans of the Abraham Lincoln Brigade.* Berkeley, CA: Heyday Books, 2005.

Berry, Faith. *Langston Hughes: Before and Beyond Harlem.* New York: Wings Books, 1995.

———, ed. *Good Morning Revolution: Uncollected Writings of Social Protest by Langston Hughes.* New York: Citadel Press, 1992.

Betten, Neil, and Raymond A. Mohl. "The Evolution of Racism in an Industrial City, 1906–1940: A Case Study of Gary, Indiana." *Journal of Negro History* 59 (Jan. 1974): 51–64.

Biondi, Martha. *To Stand and Fight: The Struggle for Civil Rights in Postwar New York City.* Cambridge, MA: Harvard University Press, 2003.

Blackwelder, Julia Kirk. *Styling Jim Crow: African American Beauty Training during Segregation.* College Station: Texas A&M University Press, 2003.

Blackwell, Joyce. *No Peace without Freedom: Race and the Women's International League for Peace and Freedom, 1915–1975.* Carbondale: Southern Illinois University Press, 2004.

Blackwell-Johnson, Joyce. "African American Activists in the Women's International League for Peace and Freedom, 1920s- 1950s." *Peace & Change* 23 (Oct. 1998): 466–82.

Blakely, Allison. *Russia and the Negro: Blacks in Russian History and Thought* (Washington, DC: Howard University Press, 1989).

Bloom, Jonathan. "Brookwood Labor College: The Final Years, 1933–1937." *Labor's Heritage* 2 (Apr. 1990): 37–39.

Bolloten, Burnett. *The Spanish Civil War.* Chapel Hill: University of North Carolina Press, 1991.

Borstelmann, Thomas. *The Cold War and the Color Line: American Race Relations in the Global Arena.* Cambridge, MA: Harvard University Press, 2001.

Boyle, Kevin. "Labour, the Left, and the Long Civil Rights Movement." *Social History* 30 (Aug. 2005): 366–72.

Boyle, Sheila Tully, and Andrew Bunie. *Paul Robeson: The Years of Promise and Achievement.* Amherst: University of Massachusetts Press, 2001.

Brier, Stephen. "Labor, Politics, and Race: A Black Worker's Life." *Labor History* 23 (Summer 1982): 416–21.

Brown, Kathleen A., and Elizabeth Faue. "Revolutionary Desire: Redefining the Politics of Sexuality of American Radicals, 1919–1945." In *Sexual Borderlands: Constructing an American Sexual Past,* ed. Kathleen Kennedy and Sharon Ullman, 273–302. Columbus: Ohio State University Press, 2003.

———. "Social Bonds, Sexual Politics, and Political Community on the U.S. Left, 1920s-1940s." *Left History* 7 (Spring 2001): 9–45.

Bryant, Ira B. *The Development of the Houston Negro Schools.* Houston: Inform-
    er Publishing Co., 1935.
Buchanan, Tom. *Britain and the Spanish Civil War.* Cambridge: Cambridge
    University Press, 1997.
Buhle, Paul, and Dave Wagner. *Radical Hollywood: The Untold Story behind
    America's Favorite Movies.* New York: Free Press, 2002.
Carew, Joy Gleason. *Blacks, Reds, and Russians: Sojourners in Search of the Soviet
    Promise.* New Brunswick, NJ: Rutgers University Press, 2008.
Carroll, Peter N. *The Odyssey of the Abraham Lincoln Brigade: Americans in the
    Spanish Civil War.* Stanford, CA: Stanford University Press, 1994.
Caulfield, Norman. *Mexican Workers and the State: From the Porfiriato to
    NAFTA.* Fort Worth: Texas Christian University Press, 1998.
——. *NAFTA and Labor in North America.* Urbana: University of Illinois Press,
    2010.
Cha-Jua, Sundiata Keita, and Clarence Lang. "The 'Long Movement' as Vam-
    pire: Temporal and Spatial Fallacies in Recent Black Freedom Studies."
    Journal of African American History 92 (Spring 2007): 265–88.
Chappell, David L. "The Lost Decade of Civil Rights." *Historically Speaking* 10
    (Apr. 2009): 37–41.
——. *Stone of Hope: Prophetic Religion and the Death of Jim Crow.* Chapel Hill:
    University of North Carolina Press, 2004.
Chateauvert, Melinda. *Marching Together: Women of the Brotherhood of Sleeping
    Car Porters.* Urbana: University of Illinois Press, 1998.
Cobble, Dorothy Sue. *The Other Women's Movement: Workplace Justice and So-
    cial Rights in Modern America.* Princeton: Princeton University Press,
    2005.
Cohen, Lizabeth. *Making a New Deal in Chicago, 1919–1939.* Cambridge: Cam-
    bridge University Press, 1990.
Cohen, Ronald D. *Children of the Mill: Schooling and Society in Gary, Indiana,
    1906–1960.* New York: Routledge, 2002.
Colodny, Robert G. *Spain: The Glory and the Tragedy.* New York: Humanities
    Press, 1970.
Crocker, Ruth Hutchinson. *Social Work and Social Order: The Settlement Move-
    ment in Two Industrial Cities, 1889–1930.* Urbana: University of Illinois
    Press, 1992.
Cuthbert, Marion Vera. *Education and Marginality: A Study of the Negro Wom-
    an College Graduate.* New York: Columbia University, 1942.
Dallek, Robert. *Franklin D. Roosevelt and American Foreign Policy, 1932–1945.*
    New York: Oxford University Press, 1979.
Davies, Carol Boyce. *Left of Karl Marx: The Political Life of Black Communist
    Claudia Jones.* Durham, NC: Duke University Press, 2007.

Davis, Benjamin J. "Why I Became a Communist." *Phylon* 8, no. 2 (1947): 105–16.

Dempsey, Terrell. *Searching for Jim: Slavery in Sam Clemens's World.* Columbia: University of Missouri Press, 2005.

Denning, Michael. *The Cultural Front: The Laboring of American Culture in the Twentieth Century.* London: Verso, 1998.

Denzer, LaRay. "Women in Freetown Politics, 1914–61: A Preliminary Study." *Africa: Journal of the International African Institute* 57, no. 4 (1987): 439–56.

Dudziak, Mary L. *Cold War Civil Rights: Race and the Image of American Democracy.* Princeton: Princeton University Press, 2000.

Faue, Elizabeth. *Writing the Wrongs: Eva Valesh and the Rise of Labor Journalism.* Ithaca: Cornell University Press, 2005.

Foster, Carrie A. *The Women and the Warriors: The U.S. Section of the Women's International League for Peace and Freedom, 1915–1946.* Syracuse, NY: Syracuse University Press, 1995.

Foster, Catherine. *Women for All Seasons: The Story of the Women's International League for Peace and Freedom.* Athens: University of Georgia Press, 1989.

Fox, Soledad. *Constancia de la Mora in War and Exile: International Voice for the Spanish Republic.* Eastbourne: Sussex Academic Press, 2007.

Friedman, Mickey. *A Red Family: Junius, Gladys, and Barbara Scales.* Urbana: University of Illinois Press, 2009.

Fyrth, Jim, ed. With Sally Alexander. *Women's Voices from the Spanish Civil War.* London: Lawrence and Wishart, 1991.

Gallagher, M. D. "Leon Blum and the Spanish Civil War." *Journal of Contemporary History* 6, no. 3 (1971): 56–64.

Gallicchio, Mark. *The African-American Encounter with Japan and China: Black Internationalism in Asia, 1895–1945.* Chapel Hill: University of North Carolina Press, 2000.

Gertz, Gwynne. "Thyra J. Edwards." In *Women Building Chicago, 1790–1990: A Biographical Dictionary,* ed. Rima Lunin Schultz and Adele Hast, 244–48. Bloomington: Indiana University Press, 2001.

Gilmore, Glenda Elizabeth. *Defying Dixie: The Radical Roots of Civil Rights, 1919–1950.* New York: W. W. Norton, 2008.

Glasrud, Bruce A., and Gregg Andrews. "Confronting White Supremacy: The African American Left in Texas, 1874–1974." In *The Texas Left: The Radical Roots of Lone Star Liberalism,* ed. David O'Donald Cullen and Kyle G. Wilkison, 157–90. College Station: Texas A&M University Press, 2010.

Gordon, Rita Werner. "The Change in the Political Alignment of Chicago's Negroes during the New Deal." *Journal of American History* 56 (Dec. 1969): 584–603.

Gore, Dayo Falayon. "'To Hold a Candle in the Wind': Black Women Radicals and Post World War II U.S. Politics." PhD diss., New York University, 2003.

Gore, Dayo F., Jeanne Theoharis, and Komozi Woodard, eds. *Want to Start a Revolution? Radical Women in the Black Freedom Struggle.* New York: New York University Press, 2009.

Graham, Helen. *The Spanish Civil War: A Very Short Introduction.* Oxford: Oxford University Press, 2005.

Green, Adam. *Selling the Race: Culture, Community, and Black Chicago, 1940–1955.* Chicago: University of Chicago Press, 2007.

Greenberg, Cheryl Lynn. *"Or Does It Explode?" Black Harlem in the Great Depression.* Oxford: Oxford University Press, pap. ed., 1997.

Gregory, James N. *The Southern Diaspora: How the Great Migrations of Black and White Southerners Transformed America.* Chapel Hill: University of North Carolina Press, 2005.

Hall, Jacquelyn Dowd. "The Long Civil Rights Movement and the Political Uses of the Past." *Journal of American History* 91 (Mar. 2005): 1233–63.

Harris, William H. *Keeping the Faith: A. Philip Randolph, Milton P. Webster, and the Brotherhood of the Sleeping Car Porters, 1925–1937.* Urbana: University of Illinois Press, 1978.

Hayden, Dolores. *Redesigning the American Dream: Gender, Housing, and Family Life.* New York: W. W. Norton, 2002.

Haynes, Robert V. *A Night of Violence: The Houston Riot of 1917.* Baton Rouge: Louisiana State University Press, 1976.

Haywood, Harry. *Black Bolshevik: Autobiography of an Afro- American Communist.* Chicago: Liberator Press, 1978.

Hine, Darlene Clark. *Black Victory: The Rise and Fall of the White Primary in Texas.* Columbia: University of Missouri Press, 2003. New edition with essays by Darlene Clark Hine, Stephen F. Lawson, and Merline Pitre. Originally published in 1979.

———. *Black Women in White: Racial Conflict and Cooperation in the Nursing Profession, 1890–1950.* Bloomington: Indiana University Press, 1989.

Hine, Darlene Clark, ed. *Black Women in America.* 3 vols. 2d ed. Oxford: Oxford University Press, 2005.

Hollis, Karyn L. *Liberating Voices: Writing at the Bryn Mawr Summer School for Women Workers.* Carbondale: Southern Illinois University Press, 2004.

Holloway, Jonathan Scott. *Confronting the Veil: Abram Harris Jr., E. Franklin Frazier, and Ralph Bunche, 1919–1941.* Chapel Hill: University of North Carolina Press, 2002.

Honey, Michael K. *Going Down Jericho Road: The Memphis Strike, Martin Luther King's Last Campaign.* New York: W. W. Norton, 2007.

——. *Southern Labor and Black Civil Rights: Organizing Memphis Workers.* Urbana: University of Illinois Press, 1993.

Horne, Gerald. *Black Liberation/Red Scare: Ben Davis and the Communist Party.* Newark, DE: University of Delaware Press, 1994.

——. *Black & Red: W. E. B. Du Bois and the Afro-American Response to the Cold War, 1944–1963.* Albany: State University of New York Press, 1986.

——. *The End of Empires: African Americans and India.* Philadelphia: Temple University Press, 2008.

——. *Race Woman: The Lives of Shirley Graham DuBois.* New York: New York University Press, 2000.

——. *Red Seas: Ferdinand Smith and Radical Black Sailors in the United States and Jamaica.* New York: New York University Press, 2005.

Howlett, Charles F. *Brookwood Labor College: The Quest for Social Reform, 1919–1937.* Jackson: University Press of Mississippi, 1989.

——. *Brookwood Labor College and the Struggle for Peace and Social Justice in America.* Lewiston, NY: Edwin Mellen Press, 1993.

Hughes, Langston. *The Collected Works of Langston Hughes,* vol. 14, *Autobiography: "I Wonder as I Wander,"* ed. Joseph McLaren. Columbia: University of Missouri Press, 2003.

——. *The Collected Works of Langston Hughes,* vol. 9, *Essays on Art, Race, Politics, and World Affairs,* ed. Christopher C. De Santis. Columbia: University of Missouri Press, 2002.

——. *The Collected Works of Langston Hughes,* vol. 10, *Fight for Freedom and Other Writings on Civil Rights,* ed. Christopher C. De Santis. Columbia: University of Missouri Press, 2001.

Isserman, Maurice. *Which Side Were You On? The American Communist Party during the Second World War.* Urbana: University of Illinois Press, 1982.

Jackson, A. W. *A Sure Foundation.* N.p., 1940.

Jackson, Gabriel. *The Spanish Republic and the Civil War, 1931- 1939.* Princeton: Princeton University Press, 1967.

Jackson, Julian. *The Popular Front in France: Defending Democracy, 1934–38.* Cambridge: Cambridge University Press, 1990.

Jackson, Thomas E. *From Civil Rights to Human Rights: Martin Luther King, Jr., and the Struggle for Economic Justice.* Philadelphia: University of Pennsylvania Press, 2007.

Jones, Martha S. *All Bound Up Together: The Woman Question in African American Public Culture, 1830–1900.* Chapel Hill: University of North Carolina Press, 2007.

Kaiser, Ernest. "Racial Dialectics: The Aptheker-Myrdal School of Controversy." *Phylon* 9, no. 4 (1948): 295–302.

Keiler, Allan. *Marian Anderson: A Singer's Journey.* Urbana: University of Illinois Press, 2002.

Kellar, William Henry. *Make Haste Slowly: Moderates, Conservatives, and School Desegregation in Houston.* College Station: Texas A&M University Press, 1999.

Kelley, Robin D. G. *Freedom Dreams: The Black Radical Imagination.* Boston: Beacon Press, 2002.

———. *Hammer and Hoe: Alabama Communists during the Great Depression.* Chapel Hill: University of North Carolina Press, 1990.

———. *Race Rebels: Culture, Politics, and the Black Working Class.* New York: Free Press, 1994.

Kirschke, Amy. *Aaron Douglas: Art, Race, and the Harlem Renaissance.* Jackson: University Press of Mississippi, 1995.

Klehr, Harvey, John Earl Haynes, and Kyrill M. Anderson. *The Soviet World of American Communism.* New Haven, CT: Yale University Press, 1998.

Knupfer, Ann Meis. *The Chicago Black Renaissance and Women's Activism.* Urbana: University of Illinois Press, 2006.

———. *Toward a Tenderer Humanity and a Nobler Womanhood: African-American Women's Clubs in Turn-of-the-Century Chicago.* New York: New York University Press, 1996.

Korstad, Robert Rodgers. *Civil Rights Unionism: Tobacco Workers and the Struggle for Democracy in the Mid-Twentieth-Century South.* Chapel Hill: University of North Carolina Press, 2003.

Korstad, Robert, and Nelson Lichtenstein. "Opportunities Found and Lost: Labor, Radicals, and the Early Civil Rights Movement." *Journal of American History* 75 (Dec. 1988): 786–811.

Kulich, Jindra. "The Danish Folk High School: Can It Be Transplanted? The Success and Failure of the Danish Folk High School at Home and Abroad." *International Review of Education* 10, no. 4 (1964): 417–30.

La Brie, Henry G., ed. *Perspectives of the Black Press, 1974.* Kennebunkport, ME: Mercer House, 1974.

Lake, Obiagele. *Blue Veins and Kinky Hair: Naming and Color Consciousness in African America.* Westport, CT: Greenwood, 2003.

Lane, James B. *"City of the Century": A History of Gary, Indiana.* Bloomington: Indiana University Press, 1978.

Large, David Clay. *Between Two Fires: Europe's Path in the 1930s.* New York: W. W. Norton, 1991.

Lasch-Quinn, Elisabeth. *Black Neighbors: Race and the Limits of Reform in the American Settlement House Movement, 1890–1945.* Chapel Hill: University of North Carolina Press, 1993.

Lavery, Jason Edward. *The History of Finland.* Westport, CT: Greenwood, 2006.

Lawson, Steven. *Civil Rights Crossroads: Nation, Community, and the Black Freedom Struggle.* Lexington: University Press of Kentucky, 2003.

Levenstein, Harvey A. *Communism, Anti-Communism, and the CIO.* Westport, CT: Greenwood, 1981.

———. *Labor Organizations in the United States and Mexico: A History of Their Relations.* Westport, CT: Greenwood, 1971.

———. *We'll Always Have Paris: American Tourists in France since 1930.* Chicago: University of Chicago Press, 2004.

Lewis, David Levering, Michael H. Nash, and Daniel J. Leab, eds. *Red Activists and Black Freedom: James and Esther Jackson and the Long Civil Rights Revolution.* New York: Routledge, 2009.

Lichtenstein, Nelson. *The CIO's War at Home.* Cambridge: Cambridge University Press, 2002.

Lieberman, Robbie. *The Strangest Dream: Communism, Anticommunism, and the U.S. Peace Movement, 1945–1963.* Syracuse: Syracuse University Press, 2004.

Lieberman, Robbie, and Clarence Lang, eds. *Anticommunism and the African American Freedom Movement: "Another Side of the Story."* New York: Palgrave MacMillan, 2009.

Malik, Hafeez. "The Marxist Literary Movement in India and Pakistan." *Journal of Asian Studies* 26 (Aug. 1967): 649- 64.

Marshall, Thelma. "The Ancestors of William Marshall." N.p. Aug. 10, 1963.

Martin, Elmer P., and Joanne M. Martin. "Thyra J. Edwards: Internationalist Social Worker." In *African American Leadership: An Empowerment Tradition in Social Welfare History,* ed. Iris B. Carlton-LaNey, 163–76. Washington, DC: National Association of Social Workers Press, 2001.

Materson, Lisa G. *For the Freedom of Her Race: Black Women and Electoral Politics in Illinois, 1877–1932.* Chapel Hill: University of North Carolina Press, 2009.

Maxwell, William J. *New Negro, Old Left: African-American Writing and Communism between the Wars.* New York: Columbia University Press, 1999.

McArthur, Judith N., and Harold L. Smith. *Minnie Fisher Cunningham: A Suffragist's Life in Politics.* New York: Oxford University Press, 2005.

McDuffie, Erik S. "Long Journeys: Four Black Women and the Communist Party, USA, 1930–1956." PhD diss., New York University, 2003.

———. "The March of Young Southern Black Women: Esther Cooper Jackson, Black Left Feminism, and the Personal and Political Costs of Cold War Repression." In *Anticommunism and the African American Freedom Movement: "Another Side of the Story,"* ed. Robbie Lieberman and Clarence Lang, 81–114. New York: Palgrave Macmillan, 2009.

———. "A New Freedom Movement of Negro Women: Sojourning for Truth, Justice, and Human Rights during the Early Cold War." *Radical History Review* 101 (Spring 2008): 81–105.

Merithew, Caroline Waldron. "Sister Katie: The Memory and Making of a 1.5 Generation Working-Class International." *Journal of Women's History* 21 (Winter 2009): 84–110.

——. "'We Were Not Ladies': Gender, Class, and a Women's Auxiliary's Battle for Mining Unionism." *Journal of Women's History* 18, no. 2 (2006): 63–94.

Meyerowitz, Joanne, ed. *Not June Cleaver: Women and Gender in Postwar America.* Philadelphia: Temple University Press, 1994.

Millender, Dharathula. *Gary's Central Business Community: Images of America.* Mount Pleasant, SC: Arcadia, 2003.

Mohl, Raymond A., and Neil Betten. "Ethnic Adjustment in the Industrial Society: The International Institute of Gary, 1919–1940." *International Migration Review* 6 (Winter 1972): 361–76.

——. "Gary, Indiana: The Urban Laboratory as a Teaching Tool." *The History Teacher* 4 (Jan. 1971): 5–17.

Moore, Leonard Joseph. *Citizen Klansmen: The Ku Klux Klan in Indiana, 1921–1928.* Chapel Hill: University of North Carolina Press, 1991.

Mullen, Bill. *Popular Fronts: Chicago and African-American Cultural Politics, 1935–46.* Urbana: University of Illinois Press, 1999.

Mullen, Bill, and James Smethurst, eds. *Left of the Color Line: Race, Radicalism, and Twentieth-Century Literature of the United States.* Chapel Hill: University of North Carolina Press, 2003.

Murray, Pauli. *Pauli Murray: The Autobiography of a Black Activist, Feminist, Lawyer, Priest, and Poet.* Knoxville: University of Tennessee Press, 1989.

——. *Song in a Weary Throat: An American Pilgrimage.* New York: Harper and Row, 1987.

Naison, Mark. *Communists in Harlem during the Depression.* Urbana: University of Illinois Press, pap. ed., 1985. Originally published in 1983.

Needleman, Ruth. *Black Freedom Fighters in Steel: The Struggle for Democratic Unionism.* Ithaca: Cornell University Press, 2003.

Nelson, Claire Nee. "Louise Thompson Patterson and the Southern Roots of the Popular Front." In *Women Shaping the South: Creating and Confronting Change,* ed. Angela Boswell and Judith N. McArthur, 204–28. Columbia: University of Missouri Press, 2006.

Obadele-Starks, Ernest. *Black Unionism in the Industrial South.* College Station: Texas A&M University Press, 2000.

Ortiz, Paul. *Emancipation Betrayed: The Hidden History of Black Organizing and White Violence in Florida from Reconstruction to the Bloody Election of 1920.* Berkeley: University of California Press, 2005.

Ostrower, Gary B. "The American Decision to Join the International Labor Organization." *Labor History* 16, no. 4 (1975): 495–504.

Ottanelli, Fraser. *The Communist Party of the United States: From the Depression to World War II.* New Brunswick, NJ: Rutgers University Press, 1991.

Padmore, George, and Dorothy Pizer. *How Russia Transformed Her Colonial Empire: A Challenge to the Imperialist.* London: Dennis Dobson, 1946.

Painter, Nell Irvin. *Creating Black Americans: African American History and Its Meanings, 1619 to the Present.* New York: Oxford University Press, 2005.

——. *The Narrative of Hosea Hudson.* Cambridge: Cambridge University Press, 1979.

——. *Southern History across the Color Line.* Chapel Hill: University of North Carolina Press, 2002.

——. *Standing at Armageddon: The United States, 1877–1919.* New York: W. W. Norton, 1987.

Patai, Frances. "Heroines of the Good Fight: Testimonies of U.S. Volunteer Nurses in the Spanish Civil War, 1936–1939." *Nursing History Review: Official Journal of the American Association for the History of Nursing* 3 (1995): 79–104.

Payne, Stanley G. *The Collapse of the Spanish Republic, 1933- 1936: Origins of the Civil War.* New Haven, CT: Yale University Press, 2006.

——. *A History of Fascism, 1914–1945.* Madison: University of Wisconsin Press, 1995.

Pitre, Merline. *In ˙Struggle against Jim Crow: Lulu B. White and the NAACP, 1900–1957.* College Station: Texas A&M University Press, 1999.

Plummer, Brenda Gayle. *Rising Wind: Black Americans and U.S. Foreign Affairs, 1935–1960.* Chapel Hill: University of North Carolina Press, 1996.

——, ed. *Window on Freedom: Race, Civil Rights, and Foreign Affairs, 1945– 1988.* Chapel Hill: University of North Carolina Press, 2003.

Rampersad, Arnold. *The Life of Langston Hughes,* vol. 1, *1902- 1941, I, Too, Sing America.* New York: Oxford University Press, 1986.

——. *The Life of Langston Hughes,* vol. 2, *1914–1967, I Dream a World.* New York: Oxford University Press, 1988.

——. *Ralph Ellison: A Biography.* New York: Alfred A. Knopf, 2007.

Ransby, Barbara. *Ella Baker and the Black Freedom Movement: A Radical Democratic Vision.* Chapel Hill: University of North Carolina Press, 2003.

Reed, Touré F. *Not Alms but Opportunity: The Urban League and the Politics of Racial Uplift, 1910–1950.* Chapel Hill: University of North Carolina Press, 2008.

Reese, DeAnna J. "Domestic Drudges to Dazzling Divas." In *Women in Missouri History: In Search of Power and Influence,* ed. LeeAnn Whites, Mary Neth, and Gary R. Kremer, 168–79. Columbia: University of Missouri Press, 2004.

Reich, Steven A. "Soldiers of Democracy: Black Texans and the Fight for Citizenship, 1917–1921." *Journal of American History* 82 (Mar. 1996): 1478–1504.

Resh, Richard, ed. *Black America: Accommodation and Confrontation in the Twentieth Century.* Lexington, Mass.: Heath, 1969.

Ritterhouse, Jennifer. *Growing Up Jim Crow: How Black and White Southern Children Learned Race.* Chapel Hill: University of North Carolina Press, 2006.

Robinson, Cedric J. *Forgeries of Memory and Meaning: Blacks and the Regimes of Race in American Theater and Film before World War II.* Chapel Hill: University of North Carolina Press, 2007.

Romano, Renee C. *Race Mixing: Black-White Marriage in Postwar America.* Cambridge, MA: Harvard University Press, 2003.

Rosenberg, Jonathan. *How Far the Promised Land? World Affairs and the American Civil Rights Movement from the First World War to Vietnam.* Princeton: Princeton University Press, 2006.

Rosenthal, Joel. "Southern Black Student Activism: Assimilation vs. Nationalism." *Journal of Negro Education* 44 (Spring 1975): 113–29.

Rosswurm, Steve, ed. *The CIO's Left-Led Unions.* New Brunswick, NJ: Rutgers University Press, 1992.

———. "The Wondrous Tale of an FBI Bug: What It Tells Us about Communism, Anti-Communism, and the CIO Leadership." *American Communist History* 2, no. 1 (2003): 23–26.

Rowley, Hazel. *Richard Wright: The Life and Times.* New York: Henry Holt and Company, 2001.

Ruiz, Vicki L. *Cannery Women, Cannery Lives: Mexican Women, Unionization, and the California Food Processing Industry, 1930–1950.* Albuquerque: University of New Mexico Press, 1987.

Rzeszutek, Sara Elizabeth. "Love and Activism: James and Esther Cooper Jackson and the Black Freedom Movement in the United States, 1914–1968." PhD diss., Rutgers University, 2009.

Sabin, Arthur J. *Red Scare in Court: New York versus the International Workers Order.* Philadelphia: University of Pennsylvania Press, 1993.

Schneider, Mark Robert. *"We Return Fighting": The Civil Rights Movement in the Jazz Age.* Boston: Northeastern University Press, 2002.

Schott, Linda K. *Reconstructing Women's Thoughts: The Women's International League for Peace and Freedom before World War II.* Stanford: Stanford University Press, 1997.

Schuler, Edgar A. "The Houston Race Riot, 1917." *Journal of Negro History* 29 (July 1944): 300–338.

Schuler, Friedrich E. *Mexico between Hitler and Roosevelt: Mexican Foreign*

Relations in the Age of Lázaro Cárdenas, 1934–1940. Albuquerque: University of New Mexico Press, 1998.

Scott, Anne Firor, ed. *Pauli Murray and Caroline Ware: Forty Years of Letters in Black and White.* Chapel Hill: University of North Carolina Press, 2006.

Sherman, John W. *The Mexican Right: The End of Revolutionary Reform, 1929–1940.* Westport, CT: Greenwood, 1997.

Sitkoff, Harvard. *A New Deal for Blacks: The Emergence of Civil Rights as a National Issue,* vol. 1, *The Depression Decade.* New York: Oxford University Press, 1978.

Sklaroff, Laura Rebecca. *Black Culture and the New Deal: The Quest for Civil Rights in the Roosevelt Era.* Chapel Hill: University of North Carolina Press, 2009.

Snow, Sinclair. *The Pan-American Federation of Labor.* Durham, NC: Duke University Press, 1964.

Solomon, Mark. *The Cry Was Unity: Communists and African Americans, 1917–1936.* Jackson: University Press of Mississippi, 1998.

Solotaroff, Ted. *First Loves: A Memoir.* New York: Seven Stories Press, 2004.

Sorelle, James M. "The Darker Side of 'Heaven': The Black Community in Houston, Texas, 1917–1945." PhD diss., Kent State University, 1980.

Stein, Judith. *The World of Marcus Garvey: Race and Class in Modern Society.* Baton Rouge: Louisiana State University Press, 1986.

Stepan-Norris, Judith, and Maurice Zeitlin. *Left Out: Reds and America's Industrial Unions.* Cambridge: Cambridge University Press, 2002.

Storch, Randi. "'The Realities of the Situation': Revolutionary Discipline and Everyday Political Life in Chicago's Communist Party, 1928–1935." *Labor: Studies in Working-Class History of the Americas* 1, no. 3 (2004): 19–44.

———. *Red Chicago: American Communism at Its Grassroots, 1928–1935.* Urbana: University of Illinois Press, 2007.

Storrs, Landon R. Y. *Civilizing Capitalism: The National Consumers' League, Women's Activism, and Labor Standards in the New Deal Era.* Chapel Hill: University of North Carolina Press, 2000.

———. "Left-Feminism, the Consumer Movement, and Red Scare Politics in the United States, 1935–1960." *Journal of Women's History* 18, no. 3 (2006): 40–67.

Streitmatter, Rodger. *Raising Her Voice: African-American Women Journalists Who Changed History.* Lexington: University Press of Kentucky, 1994.

Strong, Tracey, and Helen Keyysar. *Right in Her Soul: The Life of Anna Louise Strong.* New York: Random House, 1984.

Sugrue, Thomas J. *Sweet Land of Liberty: The Forgotten Struggle for Civil Rights in the North.* New York: Random House, 2008.

Sullivan, Patricia. *Days of Hope: Race and Democracy in the New Deal Era.* Chapel Hill: University of North Carolina Press, 1996.

———. *Lift Every Voice: The NAACP and the Making of the Civil Rights Movement.* New York: New Press, 2009.

Swerdlow, Amy. "The Congress of American Women: Left-Feminist Peace Politics in the Cold War." In *U.S. History as Women's History: New Feminist Essays,* ed. Alice Kessler-Harris, Kathryn Kish Sklar, and Linda K. Kerber, 296–312. Chapel Hill: University of North Carolina Press, 1995.

Thomas, Hugh. *The Spanish Civil War.* New York: Harper, 1961.

Thornbrough, Emma Lou. *Indiana Blacks in the Twentieth Century,* ed. Lana Ruegamer. Bloomington: Indiana University Press, 2000.

———. "Segregation in Indiana during the Klan Era of the 1920s." *Mississippi Valley Historical Review* 47 (Mar. 1961): 594–618.

Turner, Joyce Moore. With W. Burghardt Turner. *Caribbean Crusaders and the Harlem Renaissance.* Urbana: University of Illinois Press, 2005.

Vendryes, Margaret Rose. *Barthé: A Life in Sculpture.* Jackson: University Press of Mississippi, 2008.

Von Eschen, Penny Marie. *Race against Empire: Black Americans and Anticolonialism, 1937–1957.* Ithaca: Cornell University Press, 1997.

Wadelington, Charles W., and Richard F. Knapp. *Charlotte Hawkins Brown and Palmer Memorial Institute: What One Young African American Woman Could Do.* Chapel Hill: University of North Carolina Press, 1999.

Wald, Alan. *Trinity of Passion: The Literary Left and the Antifascist Crusade.* Chapel Hill: University of North Carolina Press, 2007.

Walker, Susannah. *Style and Status: Selling Beauty to African American Women, 1920–1975.* Lexington: University Press of Kentucky, 2007.

Watson, Dwight D. *Race and the Houston Police Department, 1930–1990: A Change Did Come.* College Station: Texas A&M University Press, 2005.

Webb, Constance. *Richard Wright: A Biography.* New York: G. P. Putnam, 1968.

Weigand, Kate. *Red Feminism: American Communism and the Making of Women's Liberation.* Baltimore: Johns Hopkins University Press, 2001.

Wieck, David Thoreau. *Woman from Spillertown: A Memoir of Agnes Burns Wieck.* Carbondale: Southern Illinois University Press, 1992.

Winegarten, Ruth. *Black Texas Women: 150 Years of Trial and Triumph.* Austin: University of Texas Press, 1995.

Work, Monroe Nathan, ed. *Negro Year Book.* Negro Year Book Publishing Co., 1952.

Wittner, Lawrence S. "The National Negro Congress: A Reassessment." *American Quarterly* 22 (Winter 1970): 883–901.

———. *The Struggle against the Bomb: A History of the World Nuclear Disarmament Movement through 1953.* Stanford: Stanford University Press, 1993.

Yenser, Thomas, ed. *Who's Who in Colored America.* 4th ed. Brooklyn, NY: Thomas Yenser, 1933–1937.

Zalampas, Michael. *Adolph Hitler and the Third Reich in American Magazines, 1923–1939.* Madison: University of Wisconsin Press, 1989.

Zieger, Robert H. *The CIO: 1935–1955.* Chapel Hill: University of North Carolina Press, 1995.

Index

Abbott, Edith, 73
Abbott, Helen, 31, 105
Abbott, Robert S., 31, 93, 105
Abyssinia. *See* Ethiopia
ACLU. *See* American Civil Liberties Union (ACLU)
Action Committee to Free Spain, 168
Addams, Jane, 4, 28, 29, 58, 77–78, 88
Ades, Bernard, 175, 178
AFL. *See* American Federation of Labor (AFL)
Africa, 41, 86, 96, 152, 156, 157–58
African Americans: as colonial subjects, 107–8, 182; employment of, 12, 25, 31, 80, 158, 163–65; in International Brigade of Spanish Civil War, 101, 103–4; and New Deal programs, 80; stereotypes about, 50, 78, 79; unemployment of, 77, 78–80. *See also* Civil rights; Race relations and racism; Segregation; Slavery; *and specific African Americans*
African Methodist Episcopal (AME) Church, 156
Ahlberg, Alf, 55
Almazán, Juan Andreu, 131, 145
Amalgamated Association of Meat Cutters and Butcher Workmen of North America, 84
AME Church, 156
American Association of Social Workers, 45, 115
American Civil Liberties Union (ACLU), 76, 82
American Federation of Labor (AFL): and Brookwood Labor College, 36–38; and Brotherhood of Sleeping Car Porters (BSCP), 83–84; CIO's

break with, 71; and hiring discrimination on federal public-works projects, 76; and International Labor Organization (ILO), 154–55; and interracial summer labor institutes in 1940s, 159; Master Mates and Pilots Union of, 160; and Pan-American Federation of Labor, 155; racist practices of, 19, 37, 138, 154–55; reunification of CIO and, 180; scholarship for Edwards from, to International People's College, 41. *See also specific unions, such as* International Longshoremen's Association (ILA)
American Friends Service, 95
American Jewish Joint Distribution Committee, 5, 169
American Labor Party, 112
American League against War and Fascism, 89, 112, 148, 149
American League for Peace and Democracy, 112–16, 145, 148
American Medical Bureau to Aid Spanish Democracy, 105, 108, 113–15
American Peace Mobilization, 146
American People's Mobilization, 146
American Student Union (ASU), 130
American Workers Party, 36
Andersen, Hans Christian, 47–48
Anderson, Alyse, 47
Anderson, Kai, 57, 90
Anderson, Marian, 4, 28, 47, 50, 158
Andrews, William, 96
ANP. *See* Associated Negro Press (ANP)

Poverty: in Chicago, 77–80; in Gary, Ind., 31; stereotypes about African Americans on relief, 78, 79; in Texas, 162

Powell, Adam Clayton, Jr., 5, 81, 96, 151, 152, 153, 181

Prairie View A&M College, 97, 108

Pravda, 168

Price, Melva, 131, 132

Procter and Gamble, 111

Progressive education, 24–25, 36, 37. *See also* Education

Progressive Miners of America (PMA), 38–40, 75

Progressive Writers Association, 42

Public Health Service, U.S., 147, 148

Pueblos Hispanos, 152

Puerto Rico, 152, 155

Pushkin, Alexander, 90

Quaker Society of Friends, 41, 95

Race and race relations, and internal colonialism, 107–8, 182

Race relations and racism: in Britain, 31, 42, 51; at Brookwood Labor College, 35–38; in Chicago, 40; and Communist Party, 103, 151; Denmark's race attitudes, 50–51; and Double V campaign, 144, 151, 154–65, 180, 182; Edwards on "weight of being black," 70; Edwards's early understanding of, 13–16; in Gary, Ind., 24–27, 30, 32–33; integration of Merchant Marine during World War II, 159, 160; and interracial marriage, 4–5, 50, 56, 64; in labor movement, 19, 37, 71, 72, 75, 96, 154, 156, 157, 159; in Mexico, 140–41; in Nazi Germany, 62, 65, 66, 68, 94, 95; in Soviet Union, 4, 54, 60, 93, 96, 152, 168, 180; stereotypes about African Americans on relief, 78, 79. *See also* Civil rights; Colonialism and decolonization; Race riots; Segregation

Race riots: Camp Logan Riot (Houston), 2, 19–20, 22, 84; in Chicago (1919), 29; in Longview, Tex., 22

Racial uplift, 28

Randolph, A. Philip: and Brotherhood of Sleeping Car Porters (BSCP), 4, 35, 72, 83–84, 111, 164; and civil rights generally, 4; on Thyra Edwards, 1, 80; end of extramarital affair between Thyra Edwards and, 138, 146, 181; extramarital affair of, with Thyra Edwards, 4,

35, 51–52, 56, 72, 138; and Fair Employment Practices Commission, 158, 183; health problems of, 81, 83; as mentor of Thyra Edwards, 4, 35, 41, 72, 159, 181; and National Negro Congress (NNC), 80–83, 86, 87, 96, 112, 114–15; resignation of, from National Negro Congress (NNC), 145, 181; and Spanish Civil War, 112; strain in Edwards's relationship with, 129, 181

Rasmussen, Forstander, 47–48, 49, 162

Rayside, Rosa, 81

Redmond, Sidney R., 141

Red Summer (1919), 22

Reese, Curtis, 34, 40, 59, 72, 76, 150

Refugees. *See* Jews and Jewish refugees; Spanish Loyalist refugees

Reissig, Herman F., 102, 114

Rheumatoid arthritis, 5, 129–30, 136–38, 141, 143–47, 153–54, 165–67, 171–73, 184

Rhodes, Peter, 101, 104

Rice, C. W., 106–7

Richardson, C. F., 21–22

Robeson, Paul, 4, 108, 127, 148, 158, 171, 180, 183

Rogers, Etha Bell, 52, 55

Roland, Irene, 97

Rommel, Erwin, 158

Rooks, Shelby, 177

Roosevelt, Eleanor, 156, 159

Roosevelt, Franklin D.: death of, 159; Edwards' support for reelection of, 143, 156, 158, 160–61, 181; and embargo on arms shipments to Spanish Republic, 112; and Fair Employment Practices Commission, 158; and International Labor Organization (ILO), 154, 155; and National Negro Congress (NNC), 83; New Deal of, 36, 45, 50, 74, 78, 80, 87, 147, 158–59; race-relations advisers to, 105, 158–59

Rorre, Joe de, 38

Rorre, Katie de, 38–39

Rosenwald Fund, 164

Rothier, Mrs. F. A., 110–11

Roumain, Jacques, 98

Rousseau, Imogene, 89

Ruskin Workers' School, Oxford University, 89

Russell, Bertrand, 55

Russell, Dora, 55

Russia. *See* Soviet Union

Ryan, Neva, 81, 86

Rye, Eleanor, 84–86